ENGLISH ILLUMINATION

ENGLISH ILLUMINATION

BY

O. ELFRIDA SAUNDERS

Volume I

Reprinted by

HACKER ART BOOKS

NEW YORK

1969

First Published in 1933

by PANTHEON, Florence

Reprinted 1969

HACKER ART BOOKS

New York

TO MY TEACHERS

IN MANY PLACES AND AT MANY TIMES

IN GRATEFUL REMEMBRANCE

Library of Congress Catalog Card Number 71-78356

PREFACE

I am indebted to the authorities of the following institutions for kind permission to reproduce pages from their manuscripts: the British Museum; the Bodleian Library, Oxford; the Fitzwilliam Museum, Cambridge; the Hunterian Museum, Glasgow; the Rylands Library, Manchester; the Bibliothèque Nationale, Paris; All Souls and University Colleges, Oxford; Trinity, St. John's and Corpus Christi Colleges, Cambridge; and Trinity College, Dublin: and also to the following private owners of manuscripts: His Grace the Archbishop of Canterbury, Mr. C. W. Dyson Perrins and His Grace the Duke of Devonshire. I should also like to express my hearty thanks to those who gave me help and encouragement while the book was in progress, especially to Dr. Borenius, Mr. S. C. Cockerell and my sister, Miss Grace H. Saunders.

The photographs of manuscripts at the British Museum and the Lambeth Palace Library were taken by Artists' Illustrators Ltd., those at Oxford by the Oxford University Press, those at Cambridge by Mr. W. Tams, those in Dublin by Mr. A. Carroll, those at Glasgow by Mr. D. M. Filshill, those at Chatsworth by Messrs. Bemrose of Derby, those of Mr. Dyson Perrins' MSS. by Messrs. Norman May of Malvern, and those in Paris by M. Lecuyer. Plates 8, 9, 22a, 36 and 37 are from the official photographs of the Victoria and Albert Museum, by kind permission of the Director.

CONTENTS

LIST OF PLATES

PLATE 56 Westminster Psalter. *British Museum.* Royal 2. A. XXII. Late 12th century. f. 66. Psalm LI. « Quid gloriaris ».

PLATE 57 Westminster Psalter. *British Museum.* Royal 2. A. XXII. Late 12th century. f. 12b. Annunciation.

PLATE 58a Manerius Bible. *Paris, Bibliothèque Nationale,* lat. 11534. Late 12th century. f. 6b. Initial page of Genesis, (Creation scenes).

PLATE 58b Psalter. *British Museum.* Harley 5102. Late 12th century. f. 49. Initial Q to Psalm LI. David rebuking a tyrant.

PLATE 58c Psalter. *British Museum.* Royal 1. D. X. Early 13th century. f. 62. Initial S of Psalm LII.

PLATE 59a Life of St. Cuthbert. *British Museum.* Add. 29943. c. 1200 f. 28b. An eagle provides food for St. Cuthbert on a journey, and the saint exhorts his companion to give the bird its share.

PLATE 59b Life of St. Cuthbert. *British Museum.* Add. 29943. c. 1200. f. 62b. St. Cuthbert heals a child.

PLATE 60 Life of St. Guthlac. *British Museum.* Harley Roll, y. 6. St. Guthlac carried off by demons.

PLATE 61 Psalter. *British Museum.* Royal 1. D. X. Early 13th century. f. 3b. Feast in Simon's House. Entry into Jerusalem.

PLATE 62 Psalter. *British Museum.* Royal 1. D. X. Early 13th century. f. 9b. Calendar page for February.

PLATE 63 Peterborough Psalter. *Cambridge, Fitzwilliam Museum.* 12. 1260-1270. f. 12. Crucifixion (slightly reduced).

PLATE 64 Peterborough Psalter. *Cambridge, Fitzwilllam Museum.* 12. 1260-1270. Beatus page: Christ in Glory: Mercy and Truth.

PLATE 65a Hours by William de Brailes. *Dyson Perrins Collection.* 1220-1240. f. 1. Passion Scenes.

PLATE 65b Psalter. *All Souls' College, Oxford.* c. 1250. f. 35b. Initial D of Psalm XXVI. « Dominus illuminatio mea ». Samuel anointing David.

PLATE 66 Psalter. *All Souls' College, Oxford.* c. 1250. Crucifixion. Medallions: God the Father; Adam rising from the grave; the Church; the Synagogue.

PLATE 67 Missal of Henry of Chichester. *Rylands Library, Manchester.* 24. 13th century. f. 149b. Nativity.

PLATE 68 Missal of Henry of Chichester. *Rylands Library, Manchester.* 24. 13th century. f. 150a. Virgin and Child adored by a Priest.

PLATE 69 Glossed Psalter and Hours of Robert de Lindeseye. *St. John's College, Cambridge.* c. 1220. Angels appearing to Shepherds. Three kings before Herod.

PLATE 70 Oscott Psalter. *Dyson Perrins Collection.* Latter half of 13th century. f. 10b. Apostle.

PLATE 71 De Quincey Apocalypse. *Lambeth Palace Library,* 209. Late 13th century f. 50. St. Catherine.

PLATE 72 De Quincey Apocalypse. *Lambeth Palace Library,* 209. Late 13th century. f. 40. St. Christopher.

PLATE 73 De Quincey Apocalypse. *Lambeth Palace Library,* 209. Late 13th century. f. 53. Allegory of the penitent.

PLATE 74 De Quincey Apocalypse. *Lambeth Palace Library,* 209. Late 13th century. f. 51b. Crucifixion.

PLATE 75a Bible of Robert de Bello. *British Museum.* Burney 3. 1224-1253. f. 392. Initial F before II Macabees.

PLATE 75b Bible of Robert de Bello. *British Museum.* Burney 3. 1224-1253. f. 274. Initial V before Isaiah.

PLATE 76 Bible of William of Devon. *British Museum.* Royal 1. D. I. Initial A before Judith. (Slightly reduced).

PLATE 77 Petrus Comestor from Ashridge College. *British Museum.* Royal 3. D. VI. 1283-1300. f. 3. Initials R and I before Genesis. (reduced).

PLATE 78 Petrus Comestor from Ashridge College. *British Museum.* Royal 3. D. VI. 1283-1300. f. 79b. Initial Q before Numbers (reduced).

PLATE 79 Chronica Maiora of Matthew Paris. *Corpus Christi College, Cambridge.* 26. Middle 13th century. Page at end with heads of Virgin and Child, and of Christ.

PLATE 80 Chronica Minora of Matthew Paris. *British Museum.* Royal 14. C. VII. Middle of 13th century. f. 8b. Norman Kings (slightly reduced)

PLATE 81 Collections of Matthew Paris. *British Museum.* Nero D. 1. Middle of 13th century. f. 3. The Knighting of Offa.

PLATE 82 Collections of Matthew Paris. *British Museum.* Nero D. 1. Middle 13th century. f. 3b. Battle scene from the life of Offa.

PLATE 83 Life of St. Edward. (The Confessor). *Cambridge University Library*. Ee. 3. 59. c. 1250. f. 23b. Blind beggars come to be healed, (by drinking water in which St. Edward has washed his hands).

PLATE 84 Life of St. Edward. *Cambridge University Library*. Ee. 3. 59. c. 1250. f. 27. Two pilgrims return his ring to St. Edward.

PLATE 85 Westminster Psalter. *British Museum*. Royal 2. A. XXII. Drawing added in the 13th century. f. 220b. St. Christopher.

PLATE 86 Psalter of Alphonso. (Tenison Psalter). *British Museum*. Add. 24686. 1284. f. 11. Beatus Page; David harping, David and Goliath below on border.

PLATE 87 Psalter of Alphonso. (Tenison Psalter). *British Museum*. Add. 24686. 1284. f. 3. Sts. Lucy, Mary Magdalen, Helena, and Radegund.

PLATE 88a Psalter from Huth Collection. *British Museum*. Add. 38116. 1280-1300. f. 13b. Last Judgment.

PLATE 88b Psalter from Huth Collection. *British Museum*. Add. 38116. 1280-1300. f. 119b. Initial D of Psalm CIX. « Dixit Dominus ». Trinity; Coronation of the Virgin; the Church; the Synagogue.

PLATE 89 Grandison Psalter. *British Museum*. Add. 21926. Late 13th century. f. 17. Baptism and Agony in the Garden.

PLATE 90a Apocalypse. *Paris, Bibliothèque Nationale*. fr. 403. Early 13th century. f. 15b. The armies of Horsemen. Rev. IX. 16.

PLATE 90b Apocalypse. *Paris, Bibliothèque Nationale*. fr. 403. Early 13th century. f. 20. Michael and his angels warring with the dragon. Rev. XII. 7.

PLATE 91 Apocalypse. *Oxford, Bodleian Library*. Auct. D. 4. 17. 1250-1250. f. 9. Two Angels. Rev. XII. 10. « I heard a great voice in heaven».

PLATE 92 Trinity College Apocalypse. *Trinity College, Cambridge*. R. 16. 2. c. 1230. f. 2. Life of St. John. St. John exiled, and the voyage to Patmos.

PLATE 93 Trinity College Apocalypse. *Trinity College, Cambridge*. R. 16. 2. c. 1230. f. 29. The scarlet woman. Rev. XVII. 3.

PLATE 94a Apocalypse. *British Museum*. Add. 35166. Late 13th century. f. 5b. Christ adored by the Elders. Rev. IV. 9, 10.

PLATE 94b Apocalypse. *British Museum*. Add. 35166. Late 13th century. f. 7. The Rider on the white horse. Rev. VI. 2.

PLATE 95a Apocalypse. *British Museum*. Add. 35166. Late 13th century. f. 20. The scarlet woman. Rev. XVII. 3.

Plate 95b Apocalypse. *Dyson Perrins Collection*. Middle 13th century. f. 22b. The dragon wars with the seed of the woman. Rev. XII. 17.

Plate 96a Apocalypse. *Paris, Bibliothèque Nationale*. Lat 10474. Late 13th century. f. 36. St. John on Patmos.

Plate 96b Apocalypse. *Paris, Bibliothèque Nationale*. Lat. 10474. Late 13th century. The Vintage. Rev. XIV. 17.

Plate 97a Apocalypse. 3. *Paris, Bibliothèque Nationale*. Lat. 10474. Late 13th. century. The scarlet woman, Rev. XVII.

Plate 97b Douce Apocalypse. *Oxford, Bodleian Library*. Douce 180. 1270-1300. f. 26. Fourth angel sounding. Rev. VIII. 12.

Plate 98a De Quincey Apocalypse. *Lambeth Palace Library,* 209. Late 13th century. f. 20. Worship of the Beast. Rev. XIII. 4.

Plate 98b De Quincey Apocalypse. *Lambeth Palace Library,* 209. Late 13th century. f. 25. Vintage scene. Rev. XIV. 17.

Plate 99a Apocalypse. *British Museum*. Royal 19. B. XV. Early 14th century. f. 10b. The rider on the pale horse. Rev. VI. 8.

Plate 99b Apocalypse. *British Museum*. Royal. 19. B. XV. Early 14th century. f. 45. St. John kneeling before Christ.

Plate 100 Apocalypse. *British Museum*. Royal 15. D. II. Early 14th century. The rider on the white horse. Rev. VI. 2.

Plate 101 Queen Mary's Psalter. *British Museum*. Royal 2. B. VII. Early 14th century. f. 149. Psalm LI. Presentation of Christ in the Temple. Initial; David and Goliath.

Plate 102 Queen Mary's Psalter. *British Museum*. Royal 2. B. VII. Early 14th century. f. 245. Psalm CXVIII. Passion scenes: Christ before the High Priest; Disciples fleeing; Scourging; Peter at the fire. Below: St. Edward poisoned.

Plate 103 Peterborough Psalter (and Bestiary). *Corpus Christi College, Cambridge*. Early 14th century. f. 8b. St. Andrew and David.

Plate 104 Peterborough Psalter (and Bestiary). *Corpus Christi College, Cambridge*. Early 14th century. f. 11b. Coronation of the Virgin.

Plate 105 Arundel Psalter (second part). *British Museum*. Arundel 83. Before 1300. f. 128b. Tree of vices.

Plate 106 Arundel Psalter (second part). *British Museum*. Arundel 83. Before 1300 f. 130. Christ enthroned with Evangelists.

PLATE 107 Arundel Psalter (second part). *British Museum*. Arundel 83. Before 1300. f. 132b. Passion scenes; Harrowing of Hell; Descent from the Cross; Entombment; Bribing of the guards.

PLATE 108 Arundel Psalter, (first part). *British Museum*. Arundel 83. 1300-1308. f. 55b. Psalm LXXX. Initial. David as musician, (playing bells).

PLATE 109 Ormesby Psalter. *Oxford, Bodleian Library*. Douce 366. Early 14th century. f. 55b. Psalm XXXVIII. Initial: Christ before Pilate, (reduced).

PLATE 110 Ormesby Psalter. *Oxford, Bodleian Library*. Douce 366. Early 14th century. f. 10. Second Beatus page: David harping.

PLATE 111 Gorleston Psalter. *Dyson Perrins Collection*. Before 1306. f. 146b. Psalm CIX. Initial: The Trinity, (reduced).

PLATE 112 Stowe Breviary. *British Museum*. Stowe 12. 1322-1325. f. 274b. Initial: St. Margaret.

PLATE 113 St. Omer Psalter. *British Museum*. Add. 39810. c. 1322-1325. f. 7. Beatus page, (slightly reduced). Jesse tree. Scenes in medallions from bottom left: Christ as Creator; Creation of Adam and Eve; Fall; Expulsion; Adam and Eve working; Lamech shooting Cain; Building of the ark; Entering the ark; Noah mocked by Ham; (slightly reduced).

PLATE 114 St. Omer Psalter. *British Museum*. Add. 39810. c. 1322-1325. f. 120. Psalm CIX. Initial: Last Judgment. Scenes in medallions from bottom left: Betrayal; Scourging; Christ carrying Cross; Crucifixion; Entombment; Resurrection; Maries at the Sepulchre; Ascension; Pentecost. (slightly reduced).

PLATE 115 Psalter. *All Souls' College, Oxford*. Early 14th century. f. 8. Psalms II and III.

PLATE 116 Psalter. *All Souls' College, Oxford*. Early 14th century. f. 89. Psalm XCVII. Initial: Monks chanting.

PLATE 117 Book of Hours. *British Museum*. Egerton 2781. 14th century. f. 10. Presentation of the Virgin in the Temple.

PLATE 118 Wycliffe Bible. *British Museum*. Egerton 617. End of 14th century. f. 81. Border, page of Jeremiah.

PLATE 119a Bible of Richard II. *British Museum*. Royal. 1. E. IX. End of 14th century f. 79. Abishag the Shunamite brought to David.

PLATE 119b Bible of Richard II. *British Museum*. Royal. 1. E. IX. End of 14th century f. 149b. Psalm LII. Initial S: David in the waters, mocked by his enemies.

PLATE 120 Bible of Richard II. *British Museum.* Royal 1. E. IX. End of 14th century. f. 222. Siege of Jerusalem.

PLATE 121 Bible of Richard II. *British Museum.* Royal 1. E. IX. End of 14th century. f. 234b. Initials A and Q with St. Jerome.

PLATE 122 Chichele Breviary. *Lambeth Palace Library.* 69. Early 15th century. f. 4b. Decorated page. Initial: Annunciation, (slightly reduced).

PLATE 123a Chichele Breviary. *Lambeth Palace Library.* 69. Early 15th century. f. 282. Initial: David dancing before the ark.

PLATE 123b Psalter. *Lambeth Palace Library.* 459. 15th century. f. 85. Resurrection.

PLATE 124 Psalter. *Lambeth Palace Library.* 459. 15th century. f. 19b. Page with initial and border.

PLATE 125 Hours of Elysabeth ye Quene. *Dyson Perrins Collection.* c. 1410. f. 22. Crucifixion and border.

PLATE 126 Hours of the Duke of Warwick. *Dyson Perrins Collection.* First half of 15th century. f. 29. Christ before Pilate, and border.

PLATE 127 Lectionary of Siferwas. *British Museum.* Harley 7026. c. 1400. f. 12. Page with border and miniature of the Circumcision.

PLATE 128 Epistle of Othea to Hector. *St. John's College, Cambridge.* c. 1450. f. 9. Perseus and Andromeda.

PLATE 129 Chaucer's Troilus. *Corpus Christi College, Cambridge.* 15th century. Frontispiece.

THE TEXT

CHAPTER I

CELTIC ILLUMINATION

MANUSCRIPT painting was the basic art of the Middle Ages. That is to say, it was the most general, and at the same time the most original of the forms of mediaeval art expression. It was universally practised wherever there was culture of any sort, whereas other types of art, such as sculpture, wall-painting and metal-work, were more sporadic in their appearance. It was also the principal means of the dissemination of artistic styles, ivories and metal-work coming a good way behind it in this respect.

For a single book could contain in its pages many scenes illustrating Biblical and other stories, as well as much pure ornament, and so could form a regular compendium of subjects for art work, as well as of patterns and styles for its execution. The fact that motives for wall-painting and sculpture and other arts were taken from the manuscripts is being frequently corroborated by fresh discoveries, and it is only very rarely that the opposite has been found to be the case. The iconography of the Eastern Church penetrated to the West chiefly through the Syrian and other manuscripts which found their way to Rome, and thence to the other countries of Western Europe.

Manuscripts take a particularly important part in the history of English art, because of the comparative scarcity in this country of other monuments of the mediaeval period. Wall-paintings and carvings were ruthlessly destroyed at the Reformation, and it is probable that many tendencies of English art at particular periods, and influences both given and received from other countries, would have remained entirely unknown, if it were not for the study of the miniatures, as paintings in manuscripts are generally called. The result of a closer acquaintance with these beautiful works of art is to make the student realise how very much English art in early times has been underrated. All through the mediaeval period England held a place in the forefront of art-producing countries, France being her chief rival; and at certain periods her illuminations were superior to those of any other country.

The art of manuscript painting in England was essentially a decorative art until the time of its decadence. That is to say, it did not occupy itself seriously with problems of representation such as perspective, space composition or effects of lighting, and it was only in the Gothic period that it began to make much effort at expressing solidity by shading. But this was almost equally the case with wall-painting at the same periods. And within its limitations miniature painting had serious artistic aims. The best productions of each age are the achievements of real artists who, in spite of the immaturity which makes their works look quaint to the modern eye, shew much skill in composition, in the rhythm and movement of line and in the combination of colours; while their technical dexterity in the management of the pen and the application of gold and colours, often on a very small scale, is too well-known to need emphasis.

The art flourished from the 7th to the 15th centuries, and began straight away with a brilliant period, in which the products of these islands surpassed those of any other country.

The term *Celtic,* to denote the style of manuscript painting which was practised in Ireland after the introduction of Christianity, and from there spread to the North of Britain, has been attacked by Irish writers as referring, strictly speaking, only to pre-Christian monuments in Ireland and to those in Britain prior to the Roman occupation; while English writers have wished to perpetuate in the name the fact that much of the work was done in Britain by Anglo-Saxon monks, and have therefore called the style Hiberno-Saxon. But the word Celtic has so long had a definite connotation for ordinary people, bringing to their minds the kind of ornament found on all types of early Irish work, many of the elements of which were already present in early Christian days, that it seems best to retain it. For, after all, the style was developed among peoples of Celtic origin, and even if it afterwards took root among Anglo-Saxons, its nature remained essentially the same as it had been in its original home.

Monasticism had been introduced into Ireland in the 5th century; the Book of Armagh reports that St. Patrick used to distribute books of the Law and books of the Gospel to his newly-founded monasteries, and it was no doubt not long before the copying and decorating of books became a regular part of the work of the monks. St. Columba founded a number of monasteries in the 6th century, including Durrow, Derry and, probably, Kells. St. Columba was himself an ardent copyist, and is said to have written 300 manuscripts with his own hand. Indeed, legend reports that it was a dispute over the possession of a manuscript which led to his exile to Iona in 565.

The story runs that he borrowed a psalter from his former master, St. Finian, while paying a visit to him in Ulster, and copied it secretly at night by light of the beams which miraculously shone from his fingers. St. Finian claimed that the copy belonged to him, and St. Columba refused to give it up. Diarmaid, King of Ireland, was asked to arbitrate, and decreed that, as to every cow belongs its calf, so to every book belongs its copy. This led to a bloody war, but in the end Columba retained the copy. For his part in the strife, Columba took upon himself the penance of leaving Ireland and going to preach Christianity in Scotland.

Whatever the truth of the story, that decision was fruitful for English art as well as for English Christianity, for it caused the introduction of Celtic manuscript painting into the North of Britain. Again in 635, from Iona, Irish monks under Aidan set forth into Northumbria and founded the monastery of Lindisfarne, which soon became famous under St. Cuthbert, (d. 687), and the Lindisfarne Gospels, the magnificent surviving example of the work of its monks at the end of the 7th or beginning of the 8th century, shews that they were little behind their Irish contemporaries in the practice of the art of illumination. We shall discuss this manuscript later.

Bede reports that in the latter part of the 7th century many Angles went to Ireland to study, so that by the end of that century there were, no doubt, a number of monastic artists in Britain who were trained to carry on the work of the Irish illuminators, as well as actual Irish manuscripts to serve them as models.

Two famous manuscripts stand out as representing the great achievements of the Celtic school of illumination, the Lindisfarne Gospels, (Brit. Mus. Nero D iv) and the Book of Kells (Trinity Coll. Dublin). Their decorated pages are magnificent examples of pure ornament, in which the works of this school, although so early in date, have never been surpassed. Before considering them in detail, and their place in the history of the school, it will be as well to consider the general characteristics of Celtic illumination, whether executed in Ireland or Great Britain.

CHARACTERISTICS OF CELTIC ILLUMINATION

ALMOST all the early Celtic illuminated manuscripts are copies of the Gospels, which were evidently at that time considered the only books worthy of the skill and care of the illuminator. Two psalters exist, (the Blickling Psalter, and the Salaberga Psalter in Berlin) which were decorated in Northumbria in the 8th century, but they are very much the exception at this early period.

In complete copies of the Gospels illuminated in the Celtic style the decoration includes:

Plate 3 1 Pages containing the Canon-tables (lists of parallel passages in the various Gospels) framed in ornamental columns and arches.

Plate 11 2 Full-page pictures of the Evangelists, one before each Gospel, enclosed in a border.

Plate 4 3 Initial pages to each Gospel, containing the first few words of the text, elaborately decorated.

Plate 1 4 A few full-page ornamental designs, usually based on the form of a cross.

Plate 6 5 One or more pages containing figure subjects; scenes from the Life of Christ (in psalters, scenes from the life of David are found).

Besides these, some mansucripts have ornamental pages on which the four
Plate 5 Evangelist symbols appear together. The Book of Kells has also many decorated initials, line-fillings and other ornaments in the pages of the text, testifying to the exuberant fancy of the illuminator, but it is rare to find any decoration beyond simple initials in the ordinary pages of the text.

It is in the initial pages that the full freedom of the Celtic designers is displayed. These pages contain the first words of each Gospel, elaborately decorated. In St. Matthew the initial words are; *Liber Generationis...*, but the genealogy contained in the first 17 verses is sometimes treated as a sort of preface, and a second initial page contains the first words of verse 18, *Christi* (Xri) *autem generatio:* St. Mark has *Initium evangelii;* St. Luke *Quoniam quidem;* and St. John *In principio*. The rounded uncials of the Celtic script lend themselves well to designs of sweeping curves; the large initials themselves are generally filled with panels of various lacertine and geometrical designs, and within the spaces they enclose, as well as all around them, luxuriates an intricate maze of patterns, among which spiral whorls take a preponderating place. The background is often filled in with black, but little of it is to be seen. The *Xri page* in the Book of Kells is the most elaborate *Plate 4* of any of these initial pages. Its design, although freely adapted to fill the uneven spaces of the lettering, preserves a certain symmetry; circular and spiral patterns are very much in evidence, and geometrical and animal lacertine motives are also used; but the artist does not restrict himself to these traditional themes: at least thirteen human heads are found, on close inspection, to be included in the design, and near the bottom there is a little group of cats and mice.

The designs in the Lindisfarne Gospels are somewhat simpler and more *Plates 1 & 2* orderly. The initials are balanced by partial borders, and a profusion of red dots is used to outline the main initials and form a patterned background to the lesser ones. Some of these smaller initials are filled in with plain washes of colour; this was a favourite practice at this time.

CELTIC ORNAMENT AND ITS ORIGINS

CELTIC designs are distinguished by their *all-over* quality; the object of the designers is to fill the spaces evenly with a continuous pattern, leaving little of the background exposed; what background there is, is usually black, to shew up the colours of the pattern. Gold is not used at all, nor silver, and the colours are mingled in such a way that no one colour predominates, but a soft and blended effect is produced by the many small surfaces of different colours.

In borders and initials, as well as in full-page designs, the ground is divided into panels by plain bands, and a different pattern fills each panel.

The most characteristic of the Celtic patterns are those based on spirals and on plait-work. Of the former, the *trumpet-pattern* seems to be native to *Plate 4* Ireland, and was used in a simple form even before Christian times. It consists of spirals unfolding into broadening bands of trumpet shape which connect with other spirals, either convergent or divergent, in an endless variety of ways. It is especially suitable for filling uneven spaces, such as those left in and around initials, and it adds a particular charm to the designs of the initial pages. The plaited designs vary from the simplest borders of interlacing bands to the most intricate all-over patterns of animal forms, whose legs and wings can barely be distinguished in the maze of wide and narrow bands and knots into which their bodies have been drawn out. The creatures used in these *lacertine patterns* are generally of dog or bird form; occasionally they even have human heads, as in the Book of Kells. The accurate workmanship of these incredibly complicated patterns is perhaps more to be wondered at than anything else in the whole course of illumination.

Besides these two principal types of ornament, there are several subsidiary motives which find a place in the Celtic designs. Many geometrical patterns are used, especially those founded on the key or the fret; some of these have been called Z, T and I patterns, from the shapes which they form. Red dots are also a prominent feature, used both to form background patterns and to outline initials; their skilful use in the Lindisfarne Gospels does much to lighten the general effect of the richly decorated pages.

The elements out of which the Celtic designs are built up are all common to the art of many primitive peoples. Spirals were used on Minoan pottery: the key and other fret patterns are found on archaic Greek vases, such as the Dipylon ware: plaitwork of a rough kind occurs in sculpture in various parts of Europe, especially in Dalmatia, Lombardy and the Germanic and Scandinavian countries; it is found also in the Rabula Gospels from Syria, and on Roman mosaic pavements of the first century: red dots were in early use on the Continent as a decoration for manuscripts. But spirals, zigzags and dots were used in Ireland in very early times, and may well have arisen spontaneously there, as well as elsewhere, as motives for decoration. Ireland must also, however, have received impulses from Europe, and in that way assimilated motives which may ultimately be traced back to Egypt and Mesopotamia. These external influences came to them by two main routes: the Northern one, followed by the early migrations of peoples who reached as far as Ireland, and later by successive inroads of Scandinavians; and the Southern one, which was opened by the introduction of Christianity in the 5th century. Although St. Patrick himself may never have visited the Continent, there was a close connection between the early Irish Church and the Church in Southern Gaul, and some slight knowledge of East Christian art must have penetrated to Ireland by way of Rome and Gaul. This has left but little traces in the decorative work, which seems to have borrowed at first only from Northern sources, but there is evidence of it in the figure work of the school.

FIGURE SUBJECTS

TRACES of a knowledge of East Christian art can be seen in the general arrangement and method of treatment of the scenes, such as the Crucifixion, Virgin and Child, (Book of Kells) and Christ in Glory (St. Gall Gospels). Apart from the Evangelists, the Crucifixion is the only subject which is found more than *Plate 13* once. In each case it is represented in a form which appears also on Irish stone crosses and other monuments: the body is fully clothed, and hangs straight, with the feet side by side; the only human spectators are *Longinus* and *Stephaton,* with the spear and sponge (in later mediaeval art their places are taken by the Virgin and St. John); but especially noticeable are the angels (in one case birds), which hover on each side above the arms of the cross, a detail which seems to be specifically Irish.

In the actual style of figure painting, Celtic art shews a totally different outlook from that of the East Christian artists, such as those who in the 6th century made the mosaics at Ravenna and Rome, and decorated the Rabula Gospels. There was still much of classicism in all branches of the art of the Christian East, shewing itself in a considerable knowledge of the human form, and a natural method of representation, both of people and draperies. In Ireland, on the other hand, nothing could be further from nature than the way in which the monks depicted the human body. It became in their hands little but an additional ornamental feature, to be twisted and turned into symmetrical patterns to satisfy their decorative sense.

An effect of broken colour is aimed at, even in figure representations: the clothes form either a harlequin pattern of patches or stripes of different colours, or are twisted around the body in interlacing bands like those of the lacertine ornaments. There is no attempt at the representation of solidity, and the colour is quite arbitrary. Hair may be painted blue, or even different colours in stripes.

In these Irish manuscripts, the same awkwardnesses, due to an entire ignorance of perspective, are seen, as in early Egyptian tomb-paintings: a body is represented in full view, while the sides of the feet are shewn; or a side-view of the nose is placed in a face which is turned frontwards. The eyes are always represented as seen from the front. The Book of Kells shews slightly more attention to reality than any of the other Irish manuscripts, but the distinction

Plate 6 is only relative, and the Temptation cannot be said to be more than a translation of the scene into terms of abstract decoration.

Plates 11 & 12b The Evangelist pictures in nearly all the Celtic manuscripts are as primitive and stiff as the rest of the figures. They are usually seated, but occasionally standing. In most cases the symbol of each Evangelist is represented above his head, but in the Book of Kells and the Macdurnan Gospels the symbol is omitted altogether.

The Lindisfarne Gospels, however, have Evangelist pictures which are quite different from the usual Celtic type, and were evidently copied from an East Christian manuscript. Zimmermann thinks that this was a book which was written for Cassiodorus in South Italy in the 6th century, and was brought to Lindisfarne by Ceolfrid. Part of this actual volume, containing a seated portrait of Cassiodorus, is now bound up with a manuscript called the Codex Amiatinus (Florence, Laurentian Library), which this same Ceolfrid took with him to Rome in 715 as a gift for the Pope.

But although a few manuscripts written in England in the 8th century, such as the Vatican Gospels (Barb. lat. 570), and the Cuthbert Gospels at Vienna (lat. 1224) have Evangelist pictures of a type similar to those of the Lindisfarne Gospels, the majority of Celtic Gospels, even in England and on the Continent, adhere to the old type of the Irish manuscripts, rough as it was.

One of the surprising things about Celtic illumination is the extent to which it remains unmixed with other styles, even when produced in countries where totally different ideas were prevalent. The Irish monks, however far they wandered, were very loyal to the principles of their early teachers. They founded many monasteries on the Continent, of which those of St. Gall in Switzerland and Bobbio in Italy are the most famous, founded respectively in 612 and 613. Irish monks sent or brought books to these monasteries, which kept in close touch with the parent-houses in Ireland for several centuries. A number of Celtic manuscripts are still preserved at St. Gall, and those from Bobbio are scattered in museums at Milan, Turin, and Naples. Through these and other Irish foundations the Celtic style of illumination became known and practised in many parts of the Continent.

The state of preservation in which the early Celtic manuscripts have come down to posterity is very remarkable, and forms a great tribute to the excellence of the materials used. The paints were mixed with a gummy medium which was sometimes so thick that the colours stand out perceptibly above the level of the vellum. In the early examples the colour lies evenly, but in some later manuscripts, such as the Gospels of Macregol, there seems to have been some difficulty in making the paint *take*, and it does not always exactly fill the outline. Legend says that the Lindisfarne Gospels, together with the bones of St. Cuthbert and other relics, were carried away for safety by a 9th century Abbot of Lindisfarne, fleeing from the Danes, and that the book fell into the sea when the party was shipwrecked in the Solway Firth, but that in answer to prayer it was recovered unharmed when the tide miraculously retreated far beyond its customary limit. The book bears signs of water having trickled in from the edges and settled in a few of the pages, as though it had been immersed in a nearly, but not quite, water-tight case; so that there may possibly be some foundation for the legend, though Millar points out that similar signs of damp occur also on other Celtic manuscripts. The Annals of Clonmacnois record that a custodian of the Book of Durrow in early times used to cure sick cattle by making them drink water which had rested for some time on the pages of the book, and that no harm came to the precious manuscript thereby.

Plates 10 & 11

THE PRINCIPAL CELTIC MANUSCRIPTS

THE LINDISFARNE BOOK is generally acknowledged now to be the earlier of the two Celtic masterpieces. It contains an entry saying that the scribe, (and presumably illuminator, for the two were generally the same in those days) was Eadfrith, Bishop of Lindisfarne, who wrote it *in honour of God and St. Cuthbert and all the saints in common who are on the island.* His bishopric extended from 698 to 721, so that the book must have been finished some time during those years. Millar considers that 700 may be given as an approximate date, and suggests that it might even have been begun during the lifetime of St. Cuthbert. Certainly such a book as that must have taken a single scribe a considerable time to accomplish.

Plates 1 - 3

Apart from the Evangelist pictures, it can trace a pure descent from its Celtic forerunners, no foreign motives at all being introduced in its ornament. There are no Biblical scenes or other figure subjects. The only unusual element for a Celtic manuscript is the use of gold, but this is very slight, being confined to some words of lettering at the beginning of each Gospel, and the filling of a few small spaces on two of the decorated pages. The colouring is very soft and artfully combined, and more pigments are used than in any other manuscripts of so early a date, or indeed, in any other Celtic manuscript except the Book of Kells. They include a dull chalky cobalt blue (imperfectly washed lapis lazuli, see A. P. Laurie, *Pigments and Mediums*), yellow (orpiment), a light emerald green (malachite), scarlet (red lead), and several shades of pinkish purple and buff. No praise is too high for the beauty and variety of the designs and the exquisite perfection of the workmanship in this manuscript.

Plates 4 - 7 The Book of Kells was formerly held to be earlier than the Lindisfarne Gospels, but it is now generally assigned to the late 8th, or even early 9th century. It is certainly the product of a Columban monastery, but there is no evidence to prove that it was executed at Kells. It seems to have been there in the year 1006, when *the great Gospel of Columkill* is mentioned as having been stolen, and found again later, buried in the earth. It has been suggested that it might have been illuminated at the monastery at Iona, and brought to Ireland in the early 9th century by the monks when they fled from Iona at the approach of the Danes and took refuge at Kells. This supposition would seem a reasonable one; the art of illumination must have reached a high standard in the school founded by St. Columba at Iona, since the school at Lindisfarne, which was an offshoot from it, produced such fine work by about the end of the 7th century; and it is curious that there should be no examples of the work at Iona remaining. The Book of Kells is even more elaborate than the Lindisfarne Gospels, and has a certain richness and exuberance which would seem to shew a later and, as it were, more *baroque* stage in the developement of the art. It might well shew the work of the parent house nearly 100 years later, but in the absence of other works from Iona it seems impossible to prove whether it was written there or in Ireland.

It makes use of the blue made from lapis lazuli, which was the rarest of the pigments then known, and which was seldom used in the manuscripts written in Ireland, though it appears in the Lindisfarne Gospels and other Celtic manuscripts decorated in England or on the Continent. Additional evidence of the comparatively late date to be assigned to the Book of Kells is afforded by the traces it shews in its decoration of Continental influence.

Several motives unknown in the earlier manuscripts make their appearance here: figures of birds and small animals and even a warrior on horseback are introduced in the designs, but especially note-worthy is the use of foliage, which is quite a foreign intrusion in Celtic art. This sometimes forms a scroll design filling a panel, and in a few cases the branches issue from a vase, a characteristically East Christian motive, and one which occurs in Carolingian manuscripts; some of these may perhaps already have been known to the illuminator of the Book of Kells. The rosettes which occur in the designs may also have come from this source.

Of manuscripts which are incontestably of Irish origin, (if the Book of Kells be set aside) none now remain which are of the first rank artistically. The Book of Durrow (reproduced in Zimmermann, *Vorkarolingische Miniaturen*) is the best of them, and if, as is supposed, it was executed in the 7th century, it is interesting as shewing the stage illumination had reached at that early date in Ireland. It contains all the distinctively Celtic types of ornament, and only these; it has some good full-page designs of interlacing bands and trumpet-pattern; but its decoration is relatively simple in design and colouring (red, green and yellow are the only colours used). Its Evangelist symbols are very rough and barbaric, and there are no human representations. The Durrow Book is interesting for the influence which, according to Zimmermann, it had on the artist of the Echternach Gospels, a manuscript which was written in Northumbria in the middle of the 8th century, and then taken to Echternach, where it spread the influence of Irish illumination over a whole group of monasteries in the Moselle district of Germany.

There is an important copy of the Gospels at St. Gall (codex 51, reproduced in Westwood: *Anglo-Saxon and Irish Manuscripts*), dating from the latter part of the 8th century, which may either have been taken there from Ireland, or copied on the spot from an Irish manuscript. It has beautiful ornamental work, somewhat simpler than that in the Lindisfarne Gospels, but shewing a much more developed sense of design than earlier Irish work, such as the Book of Durrow. Its two figure-subjects, the Crucifixion and the Last Judgement (or Christ in Glory), are however, quite grotesque, and illustrate the extremes to which their abstract and decorative ideals led the Irish illuminators.

Most of the other outstanding examples of Celtic work of the 8th century were produced in Britain, and probably under the influence of the work of

Lindisfarne, although of course it is possible that they may have been copied from lost Irish prototypes which had found their way to England. The St. *Plates 8 & 9* Chad Gospels in Lichfield Cathedral Library are the nearest to the Lindisfarne Gospels in their ornament; although Professor W. M. Lindsey thinks they may have been written in Wales. The Xri page is very much like that of the Northumbrian book, but bolder in design and apparently unfinished; the cruciform pages are remarkably fine; the one reproduced shews little variety of motive, but possibly gains thereby in unity and effectiveness. Its workmanship is worthy of the best traditions of Celtic art. The Evangelist pictures in this manuscript are of the grotesque and conventional Irish type, and are not borrowed, as in the Lindisfarne Gospels, from a foreign source.

A copy of the Gospels in the Vatican (Barb. lat. 570, reproduced in Westwood), and another at Petrograd (Lat. F v l. N. 8, reproduced in New Palaeographical Society, Series II), have initial pages which are again similar to that of the Lindisfarne Gospels in general design although somewhat simpler; but the Vatican manuscript introduces a foreign element in the pattern of a vine-scroll and birds pecking at fruit, which must be ultimately of East Christian origin. These manuscripts date from the latter half of the 8th century, and Zimmermann considers that they were produced in the South of England.

From the 9th century, Celtic illumination in Britain ceases, and in Ireland the style begins to shew signs of decadence. In the Bodleian Library at Oxford *Plates 10 & 11* there is a copy of the Gospels which is signed by a scribe called Macregol, who became Bishop and Abbot of Birra in the centre of Ireland, and died in 820. The execution is careful, but rather weak; and an initial page such as that before St. Luke's Gospel shews the marked inferiority of the decorative work of this period to that of the preceding century. All the different types of Celtic pattern are used in it, but they are merely arranged side by side in panels, instead of being worked up into a free and striking design. The Evangelists are very poorly drawn, their hands and feet in particular being ludicrously inadequate; St. Luke's hair is coloured red, yellow and violet in sections.

Plate 12 The Gospels of Macdurnan in Lambeth Palace Library, dating from the latter part of the century, are much superior in finish and refinement to the Macregol Gospels, and are notable for their small size, (they are written in minuscules), whereas most Celtic manuscripts are comparatively large. But they shew little freedom or originality in design, and their colouring, though tasteful, is too subdued to be interesting, consisting chiefly of purple and various shades of green, with slight touches of scarlet. In the Evangelist pictures the flesh is coloured white, instead of being left blank, as it is in most Irish manuscripts. The emblems are not represented, but the cloven feet of the ox are transferred to St. Luke himself.

Inferior work in the Celtic style was still being produced in Ireland right up to the end of the 12th century. A psalter in St. John's College, Cambridge, *Plates 13 & 14* has simple Celtic ornament, coloured in dull purple, red and yellow, and some quite grotesque figure-subjects, which cannot even be said to have decorative merit. One is a Crucifixion, and another represents David and Goliath; the figure of the giant is no doubt meant to be prostrate, but appears to be standing on its head beside David.

In Irish art, illumination led the way, and other crafts reached their full development at a later period and borrowed designs from the manuscripts. Although there had been metal-work in Ireland from a very early date, the most beautiful works of art, chased and enamelled brooches, croziers and so on, appear after the 9th century, and the famous sculptured stone crosses of Ireland date chiefly from the 10th and 11th centuries.

Reference has already been made to the wide dissemination of Celtic manuscripts on the Continent by the Irish monks. Celtic illumination was an important source of inspiration for the eclectic art movement instituted by Charlemagne in the Frankish Empire. The influence of the Celtic style is especially evident in illumination carried out at St. Denis and monasteries connected with it. St. Denis itself had been founded by the Irish, and the Scot Dungal was living there at the time of Charlemagne. The ornament in manuscripts belonging to this branch of Carolingian illumination is quite distinctly Celtic, and the school is sometimes called the Franco-Saxon School, to mark its connection with art on this side of the Channel. The work of the School of Tours also shews, but to a lesser degree, Celtic influence brought in by Alcuin of York, who was the first Abbot of Tours.

ILLUMINATION AT CANTERBURY

A STYLE of figure-painting, further removed even than the Evangelist pictures of the Lindisfarne Gospels from that of Celtic art, makes its appearance in some Southern English manuscripts of the late eighth and early ninth cen- *Plate 15* turies. Of the three principal examples, two at least, the Gospels (Royal I E vi) and Psalter (Vespasian A i) at the British Museum, were decorated at Canterbury, and the third, the Stockholm Gospels (or Codex Aureus, as it is sometimes called) may well have originated there also, for it found its way to that same city after it had been recovered by a Saxon earl from the marauding Vikings. Canterbury seems at this time to have been the centre of a shortlived attempt to fuse Celtic with Continental art in England. No doubt numerous foreign manuscripts had been brought to its monasteries by successive occupants of the See, and there was constant intercourse with Rome and the Frankish Empire.

In all these Canterbury manuscripts the decoration is predominantly Celtic, although diluted with foreign importations such as leaf-scroll patterns, rosettes and acanthus-leaf borders. But the figure-subjects in their whole setting, pose and technique shew close analogy to the manuscripts produced in the various Frankish schools of art which were springing up at this time, under the patronage of Charlemagne. Solid, roundheaded figures, ample drapery, heavy and opaque colouring, and a somewhat streaky attempt at modelling, are the main features of Carolingian work, and they appear in these pictures also.

The single fullpage miniature in the Canterbury Psalter (reproduced in E. M. Thompson, *English Illuminated Manuscripts*) represents David seated on a cushioned throne, surrounded by musicians, dancers and scribes. It is perhaps nearest to what is called the *Palace School* of Carolingian art: while the *Plate 15* Evangelist picture in the Canterbury Gospels has undoubted affinity with the Rheims School, where a swift and sketchy method of drawing prevailed. The favourite Carolingian device of framing a figure-subject by columns and an arch, occurs in all three examples, and both the Stockholm Gospels and Canterbury Psalter show the striped backgrounds of various colours which are equally typical of the school. The Canterbury and Stockholm Gospels have some pages stained purple, and gold is used for lettering and decoration in all three.

It is a problem to reconcile these apparent signs of Carolingian influence with the early date given to the manuscripts, which are all considered eighth century work. This means that they must have been executed before the Carolingian renaissance, and must be derived independently from the same sources, Eastern and Western. But it seems curious that the two schools should be so singularly alike in their borrowing, and still more unlikely that Frankish monks should turn to England for a style which had only so recently been imported to that country from the Continent. Perhaps these pictures were copied from eighth century Continental manuscripts which have not survived, but which were already foreshadowing the new style. In the case of the Canterbury Gospels, the Evangelist picture and other decoration may possibly be a later addition. In any case, it is an interesting example of the introduction into England of the Rheims style which was to have such a notable influence on the Anglo-Saxon school of outline drawing. The acanthus border with medallions, which encloses the picture of St. Mark, seems to have been the basis from which the Winchester border was evolved some two centuries later (see next chapter).

The Danes, when they raided England, plundered churches and monasteries, and probably carried off or destroyed many manuscripts, for King Alfred, in the preface to his *Pastoral of Gregory*, wrote: *I saw, before all were spoiled and burnt, how the churches throughout Britain were filled with treasures and books.* The constant fighting during the ninth century accounts for the fact that at that time, while illumination was being largely practised on the Continent, hardly anything was produced in England.

An initial from one of the rare ninth century manuscripts, a copy of Bede's *Plate 16*
History. (Brit. Mus. Tiberius C ii) will shew that the composite style still prevailed. The B is of Celtic form, but some of the panels of the decoration contain scroll work, and the conventionalised animals of the centre filling recall, if anything, the patterns on Oriental stuffs.

For the lesser initials, both in Celtic and Southern English manuscripts *Plate 22*
of the eighth and ninth centuries, light and graceful designs in black ink, sometimes picked out with red dots, and formed of interlacing and knotted strands, ending in the heads of birds or animals, are frequently used. They often shew much taste and invention, and form a suitable decoration to the very beautiful handwriting of the period.

CHAPTER II

ANGLO-SAXON ILLUMINATION

ANGLO-SAXON ILLUMINATION AND THE WINCHESTER STYLE

IT WAS not until the middle of the 10th century, when Alfred's educational reforms had had time to bear fruit, and the monasteries had been strengthened by the spread of the Benedictine Order, that illumination flourished again in England, appearing almost at once in a homogeneous and fully-developed style which was truly national. Its centre this time was in the two Abbeys of Winchester, the Old Minster and New Minster; and their influence was dominant all over the work of the country, so that manuscripts produced at Canterbury, Bury and elsewhere during the 10th and 11th centuries shew reflections of the same manner.

There is, however, one important manuscript of the 10th century which comes before the Winchester style had crystallised, and forms an interesting prelude to it. This is King Athelstan's Psalter (Brit. Mus., Galba A xviii). It was probably written in Germany, and sent as a present to the English King, but its four full-page illustrations were added after its arrival in England, some time between 925 and 940 A. D. They seem to have been copied from an original belonging to the Syrian branch of East Christian art. Two of the miniatures, which are all quite small, represent Christ (longhaired and beardless) in Glory, adored by the choruses of heaven. One of these is much better drawn than the other. A third is of the Ascension, Christ being shewn in a mandorla (or oval glory) after the Syrian fashion, with the Virgin standing below, between two groups of the Apostles: the fourth, which is now in the Bodleian Library at Oxford, represents the Nativity, and is again of the Syrian type, the bathing of the infant being introduced at the bottom of the picture. (see E. Mâle. *L'art religieux en France au 12e siècle*). The style differs in the miniatures, the second of the *Majesties* being much superior to the other; the lines of Christ's robe in it are fine and graduated, whereas in the other they are very rough. In certain respects, such as the large hands, the conventional treatment of the features, and the colouring, which is less

Plate 17a

heavy than in the early Canterbury manuscripts, they seem to foreshadow the Winchester style, but there is nothing here of the fluttering drapery, humped attitude, or extravagant gesture that are the most striking characteristics of the latter. The border has some foliage of the acanthus type, but it has not yet developed into anything approaching the Winchester border. These miniatures shew an art which has as yet little trace of life or originality, but which is borrowing from Eastern sources.

The history of the Winchester School has been treated exhaustively by Sir G. F. Warner and other writers. It did not, apparently, arise until after Bishop Aethelwold, (Bishop of Winchester 963-984) had turned out the secular canons of the Old and New Minsters to make room for Benedictine monks from Abingdon. The earliest known manuscript is the Charter of King Edgar to New Minster, (Br. Mus. Vesp. A. VIII) dating from 966, which in its one full-page miniature (B. M. Reproductions. Series I.), a dedication picture enclosed in a leaf-work border, shews the style already fully developed. Aethelwold, himself a craftsman like his contemporary, St. Dunstan, had been in close touch with the Continent while he was Prior at Abingdon, and is known in particular to have been in communication with the monasteries of Fleury and Corbie. The sudden appearance of this new style in England, with only such slight preparation, makes it reasonable to suppose that he had stimulated his monks by examples of Carolingian art imported from northern France. He must, it seems, have brought manuscripts from Rheims, for that school is the one which shews the closest analogy to the Winchester style. The fact that the Carolingian minuscule form of writing came into use in England at about this period, and appeared first in Winchester manuscripts, is a further *Plates 18 - 21*
proof of Continental influence at this centre of illumination.

An idea of the new style can best be formed by a study of the illustrations from the famous *Benedictional of St. Aethelwold* in the Duke of Devonshire's collection at Chatsworth. It stands out far above any of the other Winchester MSS. in the elaboration and beauty of its decoration, and is a proof of the great skill to which the best English artists had already attained by 980, the date at which it was probably finished. Godeman is given as the name of the writer, and he was probably the illuminator also. This same Godeman later became Abbot of Thorney, (c. 984-1012). Besides Godeman, two other Newminster illuminators, Ethric and Wulfric, are known by name; evidently at this time there was no prejudice against monks receiving credit for their work as individuals.

With the Benedictional may be classed several other MSS. which must have emanated from the same Abbey of Newminster during the first half of the 11th century, and which are closely connected with it in style, although none of them reaches so high a standard. The nearest to it is the Benedictional of Archbishop Robert, now at Rouen, which is very much like the Aethelwold MS. in the iconography of its three miniatures, but shews a less heavy type of figure, and in the borders a freer and more rounded form of foliage. Another, the Missal of Robert of Jumièges, was executed at the commission of that prelate while he was Bishop of London (1044-1050) and was sent by him to Jumièges, where he had formerly been Abbot, to be preserved as a memorial of himself. It also is now in the Rouen Library. It is an interesting testimony to the superiority of English painting at this time to find a Frenchman ordering a manuscript in England to be sent to his native country. The style of the thirteen miniatures in this Missal is, however, much inferior to that of the two Benedictionals: the figures are stiff, straight and conventional, the colouring less pleasing and the compositions badly placed, extra spaces of foreground being filled in with meaningless smears.

A lesser MS. which bears decoration of the same type, but no figure subjects, is the so-called Ramsey Benedictional in Paris, (Bibl. Nat. lat. 987). *Plate 17b* The colouring of its borders is particularly pretty and soft, like that of the Benedictional of St. Aethelwold.

Copies of the Gospels at Trinity Coll. Cambridge, (B. 10.4) and at the British Museum, (Roy 1. D. IX) probably also emanate from this same school. The latter MS. seems to have been sent by King Cnut as a present to Canterbury, where it was in 1013.

From Christ Church Canterbury comes in all probability a Psalter, (Brit. Mus. Add. 155), illuminated between 1012 and 1023, with elaborate Winchester borders in dull colours and much gold, and containing a miniature of St. Benedict giving his rule to his monks, arranged under arches, and similar to a miniature at the end of the Benedictional of St. Aethelwold. This is a rare example of a fully coloured figure subject produced elsewhere than at Winchester, although the Winchester borders were frequently copied in other centres.

THE WINCHESTER BORDER AND INITIALS

THE WINCHESTER border, as seen in the Benedictional, clearly shews its deri- *Plates 18-21*
vation from earlier MSS. of the type of the Canterbury Gospels. The acanthus
foliage is enclosed between gold bars, except at the corners, where it juts
over the framework of the medallions; the leaves are coloured in various
soft shades, and occasionally in gold. Some miniatures shew a freer type of
foliage than others; on the whole, the evolution of the Winchester border
as time goes on is towards a looser arrangement. In later examples, the struc- *Plate 29*
tural bars are generally half-covered, and sometimes almost hidden under the
luxuriant foliage, and the medallions at the corners and mid-sides are often
almost absorbed into the rest of the decoration. But this line of progression
is not always followed, for in a Winchester Psalter, (Brit. Mus. Arundel 60) *Plate 25*
of about 1060, we find a border of leaf-patterns neatly enclosed within bars,
except where the medallions occur, from which, as usual, branching foliage
springs. This may perhaps be considered as a fresh stage of development
towards the severe borders which enclose the miniatures of the 12th century, *Plate 57*
in which the medallions have disappeared, and nothing is left but shaded
conventional leaf-designs enclosed between plain bars. These are more strictly
frames to pictures than borders, and do not occur as free designs on a page
containing writing. Indeed, the free decorative border died out altogether
after the 11th century, until it was gradually revived in a totally different
form in the course of the 13th century.

The initials used in Winchester manuscripts to introduce the Gospels, or *Plate 25*
the principal divisions of the Psalms, are generally elaborately decorated with
conventional foliage, interlacing stems and animals' heads in gold and opaque
colours. The Psalter mentioned above, (Arundel 60) has figures of David and
another entwined in the B of its Beatus page, which again is a forestalling
of a favourite 12th century motive.

But besides these rich and formal initials, a freer type, developed out of
the lesser initials of the Celtic period, appears in several manuscripts of the
10th century. They use similar motives of knot-work, leaves and biting heads,
but are painted with opaque colours in a variety of tones. Examples occur
in the Codex Vossianus, at Oxford, (Bodleian Junius 27). *Plate 22 d & e*

How much did the Winchester monks take from Frankish models, and how much did they invent for themselves in forming their new style? The border may certainly be claimed as a new and original development, with its bright colours, gold bars, and free branching foliage, although the mere element of acanthus foliage in a border was not new, being seen in Metz ivories and elsewhere. Another innovation is the relation of the figure-subjects to the border, over which they frequently project; and in general, although the actual figures are Carolingian in type, there is a freedom of treatment in the Winchester work which is characteristically English. This is shewn, amongst other things, in the combination of outline figure drawings with coloured decoration, which is so frequent a feature of Anglo-Saxon illumination, both at Winchester and elsewhere.

FIGURE-PAINTING AT WINCHESTER

THE IDEA of composition in the early Winchester pictures seems to be to fill
Plate 18 every available space. In the St. John of the Benedictional, what little space round the figure is not taken up by accessories, the throne, the curtain, the desk and the eagle symbol, is filled in with zigzag ribbons, presumably meant to represent clouds, on a striped background.

In technique of drawing and colouring, as well as in iconography, the tradition followed is in the main Carolingian. The immediate inspiration was evidently taken from the work of the schools of Rheims and Metz. The Winchester artists took up all the clichés in use at these schools, the fluttering drapery with crinkled edges, the swirls below the waist and on shoulder, elbow and knees, and the sashlike arrangement of the garment around the waist. They also adopted many of the conventional attitudes which the Rheims artists had borrowed from earlier Eastern manuscripts, being especially fond of a shrugging gesture, in which the arms are held close to the sides as far as the elbow, and then raised with out-stretched hands, rather like an *orans* in early Christian art. But it is not until a slightly later date, and under the influence of the outline drawings of the Utrecht Psalter, that the attitudes are carried to a further exaggeration which is sometimes almost ludicrous. In the Benedictional the proportions are fairly correct, the hands and feet
Plate 19 being usually of normal size, although occasionally, as in the Baptism, there is an enlarged hand: in nude figures the anatomy is indicated without much

science, but without exaggeration or schematisation; and action is indicated in a quaint, but not grotesque manner. The streaked shading, and the multiplication of lines and swirls on the garments, shew the influence of the Rheims School, but there is as yet little of the fluttering drapery which has come to be considered the main characteristic of Winchester figure drawing.

The technique of the colouring in these more elaborate early examples of the Winchester School is also borrowed from Carolingian sources. The colours are opaque, and streakily shaded, the highlights being picked out with white, and the shadows emphasized with ink lines. This leads to an exaggeration of wrinkles in the face and neck, making all the people look old.

The colouring used in the Benedictional of St. Aethelwold is peculiarly soft and harmonious, and so is that of other early examples, such as the Charter of Edgar (Brit. Mus. Vesp. A. viii) and the Ramsey Benedictional *Plate 17b* (Bibl. Nat. lat. 987). A violet colour (made, see A. P. Laurie, from ultramarine ash mixed with lake,) is often used, combined with soft shades of blue, light green, yellow, and pink shading to purple. More positive colours, such as vermilion, are introduced in small touches for emphasis. Gold is used for details in the pictures, such as haloes and censers, and occasionally for the whole of an underdress, as well as for the bars and some of the leaves of the borders.

The softness of the colouring was probably partly due to the imperfect processes of refining and washing the pigments, which made it impossible to obtain pure and brilliant tones, but the taste used in their combination may be put to the credit of the early illuminators.

The tradition of colouring thus established continued for some time. The Grimbald Gospels (Brit. Mus. Add. 34890), of the early 11th century, produced at Winchester, shew a rather brighter and heavier scheme of colouring, but one which is harmonious and not too glaring: the effect of the more vivid colours is toned down by the use of neutral shades such as grey and buff.

It is in the later work of the School, such as a copy of the Gospels in Paris (Bibl. Nat. lat. 14782), that we see the crudeness into which the style could degenerate in the hands of an illuminator who was nothing but a careful workman, and had no natural sense of colour. He delights to put vermilion side by side with various shades of crimson, and to combine brilliant cobalt blue with heavy greens and purples. It needs the contrast of a manuscript such as this to bring out the extent to which taste and artifice went to the production of the apparently artless colouring of the school at its prime.

ICONOGRAPHY

THERE had been no tradition in England up to now to guide the illuminator in the way he should portray scenes from Bible history. Celtic and Northern English artists had hardly ever ventured further in their figure subjects than Evangelist pictures or an occasional Crucifixion, nor had the artists of the 8th and 9th centuries in southern England broken much fresh ground. But the Winchester artists now included in their manuscripts numerous scenes from the life of Christ, especially those connected with his Nativity and Passion, as well as a number of other subjects. It was natural, therefore, that in the portrayal of these scenes, the English illuminators should turn for ideas to the representations nearest to their own times, namely, to Carolingian MSS. of the 9th and early 10th centuries.

The iconography in Winchester manuscripts, as in Carolingian, is of a mixed type, borrowing largely from Eastern sources. These are principally Syrian, but occasionally Hellenistic traits occur which must have come by way of Alexandria and Rome. In two pictures in the Benedictional, Christ is beardless, according to the early Roman tradition; in all the others he is bearded. Veiled *Plate 19* hands are frequent as a sign of respect, e. g. the angels in the Baptism. In the same picture, it has been pointed out by Warner that the ringlike object in the beak of the dove represents the oil-vessel used for anointing, a further example of the hieratic type of art from which it is ultimately descended. The river-god of Jordan, with his pot, survives here from Hellenistic art, as he does even sometimes as late as the 12th century in France, but hardly ever after this period in England. But the water flows in a mound, a tradition which is taken from early Syrian manuscripts, and survives right through the 12th and 13th centuries for this scene, even when other pictures in the same MS. represent water in a perfectly normal manner.

Plate 20 The Entry into Jerusalem, except for the beardless Christ, has already taken the form which continues with little alteration throughout the Middle Ages and is, as Mâle has shewn, of Hellenistic origin. Christ, astride the ass, rides from left to right into the city, followed by his disciples on foot, (in this case bearing palms, and not their particular emblems). There is the usual carelessness about relative size, and the spectators spreading garments and cutting down lotus-like palm-branches are proportioned to the architecture, but not to the main group of figures.

The Ascension scene is probably the only one in an English manuscript in which the Hellenistic treatment of the subject is shewn. Christ is represented side-face in a mandorla, as though climbing up to reach the hand of God in the clouds; below, the Apostles, grouped on each side of the Virgin, point up in wonder at the miracle. The same type of Ascension picture appears in an initial in the Sacramentary of Drogon, a Metz MS. whose style may also have served as a model to the Winchester artists. In the Missal of Robert of Jumièges, and henceforth in all English manuscripts, the scene is represented with only the feet, or lower portion of the legs of Christ visible as he ascends through the clouds; there is no hand of God, nor mandorla, nor, in most cases, are there any attendant angels. In French manuscripts more variety is shewn in the portrayal of this subject. *Plate 21*

SUBJECTS FOR DECORATION

COPIES of the Gospels in Anglo-Saxon illumination usually have canon-tables, which are decorated with arches and columns in body-colours and gold, in which the Winchester type of foliage is introduced, often incongruously taking the place of bases and capitals. Figures of Christ blessing, or of saints, are sometimes introduced in the spandrils. In Harl. 76, a manuscript in which little but the canon-tables is left, the saints are of forbidding aspect, and hold their palms like birch-rods: the designs are effective rather than beautiful, and the workmanship is not nearly so careful as it had been in Celtic times. *Plate 23*

The double pages at the beginning of each Gospel are usually both decorated with Winchester borders, one containing an Evangelist picture, and the other the first words of the Gospel, the principal initial in which is more or less elaborately ornamented with foliage and animals' heads. These form the only illuminations of the book, in most cases; but the Gospels at Trinity Coll. Cambridge and at Boulogne have also full-page pictures of Christ in Glory, and the latter manuscript contains a page representing the genealogy of Christ, in which the figures are arranged in rows, the Jesse tree not yet having made its appearance.

Plate 24 The calendars of saints' days in the psalters and other service-books are sometimes decorated with drawings of the signs of the Zodiac. In this type of book, the Crucifixion and Christ in Glory are favourite subjects for full-page miniatures. David is frequently introduced into the design of the first, or Beatus, page of the Psalms, and occasionally he is shewn, as in the Canterbury Psalter, playing his harp and surrounded by musicians, to represent Asaph and his other fellow-psalmists; in one case, a juggler is introduced (Tib. C vi). The subject of David and the musicians is borrowed from Carolingian art, and soon became a commonplace of English illumination.

A few psalters are prefixed by a longer series of full-page illuminations: one in the British Museum (Tib. C vi) contains two scenes from the Creation, three from the life of David, one of the Temptation of Christ, and ten of the Passion. In the Benedictional of St. Aethelwold the repertory of subjects is still further enlarged, to include a number of Nativity scenes, several scenes from the lives of Bible saints, such as the birth of St. John the Baptist and the stoning of St. Stephen, and figures of other saints, St. Swithun, St. Aetheldreda etc.

The choice of subjects in Anglo-Saxon manuscripts shews that the English artists were interested principally in straightforward representation of Bible scenes, and not so much in the liturgical aspect of religious teaching. Symbolical subjects such as the Adoration of the Lamb or the Fountain of Life are frequent in Carolingian manuscripts, but do not occur in Anglo-Saxon. On the other hand, subjects such as St. Michael slaying the dragon, the *Harrowing of Hell* (Christ's descent into Limbo) and the Last Judgement, appealed to the English monks and ecclesiastics, as teaching the practical lessons of struggle against sin and conquest through faith in Christ, which they were anxious to bring home to their flocks by visible demonstration.

Dedicatory pictures, which are frequent in Carolingian and Ottonian manuscripts, are very rare in England: in fact they do not occur at all in the Continental form of enthroned portraits of rulers. Kings are occasionally represented, but only in the guise of worshippers — Edgar is shewn offering to Christ a charter for an abbey (Vesp. A. viii) and Cnut an altar-cross (Stowe

944). Perhaps this shews that art was not so dependent in England on the patronage of rulers as it was on the Continent.

Before going on to discuss the outline drawing which is so important a feature of Anglo-Saxon illumination, an early 11th century copy of the Gospels may be mentioned, which is particularly interesting for its historical associations, and represents a style of work parallel to that of Winchester, although probably not actually belonging to that school. This is the Gospel-book of St. Margaret (Bodleian Lat. liturg. 5). It is a small volume decorated with pictures of the Evangelists which are similar in their method of drawing, as well as in their setting and accessories, to the figures in Winchester manuscripts, but are washed in with transparent colours in soft, bright shades on a plain background. The absence of the Winchester border, which is replaced by plain bands of gold and colours, suggests that it may have originated at some other English centre of production, and been modelled directly on manuscripts of the Rheims school. *Plate 26a*

The book has an especial historical interest as having belonged to St. Margaret, the wife of King Malcolm of Scotland. Her confessor, in his account of her life, describes this book, and says that she had a particular attachment for it, more than for any of the others which she usually read. He also relates how on a journey it fell into a river, but when it was recovered some hours later, the writing and the decoration were absolutely uninjured except for a slight mark of damp on part of the outer leaves. This is recorded as a miracle, but at any rate it is again a tribute to the excellence of the materials employed by the illuminators. The gold in this manuscript is of a granulated, reddish type, not leaf-gold as in most Anglo-Saxon manuscripts.

OUTLINE DRAWING

THE HIGHLY coloured and elaborate form of figure painting which is exemplified in the Benedictional of St. Aethelwold and its companion manuscript was practically confined to Winchester, and to a few specially important manuscripts from that city, and it is the sketchy drawing of figure subjects in outline only, or in outline reinforced with narrow bands of colour, which is the more characteristic type of Anglo-Saxon illumination, or rather manuscript illustration, for it can hardly be termed illumination in the strict sense.

Even at Winchester a number of lesser manuscripts were decorated with such drawings. The very first existing Winchester manuscript, the Charter of Edgar (Brit. Mus. Vesp. A viii) is a sort of compromise between the two types of work, for its single miniature is an outline drawing lightly filled in with washes of transparent colours, and with gold, but without any shading, on a background stained light purple. Another manuscript of the 10th century from Winchester, a Psalter (Brit. Mus. Harley 2904) produced only a little later than the Benedictional, has a drawing of the Crucifixion, often reproduced, (see E. M. Thompson, *Illuminated Manuscripts,* Pl. 6) in which the outline is very slightly emphasized by bands of blue and buff.

In the early 11th century, two manuscripts with pictures in outline touched with colour were produced at Newminster. One of these, the Register of Newminster (Brit. Mus. Stowe 944) has a drawing of Cnut and his queen presenting a cross for the Abbey, and also a lively double-page drawing of the Last Judgement (see J. A. Herbert *Illuminated Manuscripts,* Pl. 13). The other *Plate 26b* is a tiny book of the Offices of the Holy Cross, (Brit. Mus. Titus D xxvii). It contains two pictures: one represents God the Father, the Son and the Virgin all seated in a row on a rainbow, the dove of the Holy Spirit being perched on the Virgin's head, a curious and original treatment of the subject; the other is a crucifixion which, although slight, is one of the most skilful of the school. The attendant figures of Mary and St. John are conventional types, but the body of Christ shews sincere drawing based on observation, and the face is also cleverly indicated and expressive. The impersonations of Sol and Luna above are interesting relics of antiquity; a sun and moon face are usual adjuncts of this scene right through the Middle Ages, and may be found even in the High Renaissance, (as in Raphael's Crucifixion in the Mond Collection, National Gallery).

It is interesting that not until the end of the period was outline drawing at Newminster used in combination with a coloured Winchester border. But in a Psalter (Arundel 60) decorated at the School about 1060, a poor tinted outline drawing of the Crucifixion does appear framed in a border of coloured foliage. This combination occurs in other MSS. not produced at Winchester, for the Winchester border very rapidly became a convention of Anglo-Saxon illumination all over the country. In a Psalter decorated at Peterborough (or Ely) *Plate 27* in the early 11th century, a miniature of Christ, illustrating the text: *The young lion and the dragon shalt thou tread nnder thy feet,* is executed in outline, the dress only being washed with light, transparent colours and edged with gold. It is enclosed in a fully coloured Winchester border of a comparatively poor design. This drawing illustrates the beginning of the decadence of the outline style, which during the 11th century became invaded by mannerisms and exaggerations, as indeed did the coloured style also, in the Missal of Robert of Jumièges.

A Psalter of unknown provenance (Brit. Mus. Tiberius C. vi) which dates probably from the early 11th century, shews the outline style at its most mannered. It is elaborately illustrated with twenty full-page drawings, (nineteen in outline slightly accented with colour, and one fully coloured), which are not without liveliness and decorative feeling, although very far removed from reality. The Harrowing of Hell shews the main elements of the subject as *Plate 28* they appear in Byzantine work such as the mosaic at Torcello — the Devil beneath Christ's feet, the broken gates of Hell, the staff in Christ's hand (in this case not a cross, but adorned with the pennant of victory), and the figures of Adam and Eve being drawn out of Hell by the arm — but there are also further modifications, which may possibly have arisen in England, especially the immense jaws to represent the mouth of Hell, which became very popular in England, and were used at a later time in other countries also. Their use in the stage setting of miracle plays would presumably be taken from the manuscripts.

THE UTRECHT PSALTER AND ITS INFLUENCE

THE EXAGGERATIONS of the style shewn in this manuscript are the final result of the very great influence which a foreign manuscript, the *Utrecht Psalter,* *see Plate 30* exercised on all the later work of the Winchester School, and in particular on the outline drawing of the period. In the picture described above, the bizarre curve of Christ's body might almost have been copied from a figure in the Utrecht Psalter (f. 8), and the thick folds and swirls of the drapery, which are emphasized by lines and blobs of colour, as well as the humping of Adam's back and the shape of his legs and ankles, are all ultimately derived from the Psalter. It is therefore worth while considering the manuscript in some detail.

Its origin and date have been much discussed, but according to the most general opinion it was written and illustrated in the 9th century in Northern France, and is a product of the Rheims School, although it probably also reflects the style of an earlier manuscript of Eastern origin. It was for a time in Sir Robert Cotton's collection in England, but is now preserved in the University Library at Utrecht.

In subject matter it differs entirely from the usual type of Western psalter; for it affords a full illustration of the text of each of the psalms, taking all their symbolism literally, and giving bodily form to each adventure of the soul related by the Psalmist. For instance, *I will wash my hands in innocency, O Lord, and so will I go to thine altar* is represented by a man washing his hands under a fountain, and then standing before an altar. A number of scenes are combined in one picture, as though they took place in the hills and valleys of a wide landscape.

The Utrecht Psalter cannot have been the only example known in England and France of this method of literal illustration, for some manuscripts, e. g. the *Hildesheim Psalter* produced at St. Albans in the 12th century, seem to have adopted it, not from this manuscript, but from other similar prototypes.

In style the Utrecht Psalter is no less distinctive than in matter, for its drawings are really sketches, which have the appearance of having been executed with great speed and lightness, and form a contrast to the usual laboured paintings of the Carolingian period. It is this quality which seems to have appealed to the English artists, and caused them to be so zealous in imitation. The Psalter was brought to England at some early date, at any rate before the 11th century, for in the early years of that century a close copy was made
Plate 30 from it at St. Augustine's Abbey at Canterbury (Brit. Mus. Harley 603). Another copy, the Eadwine Psalter, now at Trinity College, Cambridge, was made in the 12th century at Canterbury, probably, however, from a lost intermediary, and not from the original.

The style of the original Psalter may be judged from the earlier of these two copies, of which our plate shews the illustration to Ps. XII (XI in the mediaeval psalter). The Psalm speaks of the children of men, who *speak vanity every one with his neighbour,* and again of *silver tried in a furnace and purified seven times,* each of which provides a scene in the picture: *the wicked walk on every side (in circuitu impii ambulant),* appears to be represented by men walking in a circle holding on to a large dish and again turning a kind of turnstile: *now will I arise, saith the Lord* is illustrated by the figure of Christ walking out of his mandorla, and coming to help the people below.

In these sketchy outline drawings, as well as in their prototypes in the Utrecht Psalter itself, all the marked exaggerations occur which we see reproduced in the later Anglo-Saxon drawings — humped backs, necks stretched forward, shrugging gestures, thin legs dwindling to threadlike ankles. The lively action, also, the fluttering scarf-ends, and the manner of indicating rocky ground by a series of swirls, are frequent features of 11th century illumination in England.

In the Benedictional of St. Aethelwold there had been undoubted affinity with the Rheims School, but no trace of the influence of the Utrecht Psalter. Probably, therefore, it had not yet been brought to England. It may be that Godeman by his work aroused an interest in the Rheims style, which caused further examples of the work of that School to be brought to this country, the Utrecht Psalter among them.

PRUDENTIUS ILLUSTRATIONS

THE MAJORITY of Anglo-Saxon outline drawings are executed in brown ink, and are lightly touched with washes of colour. There are, however, some manuscripts in which coloured inks are used for the drawings, and there is no tinting with the brush at all. The 11th century copy of the Utrecht Psalter is of this type (although the Psalter itself had no colour); and this was the method generally used for the illustration of the *Psychomachia* of Prudentius. Many editions exist of this early poem on the conflict between the Virtues and Vices, with outline drawings interspersed in the text; they were produced both in France and Germany, as well as in England, between the 9th and 11th centuries. The Anglo-Saxon manuscripts shew distinct superiority to those done on the Continent at about the same time, which are, for the most part, drawn with a weak, continuous outline, and shew little energy, whereas the English ones have a quality of freshness and vigour which is especially suited to these narrative subjects.

The three main English examples surviving are:

1 a manuscript from Malmesbury (Corpus Christi Coll. Cambridge 23), executed about 1040-1050,

2 an early 11th century manuscript, possibly from Bury (Brit. Mus. Cleopatra C. viii),

3 a St. Alban's manuscript (Brit. Mus. Titus D. xvi), 1119-1146, in which the drawings are lightly tinted. This can hardly be classed as an Anglo-Saxon example, as it belongs to a later period.

Plates 31 & 32 The Cambridge copy, in spite of inaccuracies in the proportions and structure of the body, is the one which shews the greatest artistic merit. These drawings, in blue, brown, red and green ink, widely spaced and freely drawn in, with a firm, clear line, have something of the quality of the drawings on Greek vases. There is little of the nervous sketchiness of the Utrecht Psalter, although some of the conventions are seen here also, such as thin ankles, and swirling pen flourishes to represent the ground. But there is more than a hint of classicism in the handsome heads with their regular features, of a type quite different from the usual Winchester drawings.

Plate 33 The Bury manuscript is a typical example of the drawing of the time, and good of its kind, but compared with the Malmesbury version it seems mechanical and lacking in inspiration. The double lines indicating folds of drapery, and the zigzag edges, are repeated with irritating regularity, and the interest of the pictures depends on the vivacity of the incidents rather than on any artistic charm.

Plate 34a This is still more the case in the 12th century St. Albans manuscript, where the figures are definitely ugly, and there is no attempt at composition. It belongs really to the Romanesque period, when outline drawings were little thought of, and already, with its colour-shading, it has departed to some extent from the tradition of Prudentius illustrations.

The series of subjects is much the same in all the Prudentius manuscripts. First come a number of pictures taken from the life of Abraham, including scenes of his riding forth to battle against the kings, and of the meeting with Melchizedek. Then come the conflicts of the Virtues and Vices: Patience defends herself against the flaming darts of Anger; Pride rides forth on a horse without a bridle, meets Humility, and falls prostrate in an impossible attitude, with the horse on top; Avarice binds many victims and nourishes many vices, until she is herself bound by Generosity; Faith and the other virtues kill Discord; finally Wisdom sits enthroned in her temple, and Prudentius, the author, gives thanks to God.

For descriptive purposes there is certainly much to be said for the method of outline illustration as practised by the Anglo-Saxon artists. It has a vivacity and air of spontaneity which are lacking in finished and fully coloured illuminations, and which make it peculiarly suited to such a series of pictures as these, in which the purpose is more to teach a lesson than to decorate a page. The attention of the reader is carried on from one to another of these lively scenes.

It has been suggested that Canterbury was the centre in which the practice of figure drawing in outline first arose. Whether this was so or no, the production of these drawings was certainly widespread throughout the country from about 970 A. D. for the next hundred years: and they took such firm hold in England that they became a special feature of English illumination at several later periods also.

The rich outburst of illumination in England during the 10th and 11th centuries was not equalled by anything on the Continent at that period. English decorative work produces an effect of informal richness different from anything seen before; and the naïve vigour of the figure representation contrasts strongly with the heavy formality of contemporary Ottonian illumination in Germany, although both styles owed much to Carolingian prototypes. Later illumination in France and England far surpassed this early work in perfection of technique, elaboration of detail and depth of colouring, but there is a freshness and charm about the best of the Anglo-Saxon manuscripts, with their breadth and swiftness of treatment and their beauty of soft and varied colouring, which is missed in the more sophisticated products of a later time.

In conclusion it may be noted that the Anglo-Saxon style was not without its influence abroad. As early as 1000 A. D. an Anglo-Saxon artist, Odbertus, was employed at the Abbey of St. Bertin at St. Omer to decorate a Psalter, which is now at Boulogne; and two 11th century manuscripts, of Winchester style, now in the Earl of Leicester's collection at Holkham Hall (15 and 16) were taken by the Duchess Judith to Weingarten, where they were copied in the early 12th century, and are thought to have had an influence on the Reichenau School of illumination. (see A. Haseloff in *Deutsche Literaturzeitung*, 1905).

CHAPTER III

THE ROMANESQUE PERIOD

EFFECTS OF THE NORMAN CONQUEST

ALTHOUGH the Anglo-Saxon or Winchester type of illumination was carried on through the first half of the 11th century, this was not a period in which any new impulse was given to art. It was indeed a time of general decadence in the Church, as well as in the nation at large. The clergy were ignorant, the monks luxurious, and drunkenness and oppression were prevalent among the laity. Thus, this phase of art was already dying a natural death when the Norman Conquest came to hasten its disappearance.

William brought over Norman abbots to preside over English monasteries, and a new epoch was introduced in illumination, no less than in architecture. Winchester borders and outline drawing of the Anglo-Saxon type fell out of fashion, and by the early part of the 12th century, English manuscript painting developed on new lines, which may be called Romanesque. That is, they are parallel and in some ways analogous to the contemporary styles of art on the Continent, for instance, to miniature painting in Germany and to sculpture in France; although they have at the same time their own specifically national character.

DECORATIVE DESIGNS

IN THE decorative design of this period there is considerable similarity between English and Continental work. Elaborate decoration was applied to the principal initials of manuscripts, which became larger than they had ever been before. The characteristic form of 12th century initial is one filled with conventional leaf patterns of a well-defined type, very accurately drawn, and painted in brilliant colours on a gold background, the edges of the leaves being picked out with white lines and dots.

Plate 34b & c

Plates 35 & 48

The largest and most elaborate initials, such as the B's on the first or Beatus pages of Psalters, (so called from the first word of Ps. 1) are usually filled with a complicated pattern of spirals formed of stems from which a few leaf-forms spring, while animals and even human figures are frequently represented as if climbing in and out of the spirals. This type of design owes its origin to the Syrian, and ultimately Persian motive of the vine-scroll enclosing beasts and birds, and similar patterns are found in many German manuscripts of the same period. That this form of decoration was not confined to miniature painting is shewn by the Gloucester candlestick, in the Victoria & Albert Museum, (about 1110) which has a similar design with intertwined figures worked out in metal; it occurs also in a 12th century open-work panel in ivory in the same museum, found at St. Albans, and is found carved on capitals in French Romanesque churches.

In Psalters and other small books, historiated initials (i. e. initials containing figure-subjects) of a simple type are sometimes used, while in the huge Bibles of the time whole scenes on a large scale are introduced, sometimes two or three in a single initial. *Plate 36*

A considerable increase of technical skill over the preceding period is evident in these decorative designs. The lines are almost miraculously exact, the colours are applied thickly and evenly, and great care is shown in the laying of the gold-leaf, a raised foundation being used, formed of gesso tinted with red ochre. On the other hand, there is not much originality in the designs, which are repeated with only slight variations.

FIGURE-PAINTING

FIGURE painting in English 12th century manuscripts is characterised by a complete neglect of naturalism, and an exaltation of decorative values. The filling of a space with harmonious and pleasing lines is considered sufficient excuse for any impossible elongation or contortion of limbs. The results are at first sight grotesque to the modern eye, and yet they are not without an aesthetic charm of a highly rarefied nature when the hand of an artist is at work, though they become absolutely repellent in the hand of a mere craftsman.

Rhythm is a quality aimed at and achieved in the best work of the period. The artist misrepresents nature not so much through ignorance, as through a contempt for mere literal accuracy. In nude figures he shews, indeed, a considerable interest in anatomy, but he reduces the bones and muscles to a decorative pattern. Solidity and form mean little to him, and although fine modelling is used on faces, the definition of other surfaces is usually effected by lines rather than by tone.

Certain of these qualities of English 12th century work, especially its preoccupation with decorative pattern and its aloofness from real life, may be traced to the fresh current of Eastern influence which, during the Romanesque period, made itself felt in all the representative arts of the West, and whose diffusion in England was no doubt hastened by the First Crusade of 1095. This new influence was the reflection of the Byzantine art, (properly so called, in that its centre was Byzantium, and no longer Antioch or Alexandria), which had flourished from the 9th to the 11th centuries, during the *Second Golden Age* of the Eastern Empire.

But although the hieratic and symbolical nature of Byzantine art was to some extent reflected in these figure representations, English art never came so completely under Byzantine domination as did, for instance, German art of the 12th century. There is wide variety among the English manuscripts; some are closely copied from Byzantine models, others shew a strong admixture of the naïve dramatic sense which was fostered during this century by the growth of the religious drama; while yet others betray a love of grotesqe realism, which became more and more, as time went on, a characteristic of English artists, and which in this century accords strangely with the abstract and symbolical art on which it is grafted.

The nearest analogy to the style of figure painting in England is perhaps to be found in French Romanesque sculpture. There is considerable affinity
Plates 36 & 37 between such miniatures as those in the Winchester Bible or the Lambeth
Plates 39 & 40 Bible and the reliefs at Vézelay, Autun and Moissac, (reproduced in Michel, Vol. 1, Pt. 2) although there can probably be no question of cross-influences. But while in French sculpture the contortion of the elongated figures produces an angular effect, in England an elegant swaying line seems to be the aim of the artist. Curiously enough, the agitated and closely pleated drapery, which was such a feature of Anglo-Saxon art, occurs again in these French reliefs, while in English painting it has given way to a scheme of drapery in which the principle of the Byzantine swirl has been extended until the whole body is mapped out in a series of more or less oval shapes outlined and connected by a few folds. Usually the effect produced is of thin stuffs clinging closely
Plate 43 to the body, but the scheme is sometimes applied simply as a pattern where

the folds are hanging loose, and the design is even on occasion emphasized by the introduction of a little leaf-form in the middle of each swirl. The edges *Plate 39* of drapery, although they do not flutter wildly, are often caught up in an arbitrary way, so as to form a more varied and agreeable line.

The linear quality of 12th century illumination is further emphasized by the fact that a much stronger outline is used than was ever the case in Anglo-Saxon work. There is no trace of sketchiness or informality, but the lines are drawn with a firm and even stroke.

At the same time, there is a great increase in the brilliancy of the colours used, due, no doubt, to improved methods of preparation. The mediaeval artist aimed at this quality of brilliance above all things, but his haphazard combination of bright colours does not always appeal to the modern aesthetic sense, especially when they are applied on the comparatively large scale of the illumination of this period; and the effect, compared with the softer tints of Irish and Anglo-Saxon manuscripts, is often garish. In the choice of colouring little regard was shewn for reality, and the artist was content to paint horses blue and men's hair green if it suited his decorative purpose.

The backgrounds of figure subjects are usually of plain gold, frequently raised and highly burnished; at no other period is gold used to cover such large surfaces. In the latter part of the century a panelled type of background *Plate 59* is frequently used, in which a broad margin of some plain colour surrounds a central panel of gold, or vice-versa. Full-page miniatures are almost always framed in a straight border decorated with conventional patterns of geometrical or leaf designs in different shades of one colour picked out with white. These shaded patterns became a part of the stock in trade of the illuminator.

THE SECOND WINCHESTER SCHOOL

THE SWAYING figures and schematised drapery which have been described above are particularly characteristic of the new school of painting which had arisen at the Cathedral Priory of St. Swithun at Winchester early in the 12th century. Here the new ideas were better assimilated than elsewhere, and a more coherent and original style was formed.

Although the outline drawing of the first School, and the illumination of the second School of Winchester are quite distinct in their style, and do not merge into each other, there is an interesting example of enamelled metalwork, possibly produced at the same Cathedral Priory, which may be mentioned here, because it combines some of the characteristics of each of the styles, and seems to represent a transitional stage, of which there are no examples in the manuscripts. This is the *Masters plaque* at the Victoria and Albert Museum, representing the Last Judgment (see article by H. F. Mitchell in the *Burlington Magazine*, Oct. 1925). Although it has some of the characteristics of the Romanesque painters of the Winchester Bible, especially the *mapped-out* drapery which appears to cling to the limbs, it also has much of the fluttering and agitation of the earlier, Anglo-Saxon period, and the angels with their heads awkwardly turned up are reminiscent of the outline drawings of the first Winchester School. Mr. Mitchell suggests a date for this plaque in the middle of the 12th century, when the Romanesque style was at its height. If it were a manuscript, it would seem to belong to an earlier period, quite at the beginning of the century, and to form a link between the two schools. Possibly, however, this is another case in which other forms of art followed in the wake of illumination, and reached the same stage of development at a slightly later date.

Isolated manuscripts have come down to us which were produced during the 12th century at a number of different English monasteries, showing that illumination was practised in all parts of the country, but from no other place except Winchester is there sufficient work for us to be able to postulate a regular school of art, or a particular style. On the whole, illuminations from other centres, unless they are strongly under the influence of Winchester, tend to a more passive acceptance of Byzantine forms, although this is sometimes combined with a striving after vivacity which is more pronounced in English work than in any contemporary work produced on the Continent.

The most important products of the second Winchester school now existing are the large Bible, now bound in three volumes, which is still at Winchester in the Cathedral Library, and the Psalter in the British Museum, (Nero C. IV) which was made for Henry of Blois, Bishop of Winchester 1129-1171.

The Winchester Bible seems to have had its initials decorated at different periods during the 12th century. Many are of definitely Romanesque type, with brilliant colour, swaying line and *mapped-out* drapery, but they are not all by
Plate 36 the same hand. The initial before II Samuel is typical of the work of the

principal purely Romanesque artist. It contains three scenes connected with the death of Saul, which are full of vigour and swinging movement. The colours used are an extraordinarily bright blue, green, yellow, vermilion and purple. This artist is fond of introducing scroll designs with grapes into his initials, and he has a very strong decorative sense.

The scene of Joel preaching to an eager congregation seems to be by a *Plate 37*
pupil or imitator of the original artist, who reproduces the schematised drapery without the elegant swaying line, or the varied expressive drawing of the features which characterise his master. It is unique in having a diaper-patterned background, which only became general in the 13th century, so that it may perhaps be one of the later of the pictures, and its early style a deliberate archaism.

Besides the definitely Romanesque initials, there are a large number scattered in among the others which are in quite a different style, with clothes falling in simple folds, unaffected, if stiff, attitudes, and faces carefully modelled and shaded in grey. These are evidently transitional work of the period after 1170, and they have certain analogies, (e. g. the scowling eyebrows) with the wall and ceiling paintings in the Chapel of the Holy Sepulchre in the Cathedral. This chapel was built about 1175, but possibly not decorated until the early 13th century. The considerable use of purple, an unusual colour at this period, in the initials of the Bible, as well as in these paintings and the somewhat later ones on the ceiling of the Chapel of the Guardian Angels, is another evidence of the fact that the two types of painting at Winchester were intimately connected. Some of the initials in the Bible, both of the earlier and later styles, are left unfinished, merely drawn in in ink, or with gilding added, but no colour, presumably as the monk who was working on that particular initial chanced to be called away to different work or moved to some other monastery.

The Psalter of Henry of Blois is very rich in narrative pictures of a typi- *Plate 38*
cally Romanesque style. It opens with 36 full-page miniatures, including Old and New Testament scenes, a Jesse tree, and nine Last Judgment scenes, in which the mannerisms of the school are combined with a grotesque realism which is confined, however, to the bad men of the story. Besides these, two miniatures representing the death and assumption of the Virgin, of a different style, copied directly from a Byzantine model, have been introduced.

OTHER CENTRES OF ILLUMINATION

CLOSELY connected in style with the Winchester school are the great Lambeth Bible, and Bishop Pudsey's Bible at Durham, and, to a lesser degree, the Bury Bible at Corpus Christi Coll: Cambridge. The Cambridge MS. is known to have been illuminated at Bury St. Edmunds, and Pudsey's Bible at Durham. so that those two centres, at any rate, must have felt the influence of Winchester work.

Plates 39 & 40

Plates 41 & 42a

These huge Bibles had taken the place, during the 12th century, of the Gospels which had been so much in favour in earlier times. Each book of the Bible usually begins with a large historiated initial, or a full-page illustration including several scenes. The pictures are crude in colouring and often amusingly naïve in their attempt at dramatic presentation, but they shew careful workmanship, and at times a feeling for grace of line and balanced design.

Rhythmical line gives a special charm to some of the work in the Lambeth Bible. In the very decoratively treated Jesse tree, the tall, slim Virgin, in her deep blue dress, forms a strong axis to the design, and the long lines of her figure lead up to the medallion above containing the head of Christ; while all the swaying forms on either side draw the eye in towards these central figures. In his narrative subjects the vivacity of the artist is his most notable quality, and a scene such as the Sacrifice of Isaac is delightfully dramatic, and unintentionally humorous.

Plate 40

The Bury Bible has less of the contortions and liveliness which characterize the other examples. It shews remarkable technical skill in line drawing and the laying on of colours, and a good idea of composition and blending of tones.

Another example of work done at Bury St. Edmunds during the 12th century is the Life of St. Edmund, formerly belonging to Sir G. Holford. It is not at all similar to the Bible, but is illustrated in an ugly but vivacious narrative style; akin to it are a New Testament (Pembroke Coll:, Cambridge) done at the same monastery early in the century, and other lesser manuscripts.

Similar in some respects to the Bury Bible is the thoroughly Eastern and hieratic Psalter from Shaftesbury Abbey, (Lansdowne 383) which, with its long straight figures stiffly grouped, shews an art completely divorced from reality, and not redeemed by any grace of line or liveliness of action. It is most

Plate 42b

at home when representing, with a certain grim dignity, the beings of another world. M. Mâle has shewn the influence of the Anglo-French liturgical drama on the iconography of this MS. In style it has something in common with Spanish Romanesque painting, as seen in 12th century altar-frontals (see A. Mayer, *Geschichte der Spanischen Malerei*).

That York had become capable of producing first-rate illumination may be seen by the Glasgow Psalter (Hunterian U. 3. 2) dating from about 1170. It shews the hands of at least two artists: one of these copies in a very wooden *Plates 44 & 45*
manner his Byzantine model, while the other develops, out of the Winchester *Plate 43*
idiom, a distinctive and highly artistic style, remarkable in its strong feeling for symmetrical composition and formal decorative pattern. In spite of the doll-like faces, conventional attitudes and impossibly short arms, this artist succeeds in imparting a certain mystical feeling and a rare charm to his work.

The Benedictine Abbey of St. Albans, the premier Abbey of England, which was to become famous as an art centre in the next century, was already producing illumination, as well as goldsmith's work, in the 12th century. But the Hildesheim Psalter, the principal manuscript from that monastery, is more remarkable for richness of invention than for beauty of execution. The types of figures are extremely ugly, (like those in the life of St. Edmund mentioned above) with long upper lips, turned-down mouths, receding chins and staring eyes, and their attitudes are either quite stiff or weirdly contorted. The complicated symbolism of the initials in this manuscript is of interest for its analogies with the subjects of contemporary sculpture in various countries (see A. Goldschmidt. *Der Albanipsalter*); much of it can be traced to the bestiaries, and to literal psalm-illustrations, such as those of the Utrecht Psalter. The initials of another St. Albans MS., a copy of Rabanus Maurus in the British Museum, shew accomplished work, with varied and graceful designs in a few plain colours, of a type which occurs in several lesser books of the period and in the minor initials of the Winchester Bible.

An example of the work done at the lesser monastic centres is afforded by the Huntingfield Psalter, in Mr. Pierpont Morgan's collection (reproductions in Catalogue), which is thought to have been illuminated at Mendham Priory in Suffolk in the latter part of the century. It is prefaced by 90 scenes from the Old and New Testaments, and forms one of the most elaborate, if not the most artistic books of the period. The artist has tried, with only partial success, to put a new content of dramatic action into the outworn Byzantine forms, and his figures are awkward and childish. As usual in this century, however, the decorative subjects far surpass the narrative ones. There is, in particular, a very elaborate and beautiful Beatus page, containing a Jesse tree with 19 figures, as well as numerous other scenes.

A few manuscripts cannot be assigned to any particular centre. Among these, the *Psalter of St. Louis,* now at Leyden, deserves to be mentioned on account of the number of its illustrations. There are 23 pages of Old and New Testament scenes, before the Psalter proper; they are, however, only second-rate work, with a uniformly thick outline and streaky shading. They illustrate again the typically English combination of Byzantine conventions, (seen especially in the general treatment of the subjects and in the type of the Virgin and Child) with a naïve dramatic sense.

SUBJECT MATTER

PSALTERS and Bibles, as we have seen, form the bulk of the illuminated manuscripts of the 12th century, and of these the psalters are by far the more numerous. Besides these, there are a few editions of commentators, such as *Plates 46 & 48* Bede on the Apocalypse, and St. Jerome on Isaiah, and a certain number of *Plate 47b* lives of saints, illustrated with narrative pictures, such as the life of St. Cuthbert at University College Oxford. There are also the bestiaries, which form a class by themselves. Secular works hardly exist, although a copy of Terence at Oxford, (Bodl: Auct. F. 2. 13) contains some outline drawings of 12th century style.

In the Bibles, the initials which introduce each of the books usually contain illustrations of the stories which are found in the first chapter or chapters of the book: thus, Genesis has Creation scenes, almost invariably; Exodus the finding of Moses; I Samuel the story of Hannah; and so on. Moses receiving the Law comes before Leviticus, Numbers, or Deuteronomy, or, as in one of the Manerius Bibles, before all three. Where the book contains no story to be illustrated, as in the minor prophets and the epistles, the writer of the *Plate 42a* book is represented receiving inspiration, generally in the form of a scroll, from the hands of God, or preaching to the people.

Twelfth century psalters begin with a calendar, which is usually decorated with medallions representing the signs of the Zodiac and the occupations of the months; the latter had been used in continental MSS. since Carolingian times, and continued to be a regular feature in calendars throughout the mediaeval period. Between this and the Psalter proper, there are generally inserted some scenes from the Old or New Testament, or both. In these the life of Christ is almost always represented by stories from the Nativity and Passion, and only rarely do such scenes as the Marriage of Cana, the Raising of Lazarus, the Baptism or the Temptation, fill in the gap.

The Nativity scenes often include such minor episodes as the three Magi before Herod, or the angel appearing to them while they lie in bed, (e.g. Leyden Psalter). The Passion scenes are frequently concluded by a picture of Christ enthroned, and sometimes by a Last Judgment, introducing the Jaws of Hell.

During this century, the worship of the Virgin became more prevalent, and this is reflected in the introduction of representations of her death and assumption into certain of the psalters, e.g. the Glasgow Psalter, the Westminster Psalter, and the Winchester Cathedral Psalter. *Plate 48*

The Psalms themselves begin with a Beatus page, the design of which almost always includes a figure of David, often surrounded by musicians, or scenes from his life.

The Psalms are usually divided into ten sections, (see A. Goldschmidt. *Psalterillustration im Mittelalter*), the first of each beginning with a special historiated initial. The subjects illustrated in these are usually those which became established into a regular cycle in England and France in the 13th century: Ps. XXVI. *Dominus illuminatio mea* – David pointing to his eyes, or the anointing of David.

Ps. XXXVIII. (XXXIX in our version) *Dixi custodiam* – David pointing to his mouth.

LI. (LII) *Quid gloriaris* – David rebuking a man, or David and Goliath, or Doeg slaying the priests of Nob. *Plate 58 b*

LII. (LIII) *Salvum me fac* – David, up to his neck in water, praying to God; or Jonah scenes.

LXXX. (LXXXI) *Exultate Deo* – David striking bells with a hammer. *Plate 108*

XCVII. (XCVIII) *Cantate Domino* – Monks singing at a lectern. *Plate 116*

CI. (CII) *Domine exaudi* – David praying.

Plate III CIX. (CX) *Dixit Dominus Domino meo* — Christ enthroned beside the Father, the Dove hovering between them, and sometimes two kings beneath their feet.

The cycle is not however, invariable: for instance, the Canterbury Psalter has for Ps. LI a king, (David?) in a castle, with a woman on each side, (Wisdom and Folly?) outside the walls. There are also sometimes additional historiated initials to other Psalms, as in the Hildesheim Psalter above mentioned, where the subjects are either symbolical, or illustrate the text in a literal manner reminiscent of the Utrecht Psalter. The Glasgow Psalter has a varied collection of subjects, symbolical and humorous, ranging from the Church Triumphant and Christ trampling on the lion and dragon, to ass and goat musicians. The influence of the bestiaries is again clearly to be seen in many of these.

THE MONKS AS ILLUMINATORS

UP TO the 13th century, illumination was entirely in the hands of the monks. The monasteries vied with each other in securing manuscripts from abroad for their libraries. Thus, Aldhelm, when visiting Canterbury for his consecration in 705 A.D., hearing that ships had just arrived at Dover, hastened thither to see if they had brought any manuscripts, and was rewarded by being able to purchase a complete Bible.

Manuscripts would also be borrowed from other monasteries. Part of the librarian's duty was to keep a note of the books lent, the abbot's permission being necessary for the lending of the most precious volumes. From a nucleus of purchased or borrowed manuscripts the monks in the scriptorium would be set to make copies, and so the libraries rapidly grew.

Although in his early training a monk would no doubt copy exactly from the manuscript before him, those who had any skill or originality as artists would gradually improve upon their models, bringing their work more into line with the style prevalent at the time, and sometimes introducing original features of their own, which, if they were approved by the community, would become the general practice of that particular scriptorium. Thus the characteristic styles of different localities and periods were evolved.

Not only did the monks work for their own abbeys, but they also sometimes executed elaborate manuscripts for individual patrons, thus earning large sums of money for their community. Bishops and kings were frequent purchasers of books, either for their own use, or for presentation to abbeys in which they took a special interest.

The scriptorium in which the work was carried on was in early times a single large room, in which a number of monks worked together. Numerous miniatures shew the monk at work at his sloping desk, from which a curtain hangs. This curtain was thrown over the precious manuscript to protect it when not in use. The monk-artist is usually represented with a pen in his right hand, and a knife, (used for scraping the vellum smooth and for trimming his pen) in his left, and some pictures shew also the large closed cupboards, containing several shelves, in which the books were stored. *Plate 47 a*

After the Conquest, it became more usual for the monks, or at any rate, the more skilled among them, to be housed separately in little cells opening on to the cloisters of the monastery. That they appreciated this privilege is shewn by the words of Nicholas, the secretary of St. Bernard: *It must not be supposed that my little tenement is to be despised, for it is a place to be desired, and is pleasant to look upon and comfortable for retirement. It is filled with most choice and divine books, at the delightful view of which I feel contempt for the vanity of this world.*

A very human note is struck in some of the *colophons* in verse or prose, which were inserted at the end of manuscripts by the scribe and illuminator. Some express the hope of reward, or at least of praise, when the work is done, and one, written by an unwilling pupil, runs: *Finito libro frangamus ossa magistro!* (F. Madan, *Books in Manuscript*).

The individual names attached to certain of these early manuscripts probably refer to the monk who was both scribe and illuminator. In some cases the head of the scriptorium may have signed the work, although his subordinates helped to carry it out, for several hands may be traced in the same manuscript.

In the later phases of the art, specialisation set in. The scribe was only responsible for the actual writing, and he left spaces which were to be filled in later with decorated initials by one artist, and figure-subjects by yet another.

The life of these mediaeval artist-monks must have been a busy one. Not only the illumination, but also the craft work of the monastery was carried on by them, so that the same man might be employed for metal-work, wood-carving and fresco-painting, as well as for miniature painting. For instance, Master Hugo of Bury not only illuminated the Bury Bible, but also cast bronze doors and a bell, and carved the rood-screen, for St. Edmund's Church.

Even the decoration of manuscripts involved much more than the mere tracing of designs and laying on of colours. The vellum, the ink and the colours all had to be prepared, often by lengthy and elaborate processes. The following, for instance, is the gist of a mediaeval recipe for the making of ink, (Theophilus, *De diversis artibus,* translated by Hendrie): *Dry for two to four weeks the wood of thorn trees picked in April or May; peel the bark by beating the wood with mallets, and soak it in water for eight days; boil the water, adding bits of bark at intervals for a short time, and cook it down until it thickens; then add wine, and cook again. Place the liquid in pots in the sun, until the black ink purifies itself from the red dregs. Afterwards take small bags of parchment carefully sewn, and bladders, and, pouring in the pure ink, suspend them in the sun until all is quite dry. And when dry, take from it as much as you wish, and temper it with wine over the fire and, adding a little vitriol, write.*

As the recipes for many of the colours are equally complicated, and often require several hours of grinding in a pestle and mortar, it is clear that the scribes or their assistants must have spent much of their time over preliminary manual labour.

The following were the principal colours used, (see A. P. Laurie, *The Pigments and Mediums of the Old Masters*): ultramarine, made from lapis lazuli, (after the middle of the 13th century, copper carbonate was occasionally used as a substitute); vermilion, (sulphide of arsenic); greens made from malachite and other copper compounds; and various shades of lake, some made from the juice of the ivy and some, apparently, from dyes imported from abroad. Ochres were also sometimes used, and a grey, made from ultramarine ash, appears from the 13th century onwards. In the Irish manuscripts, Tyrian purple made from a local species of murex was used instead of lake.

The gold-leaf was applied before the colours, so that the latter might not be injured in the processes of gilding.

CHAPTER IV

BESTIARIES

THE symbolic element plays a very large part in mediaeval illumination, as it did in the whole outlook of the mediaeval mind. Many of the liturgical books have, besides their historical pictures, others which represent such themes as the tree of virtues and the tree of vices, the mirror of theology, or the six-winged cherub, each feather of whose wings is named to represent some virtue or precept.

There is, besides, one series of manuscripts of an entirely symbolical nature, which cannot be overlooked in a discussion of English mediaeval art, on which they left a very considerable mark. These are the bestiaries, or collections of moralised stories of animals, of which numerous English copies have come down to us dating from the 12th century, and a few from the 13th and 14th.

The early history of the bestiary is obscure, both as regards text and illustrations. But the idea apparently came originally, with so much of mediaeval symbolism, from the Early Christian gnostics, who drew on classical myth and fable for stories of animals, real or imaginary, to which they could apply their favourite method of allegorical interpretation. Some of the Early Fathers, especially those of Alexandria, developed the idea in their commentaries, borrowing their material from Aristotle, Pliny, Aelian and others, and making each mythical attribute of an animal illustrate some doctrine of the Church.

In course of time these animal allegories became generally current, and accepted without question among the common people, so that the phoenix and the unicorn were taken as much for granted as the wolf and the dog. The allegories were popularly attributed to *Physiologus* (i.e. the naturalist): some time in the early Middle Ages they were collected into a volume which became known as the Bestiary, copies of which, both plain and illustrated, found their way into most of the countries of Europe. Metrical versions of the book were also current in Italy, France and England.

The illustration of bestiaries has not been traced back beyond the 10th century; to this date belongs a manuscript in Brussels containing outline drawings which have little artistic merit, but shew a certain Classical element in the figures. It may be that the illustrations as well as the text, first took form in Alexandria in Hellenistic times, but this is only conjecture. The earliest existing Eastern MS. of the Physiologus with illustrations is one in Smyrna dating from about 1100 (see O. M. Dalton, *East Christian Art*).

The general treatment of the subjects and the types of the animals have become more or less fixed and traditional by the time we reach the main body of illuminated bestiaries which date from the 12th and following centuries, but their style varies according to the country and the period in which they were produced.

Some of the animals bear such curious forms that it is a problem how they could have originated. The crocodile, for instance, is often represented as a sort of red deer, with a dragon's head, bird's feet, and saw-teeth like a fish's fin, right along its spine and down its tail (see reproduction in Catalogue of Pierpont Morgan Collection). On the other hand the description written below, although vague, bears some resemblance to reality, and might have been taken from a traveller's account. It describes a four-footed animal with a hard skin, sharp nails and teeth, and so on. Where it falls short, the artist has filled the gap with his imagination, with startling results.

The pictures in bestiaries are dotted about in the text, and generally enclosed in simple borders. Sometimes a whole page is devoted to a series of scenes from the life of one animal; for instance, the lion is usually the first beast represented, and is shewn bringing its cubs to life by breathing on them, erasing its tracks with its tail, trembling before a white cock, and so on. *Plate 49a* Frequently a series of scenes representing the different days of creation, with the naming of the animals, forms a preface to the main matter of the book.

The illustrated bestiaries vary very considerably in artistic merit. The majority are crudely coloured, with no regard for nature: a horse may be painted red and an elephant green, and it is not even unknown for a man to be represented with a blue face. This arbitrary colouring is, of course, common to other types of 12th century manuscripts. But while many are the work of unskilled and clumsy artists, a number shew good decorative designs and careful line work. And there are a few which are of really high merit, and will bear comparison with any of the other illuminated manuscripts of their day.

Among the bestiaries illuminated in England there are three in which the pictures are of especial excellence. They are:

1 a late 12th century version in the Bodleian Library at Oxford (Ashmole 1511).
2 The Worksop Bestiary, illuminated about 1170 at Radford Priory, near Worksop, and now in Mr. Pierpont Morgan's Collection in New York.
3 a 14th century bestiary from Peterborough, now at Corpus Christi College, Cambridge, bound up with a psalter of the same date and origin.

The Oxford bestiary is particularly noticeable for its love of symmetrical pattern, as for instance, in the beautiful design of the Perindens tree and dragons. The Creation scenes with which it is prefaced are very Bysantine in type, with their tall, thin and dignified figures, the folds of the drapery being finely shaded, and slightly touched with white in the high lights. The rest of the figure subjects are of the usual 12th century style, with ugly faces and animated, though awkward action. The workmanship throughout is exceptionally fine, and is quite equal to that of the best psalters of the day. The borders to the pictures are filled with shaded patterns, and many of the backgrounds are of plain gold, raised and highly burnished, but some have tooled designs, and a few shew the coloured diaper patterns which were in general use in the next century. The small red and blue initials decorated with pen flourishes also shew that the work must have been produced late in the century. Its origin is not known, but it must certainly have come from an important centre of illumination. A pattern of groups of three white dots occurs often on the draperies, and this might perhaps point to St Albans, where that seems to have been a favourite design. *Plates 49 & 50*

The Worksop Bestiary looks, and probably is, a little earlier than the Oxford manuscript. The backgrounds of its rectangular or circular pictures are of the panelled variety, having a broad coloured band, often decorated with dots or rings, round a gold centre. With its brilliant and arbitrary colouring, and its thick outlines, it is a fine specimen of the rich and careful illumination, on a large scale, which is characteristic of the 12th century as a whole.

Besides these two 12th century bestiaries, there are a number of others of the same period in the British Museum, three of which are of good, if not superfine workmanship. These are:

1 Harley 4751, a fully-illustrated and brightly coloured example dating from the end of the century. *Plate 51a*

Plate 52 2 Royal 12 c. xix, which is similar in style to the Worksop Bestiary and of about the same date, but inferior to it in execution.

Plate 53 3 Royal 12 F. xiii, which contains an exceptional number of scenes, including such rare ones as the raising of the fallen elephant, as well as a number of birds, and stories connected with them, but is of clumsy workmanship.

Plate 51 b Another, Harley 3244, among a number of rather primitive drawings washed with transparent colours, has a few good designs, such as that of the phoenix.

Plate 54 Thirteenth century English bestiaries are rare. A manuscript in the University Library at Cambridge (Ii.4.26), contains good outline drawings, a few of which have been roughly coloured. It shews an accomplished use of line, and is probably a work of the school of Matthew Paris at St. Albans in the middle of the century. It contains a number of effective symmetrical designs, one of which, the Peridexion tree, appears to be copied from the Oxford Bestiary.

There is another 13th century example at Trinity College, Cambridge, which is probably English, and which contains 106 pictures on a very small scale.

Plate 55 Still less frequent are copies dating from the 14th century. The Peterborough bestiary mentioned above is, however, a magnificent example of that period. It has initials and partial borders of the East Anglian style, as well as numerous pictures of animals dotted about in the text. These are very small and daintily finished, and form a contrast to the relatively rough and crude illustrations of the 12th century bestiaries, but they are not very much more true to life than were these. The crocodile here is more like a large shaggy dog than anything else: it is preparing to swallow a man, the story being that it swallows men whole and afterwards disgorges them, thus typifying the Resurrection. At the bottom of the page the crafty fox is depicted. He is supposed, when hungry, to feign death, smearing himself with red mud to imitate blood: then, when the crows fly down to peck at him, he catches and eats them. He is a picture of the Devil.

Plate 49 b Among the other stories illustrated in bestiaries are: The unicorn. It can only be caught be means of a stratagem. If a maiden is set to sit in the wood where it lives, it will run and rest its head in her lap, and thus the huntsmen can catch it. This is interpreted as an allegory of Christ, who was born of a pure virgin.

The perindens or peridexion tree. In the branches of this tree, or under its shadow, doves are safe from the attacks of dragons. This typifies the Church, or God the Father, the shadow being God the Son. *Plate 50*

The caladrius. This pure white bird appears to sick men, and if they are to recover, it will look towards them, but if they are to die it will turn its face away. So Christ looked away from the Jews and towards the Gentiles. *Plate 51a*

The phoenix. At the end of 500 years, this beautiful bird sets fire to its nest, and three days later rises from it again with renewed youth, as Christ did from the grave. *Plate 51b*

The elephant. The Indians in their battles fight from a castle which is carried on an elephant's back: when an elephant falls, it can only be raised by the trunk of another, which is inserted under its back. It typifies Adam, who fell, and could only be raised by Christ. *Plate 53*

The whale. Sailors take the back of the whale for an island, and anchor their ship to it. Then suddenly it plunges, and takes them to the bottom of the sea. Thus the Devil drags those who trust in him down to Hell. *Plate 54*

The salamander. The salamander is not burned by fire. It has a strong poison in its mouth, and when it climbs a tree, it poisons all the fruit, so that whoever eats of it dies. The salamander stands for the Christian, who passes unscathed through the fires of passion. *Plate 52a*

The manticora, with the body of a lion and the head of a man, is one of the numerous fabulous monsters which are described in the bestiaries, and found their way from them into the decoration of manuscripts. Others are the centaur or sagittarius, the syren, and the serra, which has the body of a lion and the tail of a fish. (for stories of these and other animals see G. C. Druce in *Journal of the Brit. Archaeol. Association* 1919 and 1920). *Plate 52b*

The principal importance of the bestiaries for the history of art lies in the fact that they were one of the most fertile sources of subjects for sculpture and painting, in England and elsewhere, from the 12th century onwards throughout the mediaeval period. They gave the initial ideas for the grotesque monsters which came more and more into favour in the decoration of English manuscripts, their popularity culminating in the East Anglian work of the 14th century.

Besides this they provided much material for church sculpture. The animal subjects which seem at first sight so incongruous as carvings on choirstalls or reliefs round church doors, are really borrowed from these moral books, and had for the mediaeval mind a symbolical significance. Single figures of animals or small scenes were peculiarly suited for filling circumscribed spaces, and thus it came that they were especially popular as a decoration for the misereres, or folding choir seats of the 14th and 15th centuries. For example, the fox is carved on a miserere in Chester Cathedral, the unicorn occurs at Chester, Ely and Lincoln, the elephant and castle at Beverley Minster and Gloucester Cathedral.

From the stories in the bestiaries we get an idea of the far-fetched symbolical and allegorical meanings which underlie so much of mediaeval art, since the subjects were always dictated by churchmen trained in the subtleties of mediaeval theology.

CHAPTER V

THE TRANSITION FROM ROMANESQUE TO GOTHIC

THE TRANSITION TO GOTHIC

THROUGHOUT the 12th century there was, no doubt, considerable interchange of artistic ideas between England and France. That this was not only receptive on the English side is shewn by the fact that some religious houses in France, e. g. the Priory of Ste. Barbe-en-Auge in Normandy, are known to have been in the habit of importing psalters which had been illuminated at their branch establishments in England (see L. Delisle, *Livres d'images*).

Towards the end of the century, from about 1170 onwards, a first wave of the Gothic movement which was already well established in France began to make itself felt in English illumination. But whereas in France the Gothic style developed quickly, under the great artistic impulsion of the cathedral building period, in England the transition from the Romanesque to the Gothic style was slow, extending over a period of some 50 years, and the inadequate equipment of the painters for their new tasks was at first painfully apparent.

In purely decorative work there was no great change before the end of the 12th century, although a few new features were introduced. The large initials continued to be decorated with the leaf and scrollwork patterns which had been in vogue through the century. But the smaller initials were sometimes coloured plain red or blue, and decorated with fine pen flourishes in the same colours. Patterns in coloured pen-work were also used to fill in the spaces left at the end of the lines. These pen-flourishes and line-endings became regular features of illumination in the next century. *Plate 56*

The diaper-patterned background, in blue, lake or other colours, also makes a tentative appearance towards the end of the 12th century, but it is only rarely used for miniatures, and a gold ground, either plain or decorated with incised designs, is still usual. The borders of miniatures continue to be formed of frames decorated with shaded patterns.

It is particularly in regard to the whole conception of figure representation that there is a break with the conceptions of the Romanesque period. Liveliness of action and decorative pattern had been the qualities aimed at so far; but now there is a sudden reaction in favour of simplicity and natural representation. People are shewn as far as possible in their true proportions, and with no exaggeration of posture or action. Lack of knowledge of the structure of the body betrays itself still in a certain awkwardness and woodenness, but there is a restful quality which had not been known in Anglo-Saxon or Romanesque figure-drawing. Draperies fall in simple and natural folds, instead of fluttering wildly, or clingly tightly to the body, and the shading is no longer effected by means of lines, but by soft gradations from colour to colour. This is especially noticeable in the treatment of the faces, which are modelled carefully, while the hair is represented in a natural manner, and not, as before, by conventional patterns. Colouring is chosen with regard to harmony and general effect, and is no longer garish, although some colours, especially the blue, have attained a greater depth and richness than ever before. On the other hand, linear design is somewhat neglected during this transitional period. The rhythmic pattern which characterised the Romanesque style has been discarded, and Gothic grace of line has not yet been achieved.

Plate 57 The style is seen clearly in the full-page miniatures of the Psalter from Westminster Abbey (Roy. 2.A.XXII); it is hard to believe that the Annunciation is but little later than the Pentecost in the Glasgow Psalter, or the pictures in the Lambeth Bible. Although the traditional way of representing the subject is still followed, the types of figures are much more human than before, and there is at times a certain restrained emotion in their expressions which does not appear in earlier work. This is still more noticeable in the Virgin and Child in the same manuscript (see B. M. Reproductions, Vol. 1); the whole setting is in the Byzantine tradition, and the Child is a small man, but the Virgin turns towards him with an altogether human expression of yearning tenderness. It has been suggested that the Psalter may be St. Albans work, but there is no definite clue to its origin.

The classical tinge which is noticeable in French Gothic sculpture had clearly had an influence on the type and modelling of the figures. The head of the Annunciation angel might be that of an Apollo, with its clustered curls and healthy roundness. There is nothing here of the diluted Eastern classicism of the Byzantine Empire, but rather a fresh life coming from Hellenistic or earlier models, whatever may have been the channels through which it found its way to England. At the same time, the heavy, even outlines give more than a suggestion of the technique of stained glass, which was already being made in England. The figures in some of the early 13th century glass at Chartres are of very much the same type as those in the Westminster Psalter, only a little more sophisticated. The illuminator may possibly have worked also in stained glass, for the artists often practised more than one craft, and he was probably in touch with the art work which was being carried on in the French Cathedrals.

A psalter in the British Museum (Harley 5102), very finely executed, has decorative initials of the usual 12th century style; but the figure-work in the historiated initials is without any exaggerated mannerisms, and pays some attention to proportion, and to the shading of faces and drapery. Grotesque monsters are now beginning to be used as decorative motives, under the influence of the bestiaries; and the initials are enclosed in square frames of blue or lake, picked out with white patterns. *Plates 34b & c, 35, 58b*

The illumination produced at Canterbury towards the end of the 12th century shews less of a break with the Romanesque tradition, but it is at the same time not uninfluenced by the new movement, as is only natural in the city which had been the first to welcome Gothic architecture to England. Something of the new Gothic influence in figure work may be seen in the Bibles signed by Manerius of Canterbury (Ste. Genevieve 8-10, Bibl. Nat. lat. 11534 and 8823). This is a case in which the monk whose name is given cannot have been the sole person employed on the books, but was probably responsible for the principal illustrations: in one manuscript he gives, besides his own name, the names of his parents and grandparents, all apparently English. The style of the principal miniatures is not comparable to first-rate work, such as that of the Westminster Psalter, but there is careful shading and restrained, harmonious colouring in the large historiated initials of these Bibles, and the figures are well proportioned, although often faultily drawn. Two special idionsyncracies are characteristic of the work of Manerius: a wearisome use of large scrolls in his compositions, whether they are appropriate to the subject represented or not (Moses giving the Law has five huge scrolls, Elkanah and his two wives have four scrolls between them), and a predilection for grotesque animals, particularly asps and other snaky creatures, borrowed from the bestiaries. *Plate 58a*

Plate 59 A life of St. Cuthbert (B. M. Add. 39943), illuminated at Durham at about the turn of the century, is in marked contrast to the earlier work of the same monastery, as exemplified in Pudsey's Bible (see Chap. 3), and shews that the new ideas had now spread to the North of England. Some half-erased wall-paintings in the Galilee of the Cathedral are similar in style, and might possibly have been executed by the same artist. The manuscript, which is small, contains a large number of fullpage miniatures, which are straightforward representations of scenes from the Saint's life, and although they are unpretentious, they are not without a certain simple dignity. Conventions such as the swirling ground are still used, but there is no artifice or exaggeration in the attitudes and gestures of the people represented, and their draperies fall in simple folds and give some effect of solidity. The colouring is natural and bright, but not crude, and the faces are carefully modelled. It may be noted that in some places the shiny upper surface of the paint has peeled off, shewing an unglazed solid underpainting; evidently the final coat of paint in this and most other 12th century MSS. was put on with some gummy medium, though a few MSS.,
Plate 48 such as the copy of St. Jerome's Commentary on Isaiah, now at Oxford, have a dull surface and chalky colouring, to which no final glaze has been added.

Outline drawing, which had held only a very minor place in English Romanesque illumination, began to come into favour again towards the end
Plate 60 of the century, as is proved by the very fine example, the life of St. Guthlac, probably from Croyland (now Crowland) Abbey, Lincolnshire, which is now in the British Museum (Harley Roll Y. 6). These 18 scenes, forming a series of circular medallions on a roll of vellum, are principally in outline, although some of the shadows are washed in with green or grey. They shew a new development in line-drawing, which is more akin to the 13th century work of St. Albans than to any of the outline drawings which had preceded them. The figures are still stiff, and tend to be elongated, and the eyes are staring, owing to the relative smallness of the pupils, as in most 12th century work, but the artist is aiming at natural representation with fair success. The sureness of his technique shews that the careful workmanship of the decorative designs of the period had prepared the way for a great advance in outline drawing. In some of the scenes, particularly those in which the Saint is carried off by the demons from the fens, the artist gives free rein to his imagination in the invention of grotesque details.

THIRTEENTH CENTURY

THE transitional period may be said to extend also over the first twenty years of the 13th century. This was not a fertile period, but produced a few notable manuscripts. Two books decorated at St. Albans early in the century, and now at Corpus College, Cambridge, (a glossed Psalter and glossed Gospels of St. Mark and St. John), have fine initials, shewing that the monks at that important Benedictine Abbey, were already beginning to deserve a reputation for their artistic work. It is interesting to note in this Psalter that the enterprise of these cultured artists is again shewn (as in the 12th century, in the Hildesheim Psalter), in the choice of an unusual series of subjects for the historiated initials.

The main problem of the early 13th century is presented by the Psalter of Queen Ingeborg (reproductions in D'Aumale, *Cabinet des Livres du Musée Condé à Chantilly*), a beautiful manuscript now at Chantilly, which was written for Ingeborg of Denmark, the wife of Philippe Auguste. It has been claimed by Warner and other authorities to be English, but is pronounced French by Delisle. The latter supports his opinion by pointing to the pure French, (not Anglo-Norman) language in which the titles of the pictures are written, as well as to the choice of saints in the Calendar, which, however, contains several English ones as well. Considering the known practice of importing psalters from England into France at this period, it seems not impossible that the psalter might have been decorated in England especially for this French queen, in honour of whom such feasts as the *Invention of St. Denis* would have been included in the calendar.

But it is perhaps more likely that it was written in France, the miniatures being copied by a French illuminator from an English manuscript. A group of definitely English manuscripts (Roy. 1. D. X., Arundel 157 and Lansdowne 420 *Plates 61 & 62*
in the British Museum, and Cod. lat. 835 in Munich), of about the same period, all have full page miniatures of the Life of Christ, which are so similar to each other and to those in the Psalter of Queen Ingeborg, that they seem to be derived from the same originals (see J. A. Herbert in *Walpole Soc. Annual,* 1914). It would appear, therefore, that they were all copied from some English psalter which is now lost.

The Chantilly manuscript is distinctly better work than any of the others in the group, although its style resembles theirs in general. The chief difference to be noticed is a more distinctly classical tinge of feeling, especially in the statuesque treatment of the voluminous folds of drapery, which recalls, though to a lesser extent, the sculptured group of the Visitation by the most classical of the sculptors who worked at Rheims. As we have seen, the classical note is not absent from English work of the transitional period, but it is likely to be more strongly marked in French illumination.

The figure drawing in the Psalter of Queen Ingeborg shews the stiffness and over-emphasis on modelling which are characteristic of the transitional period: the figures are tall and thin, the faces have a serious expression, the muscles of the neck are exaggerated, and each cheek has a conventional spot of red. All these features reappear in Roy. 1. D. X. and the best of the allied manuscripts in the British Museum, but the drawing of the faces is far superior in the French psalter, where the features are varied and expressive, while in the English manuscript they are all on a pattern, the brows evenly curved and the mouths straight. All the manuscripts of this group shew a new interest in the modelling of bodies and draperies by gradations of tones, instead of, as in the Romanesque period, by ink lines. The shading is, however, frequently streaky and exaggerated, and the structure of the body overemphasized.

Plate 61 The naïve outlook of the period is apparent in the way subjects are treated, Thus in the feast scene in Roy. 1. D. X., there is a pool, presumably meant to represent the tears in which the woman has bathed Christ's feet before wiping them with the hairs of her head. The foreshortening of objects on the table is treated in an altogether haphasard manner. The entry of Christ into Jerusalem is represented in the traditional way, although the usual boys picking palm-branches from the trees are not present here. The meek expression of the ass is both amusing and appropriate.

Plate 58c The careful finish of the decorated and historiated initials and line-endings in this manuscript, and the great richness of its colouring make it a very beautiful volume.

Plate 62 A page from the calendar shews the normal decoration for this portion of a psalter in the 12th and 13th centuries. Each page is headed by a KL in gold on a coloured background, more or less handsomely decorated. The names of the saints are entered in writing of various colours and occasionally of gold, and medallions on each page represent the appropriate sign of the Zodiac and an occupation suitable to the month. Thus in February a man is seen warming his feet at a fire, having first hung up his boots behind him. There was a regular fixed series of these occupations or labours of the months, which recur almost uniformly in French and English manuscripts, and also frequently in sculpture, as, for instance, on the West front of Amiens Cathedral.

The place of origin of the group of manuscripts we have been considering is not definitely known, but Roy. 1. D. X. has been conjecturally associated with Winchester or Oxford, Arundel 157 with Oxford, Lansdowne 420 with Chester, and the Munich manuscript with Gloucester. This would shew a very wide distribution of kindred work during the transitional period. Indeed, there is no definitely local style which can be distinguished between the years 1170 and 1220, whereas both in the earlier 12th century and again in the later 13th, the styles of the different monasteries and schools of art diverge considerably one from another. Apparently during this transitional period, the efforts of all illuminators were concentrated on getting rid of preconceived ideas and assimilating the new principles of directness and truth, so that no room was left for the airing of local or personal idiosyncrasies. It is this which gives to the painters of the period, for all their stiffness and lack of polish, a dignity and wholesomeness such as is found in the sincere beginnings of any new phase of art.

CHAPTER VI

THE GOTHIC PERIOD

THE broad distinction between the Romanesque and Gothic styles of illumination has been summed up by Vitzthum when he says: *Only in England was there an organic development from the Romanesque drawing style to Gothic painting.* It is indeed in the Gothic period that manuscript illumination for the first time becomes more interested in the problems of the painter than in those of the draughtsman, i. e. in the variety of colouring, the modelling of form and the rendering of reality, rather than in the evolution of flowing line and decorative pattern. But as England had had a more developed linear style in illumination during the Romanesque period than had any of the other European nations, so it is only natural that there should be a more pronounced linear quality about some of the best work in England, even in the 13th century, than there was in any French illumination of the same period.

It is becoming customary to speak of a *Channel School* of art in the 13th century, in the same way as the name *Rhine School* is given to the Flemish-German school of painting in the 15th century; this is perhaps the best way of expressing the essential unity and interdependence of art work, and particularly manuscript illumination, in Northern France and in England during this period.

The Gothic schools of art in France, such as the school which had been established by Abbot Suger at St. Denis about 1140, when he set to work to build the Abbey there, had produced not only architecture, but much work in sculpture, glass-painting and illumination, and their fame and influence were already spread far and wide. For instance, glass on the pattern of St. Denis had been put into Canterbury Cathedral in 1180.

The reign of Henry III (1216 to 1272) coincides with the great period of Gothic art in England. The King's visits to France aroused in him an enthusiasm for the Gothic style, and he sought to emulate his contemporary, St. Louis, in patronage of the arts. This helped to deplete his treasuries and cause discontent among his poorer subjects, but, at the same time, it undoubtedly did much to foster production and stimulate appreciation of architecture, sculpture and painting in all its forms throughout the country. This was especially the case through the gathering together at Westminster of a group of artists, both English and foreign, to work at the decoration of the new Abbey, which was begun in 1245. This produced what may be called the Court School of art, the first instance in England of a school of craftsmanship which was not wholly monastic.

But already, before the King was of age to have a personal influence on the trend of art, the intercourse between the two countries had led manuscript painting, which, owing to the easy interchange of products, was always quick to respond to outside influence, to reach the final stage in its development from Romanesque to Gothic. It may fairly be said that by 1220 the Gothic style of illumination was firmly established in England. It was not, however, uniform in its manifestations. For as in political and ecclesiastical matters there were throughout the reign two conflicting parties, the one national and the other in favour of the French connection, so in matters of art there seem to have been some centres of production where a more definitely national style was preserved and developed, while others fell entirely under foreign domination. Thus in manuscript painting, Salisbury and St. Albans, although undoubtedly influenced by France, both produced work of a marked individuality, and which is unmistakably English in the gravity and simplicity of its feeling and in its emphasis on beauty of line.

The Court School and the Abbeys of Canterbury and Rochester, which were under its influence, belonged naturally to the Anglo-French party. French influence is equally strong, and used with less discrimination, in the illumination produced at lesser centres, such as Peterborough, York and the monasteries of the Midlands. Much of the delicacy and charm of the French models is usually lost in this provincial work, while the English element is shewn in touches of realism and grotesque humour.

The principal schools of illumination will now be dealt with in turn, as well as some special types of manuscripts not connected with any particular school.

PETERBOROUGH

THE monastery at Peterborough seems to have had some special connection with St. Denis. Mâle has pointed out that some paintings of about 1160 which were formerly in the choir of Peterborough Cathedral, but are now known only by later copies of them in the Peterborough Psalter at Brussels (see Chap. 8), contained some unusual subjects which are also found in the stained glass at St. Denis, and it is likely that the English paintings were inspired by the French designs.

The style of manuscript illumination which was prevalent at Peterborough in the 13th century may be seen from two well-preserved psalters; the Psalter of Robert de Lindesey at the Society of Antiquaries (reproduction in Michel,
Plates 63 & 64 Vol. II pt. 1) and a psalter at the Fitzwilliam Museum at Cambridge (no. 12). A few leaves of a psalter, which are now bound up with the earlier manuscript Vespasian A i at the British Museum, also shew the same manner of painting, and must clearly emanate from the same source. There is considerable charm about the Peterborough work, great delicacy of execution and beauty of colour; undoubtedly the artists were among the most accomplished of their day, and it is a delight to turn over the pages of their richly decorated books. But it must be confessed that in depth of feeling and monumental quality they fall behind other work of the period, especially that of the Salisbury school. Even the most sublime figures, such as Christ enthroned, (who appears in all three MSS.,) have a doll-like quality which gives little impression of majesty; while depth of grief, as in the spectators of the Crucifixion, is represented by affected attitudes and conventional raising of the eyes. These attitudes are, of course, traditional, and would, with the exaggerated curve of Christ's body, be familiar to all students of the French ivory carvings and other work of the period. They appear again in a 13th century wall-painting on a pier in St. Alban's Abbey.

Altogether, we must conclude that there is something a little mechanical and derivative about the work of the Peterborough monks, in spite of its gay charm and exquisite finish. The psalter in the Soc. of Antiquaries, executed for Robert de Lindesey in 1220-22, was probably the prototype from which the others were copied and adapted. It only contains two full-page miniatures, Christ in Glory and the Crucifixion. They are heavier in colouring and depend less on fine gradation of line for their charm than do those of
Plate 64 the Fitzwilliam Psalter, which has been dated 1260-70. The Beatus page of the latter MS. is unusual and somewhat weak in design, with its B formed of stems and light conventional foliage; it is filled in with two scenes, above, Christ in Glory holding the cup, and below, crowned figures of Mercy and

Truth, a subject which occurred, as we saw, in the Jesse tree of the 13th century Bible at Lambeth.

It has been suggested that the school of Peterborough had considerable influence in France. Perhaps the action was mutual, and the style which, in Peterborough, was fed on the early Gothic work of St. Denis, in its turn inspired some of the band of painters who gathered in Paris to study and practise the art of illumination in the middle and later years of the 13th century.

WILLIAM DE BRAILES AND HIS WORK

SOME interesting recent discoveries have resulted in the emergence of a definite personality among all the anonymous artists who practised illumination in the 13th century. This is a certain monk called William de Brailes, who in several cases actually signed his work with a portrait of himself and his name written beside it. Unfortunately, it has not proved possible to decide definitely where he worked. London and the Midlands are among the suggestions which have been made. The MSS. which can be definitely assigned to him are four in number: a Book of Hours, belonging to Mr. Dyson Perrins; a psalter at New *Plate 65* Coll. Oxford; a smaller psalter belonging to Mr. Cockerell; and six pages of MS. discovered by the latter in America, and now in an English private collection. Besides these, a small Bible in Mr. Perrins' collection, (No. 5) has some initials which seem to be by the same hand, although possibly done before the artist's style reached its highest development.

W. de Brailes worked, apparently, in the period 1220-40, and his figures still have some of the awkwardness of gesture and roughness of shading which are characteristic of early Gothic work; at the same time, they shew great finish in the minute pen-work of faces, toes, and folds of drapery. If they lack the grace and fluidity which we associate with French Gothic illumination, and the faces are sometimes ugly and banal, they have the English liveliness, and are free from the affectation which so often spoils French work of the 13th century. The colours are light, much use being made of blue and an orange vermilion. Some initials are decorated with the 12th century type of scrollwork in which animals are intertwined; dragons are frequently introduced in the borders, as was often the case at this period, (cf. Bible of Robert de Bello, Plate 75). The grouping of the miniatures in medallions suggests a comparison with the medallion glass of Chartres and other French cathedrals, or with the *bibles moralisées* produced at this period in France, with the pictures in which the style of de Brailes' work has, indeed, a good deal in common. On the whole, the books of William de Brailes seem to be characteristic examples of work done at the period when contact with France had refined the technique of the English illuminators and not yet imparted mannerisms to their style. His work is not, however, comparable with that of the Peterborough School; his colour is not nearly so attractive, and although his figures are less sophisticated, they shew no greater depth of feeling. So that, if it were not for the interest aroused by the fact that his name is known, de Brailes' work would perhaps only deserve a passing mention, as bridging the gap between the Peterborough work of 1220 and the fully developed Gothic art of the latter half of the century, as it flourished in the schools of Salisbury and St. Albans and in the Court School.

SALISBURY

SALISBURY, by the middle of the century, must have become a notable centre of art work, for it produced about the year 1250 several manuscripts whose figure-paintings rank among the most beautiful miniatures ever executed in England. It is as though the mantle of Winchester had fallen upon the other great city of the south, whose Gothic cathedral began to rise in 1220 and was dedicated in 1258.

Plates 65b & 66 *Plates 67 & 68* The principal MSS. ascribed to this school are the Psalter at All Souls' Coll. Oxford; the Missal of Henry of Chichester, in the Rylands Library at Manchester; and the Psalter belonging to the Royal College of Physicians, London. The Rutland Psalter, an elaborately decorated book formerly at Reading Abbey, and now belonging to the Duke of Rutland, is also thought by Mr. Cockerell to have been produced by the same school during the third quarter of the century.

The All Souls' Psalter and the Missal are evidently by the same artist, and are closely related in style to the Psalter at the Roy. Coll. of Physicians, although superior to it in workmanship. The latter MS. is known to have been made for use at Wilton Abbey, near Salisbury. It is therefore probable that all three MSS. were produced at the workshops at Salisbury.

The All Souls' Psalter seems to have been written for a nun at Amesbury, whose kneeling figure appears in one of the miniatures. Four of these, each filling a page, and representing respectively the Annunciation, the Madonna and Child, the Crucifixion, and Christ enthroned, form a preface to the book. *Plate 66* The backgrounds are of tooled gold, and the colouring is varied and charming, although shades of blue and lake predominate, as was usual at this period. The line drawing is particularly fine, being both strong and delicate, without the heavy accentuation of outline which had marked the transitional period. In the historiated initials to the principal psalms, beautiful foliage work of the traditional type, with some interlacing of stems, is used, and white arabesques on a coloured ground fill in the spaces of the frame.

A comparison of the Crucifixion in this Psalter with that in the Fitzwilliam Psalter from Peterborough (Plate 63) will shew that similar attitudes in the spectators and an even greater regard for technical perfection are combined in the Salisbury example with a truly devotional and impressive rendering of the scene. The contrast between the two MSS. is particularly striking in the figure on the cross, for whereas the Peterborough artist is content with a gentle and almost pleasing treatment of the subject, in which the thinness of the arms and the blood upon the feet are the only painful touches, the artist of the All Souls' Psalter is relentless in his realism. The body no longer has the graceful French curve, but hangs erect, and its emaciated structure and bleeding wounds are painfully accentuated. The drawn face is a piece of sincere feeling, and makes other representations seem light and empty in comparison. In composition, too, this artist shews his superiority in the ease with which his figures fill their spaces, whereas in the Peterborough picture St. John is pressed into the same position as the Virgin with regard to the corner, making no allowance for the alteration of balance caused by the strong curve of the figure on the cross. Attention may be drawn, again, to the graceful lines of the censing angels in the medallions at the corners, and to the fine half-figure of God the Father above, (represented, curiously enough, as no older than the Son), holding the dove between his hands. Below is the symbolical figure of Adam rising from his grave, out of which the cross grows, and at the sides are figures representing the Synagogue and the Church, or the Old and New Dispensations; the latter bears an overturned vessel and a banner with a broken staff, but is not, as usual, blindfolded. It may be noted that the cross is coloured light green, as in many representations of the period; in some cases it is a living and branching tree. Where the artist fails is in the over-accentuation of the structure of the nude body; but at least he is much more correct in his rendering than were the illuminators of the preceding century.

A technical peculiarity which is distinctive of the school is the hatching with white lines which is frequently used as a method of bringing the highlights into relief (see David's dress in Plate 65b). The artist of this psalter and of the missal seems also to have a predilection for a particular pattern in white on the draperies, consisting of a small ring surrounded by dots (see the Virgin and Christ in Plate 66 and Samuel in Plate 65b): this is used also in drawings of the Canterbury and St. Albans Schools, but not nearly so frequently. In the same way, Mr. Lethaby has pointed out that the St. Albans artists appear to have had a special affection for a triangular pattern of three dots.

The Missal of Henry of Chichester has also several beautiful full-page illuminations, including a Nativity; a Virgin and Child adored by the owner of the book; the Betrayal, a crowded composition in which the beautiful expression of Christ's face contrasts strongly with the dark and devilish faces of the soldiers; and a Crucifixion which is very similar in style to the one in the All Souls' Psalter. Altogether the hand of the same artist is clearly shewn in these two manuscripts, in the similarity of general effect and of detail, and particularly in the delicate curves of the eyebrows, by which much of the expression is given to the faces. In the 13th century frescoes in the Chapel of the Holy Sepulchre in Winchester Cathedral similar eyebrows may be seen.

Plate 67 The Nativity scene shews, almost to excess, the undulating line which is characteristic of the school. Curtains and draperies are arbitrarily caught up into rippling folds, and a restless, if animated effect is produced. The treatment of the subject combines the hieratic with the natural. An archway with censing angels and ceremonial curtains forms the setting, but the crib is no altar-like structure, as is sometimes the case, but a natural manger out of which the ox and ass are eating; the mother gives suck to her child, while an attendant covers her with a cloak, and Joseph sits by and ponders the scene, leaning on his staff.

Plate 68 The Virgin and Child shews the particularly tender and gracious type which appears in all the manuscripts of the Salisbury School. While Italian artists were still painting only rigid and forbidding Madonnas on the Byzantine model (for even Cimabue was not born till 1240), these English painters were depicting the Virgin as a beautiful woman leaning down sweetly to caress the infant, who reaches up towards her with a natural gesture. Already in 1228 this human presentment of the Madonna and Child had appeared on the reverse of the seal of Robert de Bingham, Bishop of Salisbury, a fact which shews that the tradition was not inaugurated by these manuscripts. The type is so unusual for the period that it seems not unreasonable to suggest a Salisbury origin for the roundel of the Virgin and Child in the Bishop's Palace at Chichester, which, moreover, shews a line as graceful, if not as flowing, as these illuminations. The fresco is at any rate nearer in feeling to the Salisbury. School than to any other.

The Psalter of the Royal College of Physicians seems to be the work of a less skilled artist, but trained in the same school. It has no full-page miniatures, only a number of historiated initials of the same type as those in the preceding manuscripts, but less finely executed, and enclosed with roughly drawn bands.

The Rutland Psalter shews affinities both with the All Souls' Psalter and with that of the Roy. Coll. of Physicians: details such as white hatching and the use of spiral whorls to indicate the ground (which appear, however, also in Peterborough MSS.), reinforce the general similarity of style in attaching it to the Salisbury School. It is, however, later in date than the other three manuscripts, and the type of grotesque scenes which abound in its borders are similar to those found in the work of the East Anglian artists of the latter part of the century. In particular a group of a half-naked woman with a devil on her back, and a man behind pointing at her (reproduced in Michel Vol. II, Pt. 1) is almost identical with one in Queen Mary's Psalter (see Chap. 8), although reversed. Apart from the full-page miniatures, the pages of this Psalter are more elaborately decorated than those of the earlier Salisbury manuscripts. Dragons and scrollwork borders connect the larger initials and partially frame the writing, thus again shewing the development which was in progress towards the rich decoration of the East Anglian style.

To sum up, the particular characteristics of the work produced at Salisbury in the 13th century are:

a] a feeling for decoration, both of line and mass;

b] sincere emotion expressed in the faces, although the figures are not without affectation;

c] a delicate and rippling line, seen especially in the edges of draperies;

d] a particular grace and tenderness in the representation of the Virgin;

e] the use of white hatching to emphasize high-lights.

The School makes an individual contribution to the period, although it does not seem to have survived after the century in which it arose.

LONDON

TWO manuscripts dating from the early part of the century, 13 th and illuminated in London, shew the sort of work that was being produced in the capital before the organisation of the artists connected with the Court into a definite school. They are neither of them of especial merit, but are an interesting prelude to the achievements of the Court painters.

Plate 69 The first is a glossed Psalter, now at St. John's College, Cambridge, which was made for Robert de Lindesey, (the same Abbot of Peterborough who owned the much more important psalter which is now in the Society of Antiquaries). It belongs really to the transitional style, and seems from its heavy outlines and formal shading to be the work of an artist in stained glass. A small range of rich colours, blue, brown, green and pink, is used, put on in flat washes, and the shading on the draperies is executed by penstrokes, one thick line being regularly bordered by two thin ones, a technique which is akin to the stained glass at Chartres and other French Gothic Cathedrals; although here the method has degenerated into a mere mechanical formula.

The second Psalter produced in London early in the century, was written for a nun at St. Mary's Abbey, Winchester, and is now at Trinity College, Cambridge, (B. 11.4). It has miniatures of a lighter and more anecdotal type than those of the transition, and the design and drawing are sometimes free and attractive, but the painting is very rough and inferior. It shews distinctly the coming of the Gothic period, although it was probably written before 1220. It includes some subjects not often found at this period, such as the blessing of Ephraim and Manasseh by Jacob, Lot's wife fleeing from Sodom and, in the New Testament, the Transfiguration and the appearance to Thomas, (a scene which became very popular in manuscripts in the course of the century, and a little later in wall-paintings). Some of the pictures are regular genre scenes of mediaeval life, such as that of Joseph riding in a country cart past a barn filled with corn, (reproduction in New Paleographical Soc. Vol. II). The decoration shews a more finished technique than the pictures, and a new element is introduced in the hunting-scenes which appear as line-endings.

THE COURT SCHOOL

MANUSCRIPT painting was still during the 13th century practised in connection with wall-painting and other arts by the same artists. The fact that Ralph de Dungun, *custos librorum regis,* is recorded to have given colours in 1251 to *Master William,* the King's painter, would seem to shew that the illumination of books was included among the activities of Henry III's artists. But although the names of several of the painters and sculptors who worked at Westminster, have been preserved, (e. g. Master William of Westminster, Master Walter of Durham, and Master Thomas) and their works on wall or panel have at least conjecturally been identified, no particular manuscript paintings have so far been allotted to any of them, or even to the School in general.

There is, however, a manuscript which bears such a striking resemblance to some of the work of the Westminster painters that it must certainly be considered a product of the Court School. This is the Oscott Psalter, which *Plate 70* belonged for many years to Oscott College, near Birmingham, and is now in Mr. Dyson Perrins' collection. It dates, according to Sir G. Warner, from the latter half of the century. Its calendar is not monastic, and the only slight indication of local connection would point to a priory in the Midlands, but Mr. S. C. Cockerell thinks that the MS., which is exceptionally rich and finely executed, was probably produced at some important centre of illumination. The whole style of figure painting would point strongly to a connection with the paintings at Westminster Abbey. In the fullpage pictures of apostles, there is much of French daintiness in the drawing of the heads, which shew often an exceptionally large cranium and a protruding chin, like the figure in the Tenison Psalter, a Court work of 1284. This is combined with a broad *Plate 86* treatment of drapery, which is finely shaded and touched in with bold pen-strokes, and falls in rather hard, ample folds, resting, in the case of the womens' dresses, on the ground, in the manner of the St. Faith painting in Westminster

Abbey. But the resemblance is still stronger with the paintings on the much-injured Westminster re-table, whose origin has been debated, but which is probably a work of the English Court School of about 1260 and may be by Master Walter of Durham, a lay artist who was painter to the King from about 1262.

The colouring of the manuscript is more varied than that of the altar-piece, in which hardly any colours but dull green and red can be seen; and in the psalter the flesh parts are hardly tinted, whereas in the re-table they are a yellowish colour, with grey shadows and white highlights. Allowing, however, for the difference in destination and medium between the two paintings, it would seem that the illuminator of the Oscott Psalter must certainly have belonged to the Court School of painting, and may have been a pupil or assistant of the *Master of the Westminster Altarpiece*. The series of Biblical scenes contained in medallions shews a more popular type of art, and one clearly inspired by the French *bibles moralisées*.

CANTERBURY

ST. AUGUSTINE'S Abbey at Canterbury was again, in the 13th century, as it had been in the early days of the Church in England, a centre particularly open to influence from the Continent. It was also under the patronage of the King, and in touch with developments at Court. There is a series of manuscript paintings, executed in all probability at St. Augustine's Abbey towards the end of the 13th century, which shew very clearly the influence of Henry III's painters on the art work of Canterbury. These are the 28 tinted full-page drawings of saints, scenes from the life of Christ and St. John, and other subjects, which come at the end of an illustrated Apocalypse in the Archbishop's library at Lambeth. (No. 209, see Chap. 7). These pictures shew again the unmistakeable type of drapery, falling in severe and ample folds of an almost metallic quality, which is associated with the work of the Westminster painters. In particular, a figure of St. Catherine, with flowering sceptre and a wheel, might almost, except for the emblems, be copied from the fresco of St. Faith still existing on the wall of her chapel in Westminster Abbey. There is the same exaggerated stature, with short arms and small head, and eyes set close together, and the pose of the neck is similar. The garment falls in

Plate 71

the same way over the feet, and the cloak is in each case lined with *vair*. But a comparison of photographs of the miniature and Mr. Tristram's restoration of the wall-painting (reproduced T. Borenius.) shews that the St. Catherine is a weaker imitation of the St. Faith. The face, with its rather silly smile, has none of the dignity of the larger painting, and the drawing and shading of the hair, hands and dress is rougher. But the illuminator, even if he was not the Master of the St. Faith painting, was certainly a pupil or close imitator of that artist. This is another of the comparatively rare cases in which miniatures were inferior to and derived from more monumental work.

Apparently, several different illuminators worked at the illustrations to this Apocalypse, and of these miniatures at the end of the book, it is possible that the earlier ones, such as St. Christopher, which have a panelled background of blue and brownish buff, are by a different hand from the later ones, which are on a plain ground. The drawing of St. Christopher's legs shews a finer line than is usual in the other series. But in essential characteristics all the pictures are the same, and equally allied to the Anglo-French work of the Court. A Virgin embracing her Child, with a nun kneeling below, recalls the treatment of the subject at St. Albans and Salisbury, but with more majestic draperies and less charm of line.

Plate 72

An unusual and interesting picture is the allegory, of the penitent, represented by a young and graceful woman, warding off the attacks of the devil with a shield, on which are inscribed the names of the Trinity: evil thoughts in the guise of huge flies hover above her, but are chased away by an angel with a fly-whisk: another angel holds a sword, the fear of judgment, over her head: a peasant is laying an axe to the root of the tree under which she sits, which represents the world; on its topmost branch is perched a cock, to signify the preacher, crowing to empty air: under the lady's foot is the vanquished serpent. This picture is another example of the symbolic method of teaching which was so dear to the mediaeval mind, and which is evidenced in so many pictures and diagrams in illuminated manuscripts.

Plate 73

The Crucifixion shews a quite different treatment of the subject from those already studied: the scene is represented in a naturalistic, rather than a devotional spirit. The spectators are no longer confined to the Virgin and St. John, but are crowded in, to the detriment of the artistic effect. All the incidents are represented together, the hammering of the nails, the affixing of the su-

Plate 74

perscription, (by a figure whose small size is conditioned by exigencies of space), the piercing of the side and the giving of the sponge. The figure on the cross is realistically drawn, without the exaggerated anatomy of the Salisbury picture, or the softening down of the Peterborough ones: the drawn expression and the agonised stretching of the toes give it force and pathos. With its realism, its emotional content, its crowded composition and its broad, stiff draperies, this picture seems like a foretaste of the painting of the 15th century.

The artistic merit of this series of paintings is not particularly great; the tinting is chiefly in dull shades of grey, green and brown, and the drawing shews signs of haste. But the style is formed on good models, and these must undoubtedly have been the works of Westminster painters.

The other books which can be definitely connected with Canterbury and its affiliated Abbey of Rochester are illustrated Bibles, and as these form a class by themselves, more or less independent of local differences of style, they will be treated separately.

ILLUSTRATED BIBLES

Plates 75 - 78 AN astonishing number of complete illustrated Bibles of the 13th century has been preserved to us; almost every collection of manuscripts contains at least one of these books. They are the typical products of the Anglo-French school of illumination, and there is little difference between those written in England and on the other side of the Channel. Their average standard of workmanship is a very high one, especially in view of the minute scale on which the historiated initials and other decorations are carried out. They are in marked contrast to the 12th century Bibles. Instead of bulky volumes with brilliant and sometimes crude illuminations on a large scale, the whole text of the Bible, including the Apocryphal books, is contained in one volume of some 12 x 8 inches, or even less, written in a neat, clear hand, with two columns to the page, on the finest vellum, and decorated with borders and miniatures which are jewel-like in their exquisite detail and glowing richness of colour. The lesser features, such as the smaller flourished initials and line-endings in red and blue ink, are often of a marvellous delicacy and precision.

The development of decorative design in this period may be well studied in these MSS. A special feature of Gothic illumination was the evolution ef the partial border. The complete leaf-work border of the Ango-Saxon period had given way in the 12th century to decorated initials, often of large size, but not connected together in any way. In the Gothic period the initials were still often filled with foliage patterns, akin to those of the 12th century, but developing freer and more natural forms as the 13th century progressed. They were much smaller in size than those of the Romanesque period. But in all important MSS. the main initials were historiated, i. e. filled in with scenes, usually on a very small scale. These scenes were often on a coloured background covered with a diaper pattern. The colours used for the backgrounds and for the initials themselves were almost always blue and lake. Indeed, although in the miniatures other colours are used incidentally, for the decorative parts of Gothic illumination the changes are rung on blue, lake and gold with a somewhat monotonous insistence.

The *diaper background* mentioned above made its appearance, as we have seen, towards the end of the 12th century, and became an established feature of illumination in the 13th century, both for small initials and for full-page miniatures, although tooled gold backgrounds were also frequently used. Chess-board patterns had appeared as backgrounds in some late Ottonian MSS., and patterns divided into squares occur still earlier in Celtic work (e.g. in the panels round the evangelists in the Macdurnan Gospels); but it is possible that the new idea of replacing a gold background by a coloured diaper may have originated in the later 12th century from the example of stained glass, where gold was, of course, not available. A diaper pattern appears filling the space between medallions in the Romanesque 12th century windows of the choir of St. Denis, (finished 1154) so that this may well have been one of the new ideas which spread from that fertile centre. *Plate 76*

In the Bibles it was the general practice to begin each separate book with a historiated initial representing an appropriate scene, and if, as was usually the case, the preface of St. Jerome preceded each book, this was ornamented in addition with a smaller initial containing foliage decoration.

But the initials were not the only ornament of Gothic MSS. They began to be considered as part of a general decorative scheme for the enrichment of the page. From the frames in which they were contained, bars of colour edged with gold were continued down the side of the page, and sometimes round the corner, so as partially to enclose the writing. These were embellished with branching foliage and other decorations, which changed in type as the century proceeded, as may be seen in the three MSS. illustrated in Plates 75-78. The scrollwork and dragons which were familiar features of 12th century ornament appear in the earlier bar borders, but give way later to more natural leaves, and a greater variety of grotesque figures, which are frequently perched on the jutting out portions of the borders. The bars also develop in shape from the simple vertical and horizontal lines to curving and branching forms with cusped edges.

Besides the bar borders, subsidiary borders were frequently formed, especially in the later MSS., by the continuation of the fine blue and red flourishes which form the ornamentation of the lesser initials, as well as of the titles at the head of the pages. These form a very dainty and charming minor decoration of these MSS., and are used also to fill in the spaces of incomplete lines.

Three examples at the British Museum may be taken as typical of these Bibles at the various stages of their development. The earliest of the three *Plate 75* is the Bible of Robert de Bello, who was Abbot of St. Augustine's, Canterbury, from 1224 to 1252. The pictures in its historiated initials have naïveté and considerable charm and, compared with the work of the previous century, their execution on such a small scale is surprisingly fine, although it was surpassed by the other, later MSS. It is the most English of the three examples; a somewhat grotesque realism and energy appear in certain of these minute compositions, e.g. the fighting scenes which preface the second Book of Maccabees. In others, such as the figures of the man and woman which occur in the opening initial of Isaiah, a simple grace and seriousness is found, but there is nothing of the trivial charm which characterises many French illuminations of this period. As is usual in these Bibles, the first page of Genesis is decorated with a large initial I filled with medallions representing Creation scenes; in the last medallion of this series, the Trinity is represented, and below are six smaller ones containing other scenes, from the Fall and Expulsion, to the Sacrifice of Isaac. In these, the colours used are blue, brown and green, the blue predominating. In the whole MS., the colouring tends to heaviness rather than brilliancy, and is often of a chalky appearance, as though mixed with body-colour. The following are a few of the subjects illustrated within the initials:

EXODUS: Moses leading the Israelites. DEUTERONOMY: The burning bush. I KINGS: Anointing of Samuel. II KINGS: Death of Saul. JUDITH: Judith cutting off the head of Holofernes. BEFORE THE NEW TESTAMENT: The Jesse tree: a very favourite subject in the 13th century. ST. JOHN: The Evangelist (eagle-headed) and three scenes from his life.

The design of the bar borders in this MS. shews an early stage in their development, the whole being awkwardly enclosed in a gold band which follows the shape of the decoration; the workmanship is roughly effective rather than careful. The decorative elements used are scrollwork and dragons, as in Romanesque initials; these, as we have said, gave place later to more varied and freer motives, but the Grandison Psalter, of the late 13th century, is a late example of a somewhat similar form of rough border decoration.

The beautiful Bible (Brit Mus. Roy I. D. 1) illuminated by William of Devon, *Plate 76* probably for a Bishop of Rochester, between 1251 and 1274, represents the same form of decoration at a stage when it is already sure of itself, and when the craftsman has attained a very high pitch of dexterity (see reproduction, J. A. Herbert, *Illuminated Manuscripts*). The flourishings of the headings and smaller initials, in red and blue ink, with touches of gold, are very exact, and the drawing of the outlines in the figure-work and decoration is finely graded. Every face, however tiny, has expression, and although the style is clearly influenced by French work, it has an individual charm of its own, and its grace has not degenerated into mannerism or affectation. The borders branch out from the initials at right angles and are still severely vertical or horizontal in their main lines, although an occasional cusped edge varies their straightness, and they dwindle at the ends to fine bars, finished off with curved foliage ornaments. They are noteworthy for the large number of grotesque creatures, as well as natural birds, which are perched on them, wherever there is foothold. Grotesque heads occur also in the foliated initials, and small circular gold bosses are a favourite feature of the borders.

The third Bible, (Brit. Mus. Roy. 3. D. VI) which contains the commentary *Plates 77 & 78* of Petrus Comestor, is a particularly beautiful example of the work done towards the end of the century; it does not date before 1283. The rigid lines of the earlier bar borders have here given place to a great variety of graceful curved bands, varied by cusped edges and extra scrollwork at the springing of the branches, and ending in small sprays of foliage, — some heart-shaped,

some like ivy, vine or maple leaves. The flourished patterns in the smaller initials and headings have reached a marvellous degree of minuteness and finish (note the small L on Pl. 78). But one of the chief charms of the decoration lies in the exquisite and life-like little paintings of birds which appear in the borders: the Genesis page has a stork pecking at its wing; on other pages there are a jay, a sparrow, a bullfinch, a woodpecker and a peacock, in fact all the birds with which the illuminator and his public would be familiar. Such paintings of birds were quite a usual element of decoration towards the end of the century, both in France and England, but these are among the most charming of their kind. Other examples may be seen in the
Plate 86 Tenison Psalter, which is one of the manuscripts produced for, and possibly at the Court, during the reign of Edward I. The style of the figure paintings in the Petrus Comestor would also seem to attach it to that group of manuscripts.

These are only a few representative examples of English 13th century Bibles. There exist many others, of varying merit, but all decorated more or less on the same lines. Possibly they were made on the models set by the illuminating workshops in Paris, which by the middle of the century were turning out a large quantity of such books.

ST. ALBANS

MORE authentic information is available about the great school of art at St. Albans, which flourished throughout the 13th century, and of which Matthew Paris became the principal glory, than about any other. The school was founded by Paul of Caen soon after the Norman Conquest, and fostered by the *building abbot,* John de Cella (Abbot from 1195), who aimed at rivalling Abbot Suger of St. Denis. Under him all the arts, — fresco-painting, metal-work, carving in wood and stone, as well as the illumination of books, — were practised in connection with the Abbey. It is significant that not only monks, but also some laymen were employed; the first three craftsmen mentioned by name are: Master Walter of Colchester, a monk; Master Simon, his brother, a layman; and the latter's son, Master Richard, who was also a monk. The fact of a layman being employed shews that already the secularisation of art was beginning, which a little later transferred much of the illumination, as well as other art work, into the hands of members of guilds, not connected with the monasteries in which, or for which, (as well as for lay patrons) they worked. The high reputation of the art school at St. Albans, even in the early years of the century, is shewn by the fact that the shrine of St. Thomas in Canterbury Cathedral, which was already in place there in 1220, was commissioned from Walter of Colchester, the St. Albans goldsmith and painter.

No manuscript illumination is known to have been done by either Master Walter or his brother or nephew, although it is by no means impossible that they may have practised that branch of art work among their other crafts. But the famous historian Matthew Paris, who was born about 1200, became a monk in 1217 and by 1236 had risen to be the head of the scriptorium, reintroduced the art of outline and tinted drawing into English book decoration, and gave St. Albans a great reputation for work of that type. A considerable number of MSS. remain, with drawings in his distinctive style, and *Plates 79 - 84* they reach such an even level of excellence that it is tempting to attribute them all to the great man himself. But considering his duties as historiographer to the king, as well as the fact that he was employed on at least one diplomatic mission to Norway, connected with the affairs of the Benedictine Order, it seems only reasonable to suppose that some of the drawings attributed to him must have been carried out by other members of the scriptorium under his direction. We have only one drawing which can definitely be assigned to another artist; this is a pen and wash drawing of Christ among the candlesticks, (see W. R. Lethaby in the *Burlington Magazine* 1917) which is inserted in the volume containing Matthew Paris' Lives of the Offas and other writings. (B. M. Nero D. I.) Beside it is a contemporary note to say that it is the work of Brother William the Franciscan, an Englishman. This Friar William, the second Franciscan to be admitted into that Order on its introduction into England, became famous for his learning and sanctity and was buried near St. Francis at Assisi on his death in 1232. Paris gives a drawing of him in the margin of his account of the life and rule of St. Francis in the Chronica Maiora. How he came to be working at the Benedictine monastery of St. Albans is not explained, but his style is so closely akin to the rest of the St. Albans work that he must clearly have learnt it there, and may well have been studying in the scriptorium before he joined the Franciscans in about 1225. His single drawing shews him an accomplished artist; the drapery, in particular, is beautifully treated, with softness of texture and variety of folds, and the whole figure is dignified and well-proportioned, although a little lacking in emphasis.

Besides the artists whose names are known, there were no doubt a considerable number of anonymous workers who carried out the decoration of the St. Albans books under Matthew Paris' supervision. Although the general style of all the St. Albans books is the same, especially with regard to the treatment of the drapery, there are many minor variations, principally in the type of face, which point to different hands. And if all the MSS. which are said to shew affinities to the St. Albans style, including several Apocalypse MSS., really emanate from that Abbey, they cover a considerable range; nearly all, however, seem to have been either in pure outline, or lightly tinted on a plain background. The Trinity Coll: Cambridge Apocalypse is the only heavily coloured series of illuminations of this period which has been attributed to St. Albans.

The fact that Matthew Paris stood in an official capacity to King Henry III as historian makes it natural to suppose that he would have had influence in art matters at the Court. Henry III caused a Mappa Mundi to be painted on the wall of the King's Chamber in Westminster Palace, according to the directions of Matthew Paris, who had introduced these maps into several of his writings, and it is even possible that monks from St. Albans may have worked at Westminster, although it is not until the middle of the next century that a Hugh of St. Albans is mentioned by name among the King's painters. In 1248 Henry caused the new lectern for Westminster Abbey to be made in imitation of the one at St. Albans.

Plate 79 The Chronica Maiora, (of which the principal copy is at Corpus Christi Coll. Cambridge, and an inferior copy in the British Museum, Nero D. 5)
Plate 80 and the Chronica Minora (B. M. Roy. 14 C VII), are the works which are most indubitably associated with Matthew Paris, as having been composed by him, and also probably written by his own hand. The few larger pictures with which they are decorated are generally accepted as being Matthew Paris' own work, and may be taken as the norm of his style. We reproduce here a page of large heads from the end of the first volume of the Chronica Maiora, and a page shewing portraits of the four Norman kings, each holding a model of an institution he founded — William I with Battle Abbey, Rufus with West-

minster Hall, and so on, — from the Chronica Minora. In both cases the drawings are outlined in ink and then lightly tinted with various colours. It was not unusual to have a drawing of the head of Christ on a large scale, (sometimes called a St. Veronica head) at the end of a MS. of this period, and the customary method of representing the eye with a very small black pupil gives these drawings a very staring and forbidding aspect; such heads occur in the Lambeth Apocalypse and in the 13th century additional drawings at the end of the Westminster Psalter, (Roy. 2 A XXII). The addition of heads of the Virgin and Child and of the dying Christ in the Chronica Maiora is, however, unusual. The latter picture recalls forcibly a head of Christ from a Crucifixion in a 12th century glass window at Chartres. These drawings shew Matthew Paris' own technique, with its astonishing sureness and delicacy of line, as well as his tenderness of feeling. The latter quality comes out even more clearly in the well-known Madonna embracing the Child, with Matthew Paris himself kneeling below (reproduced Michel Vol. II Pt. I) which, apart from the gallery of kings, is the only full-page illustration in the Minor Chronicles. The heads of the Virgins in the two cases are closely similar, and evidently by the same artist. The figures of the kings shew the distinguishing qualities of Matthew Paris' drawing of drapery, in which he may be said to have excelled all predecessors. He is an adept at arranging cloaks and robes in natural and easy curves, falling in soft folds round the feet. Although these four kings are all in similar attitudes, the arrangement of their garments is different in each case. The small folds are indicated by fine, sketchy penstrokes, emphasized slightly by tinting. The heads do not show so much variety. The backgrounds of the figures are painted in opaque blue and red.

Turning from these unquestioned works of Matthew Paris to the outline illustrations of a Life of Offa which comes at the beginning of the volume *Plates 81 & 82* of *Collections of Matthew Paris* preserved in the British Museum, (Nero D I), we find in the first seven pictures, which are far superior to the rest, a style which is certainly closely akin to that of the great historiographer, to whom they are generally attributed, and yet in some points diverges from it. The quality of the drapery might lead one to infer they were by the same hand as the drawings of the kings, but the faces are of another type, the mouth, in particular, being treated differently. The line of the lips is invariably a simple one, either straight or curving slightly downwards, whereas, in all the drawings of the kings, the large heads and the Virgin and Child, it is broken by a second curve or dip in the middle.

There is a strong resemblance to the drawing of heads in some of the small tinted marginal drawings in the Chronica Minora, and horses introduced in these are the exact counterpart of those in the Life of Offa, so that there seems no question that these two series are by the same hand. As one of the marginal drawings represents the death of Paris, this hand cannot be his own. Otherwise these two series of drawings might have been by Paris at a different period from those in the Chronicles, but as it is they are probably by some artist thoroughly imbued with his style.

The battle-scene from the Life of Offa, illustrates the astonishing steadiness and grace of line which were characteristic of the artist and his school; the horses might have been traced from some Greek vase. As a matter of fact, there is an interesting detail in the latter part of this same MS. which shews that certain relics of Roman, if not of Greek antiquity had come down to the St. Albans monks. It is an illustration, inserted in an inventory of gems, of an oval cameo with a picture of Mercury leaning on his staff and holding a small image of Victory on his left hand. The drawing, which is about 4 x 3 in., is executed with a firm and graceful line, and brings an unexpected flavour of antiquity into a mediaeval MS. One writer has suggested that this Inventory is the only part of the MS. that can be attributed to Matthew Paris himself.

Besides these MSS., there is a series of illustrated lives of saints which were certainly executed by the St. Albans school, and have been assigned to Paris himself; these are: the life of St. Edward, now at the University Library, Cambridge, (Ee 3.59); the Life of SS. Alban and Amphibalus, at Trinity Coll: Dublin, (E. i. 40, reproduced with an introduction by Dr. M. R. James), and some pages from a Life of St. Thomas of Canterbury, which are now in a private collection in Belgium. These contain tinted outline drawings, delicately executed but more roughly coloured, in a narrative style of great charm. A humorous realism plays a larger part in these MSS. than in the other authenticated works of Matthew Paris, and the line drawing is somewhat weaker, although equally varied and exact. The style has much in common with some Apocalypse MSS. which are connected with St. Albans, and will be discussed in the next chapter.

Plates 83 & 84

The strongest argument in favour of the attribution of these three MSS.

to Matthew Paris is the fact that William of Walsingham mentions his having illustrated some Lives of SS. Alban, Amphibalus, Thomas and Edmund. But the style differs so distinctly from Paris' own works that it seems possible that the chronicler was committing the not infrequent error of classing all the work of a school under the name of its principal master.

Another MS. from St. Albans (B. M. Roy. 2 B VI.), dating from about 1250-60, shews the rougher work of the school. It has a series of tinted scenes from the life of Christ and pictures of martyrdoms of saints, which are lively and not without charm, but compared with the other work of the school they seem a trifle weak and sentimental. There is a distinct analogy between the heads of some of the figures and those in the famous Apocalypse at Trin: Coll: Camb:, and it has been suggested that the Psalter is by one of the artists who worked on the latter MS. The style is, however, markedly inferior to that of any of the pages of the Apocalypse, and it does not seem as though the connection could be as close as that. A full-page tinted drawing of the Virgin and Child in the Psalter, (reproduced in the Brit. Museum catalogue) is more hieratic in conception than that of M. Paris' Madonna, and would seem to have something in common with the Madonnas painted on the piers in the Abbey of St. Albans.

The last paintings to be discussed in connection with the St. Albans school are the series of tinted drawings of the middle or latter part of the 13th century, which were added to the 12th century Westminster Psalter, (Roy. 2 A XXII) mentioned in the last chapter. They are exceptionally beautiful drawings, suggesting, in the thickness of their outline, designs for stained glass. They represent a king with fleur de lys on his robe, to whom a knight is doing homage: St. Christopher: a bishop or archbishop, represented in the attitude *Plate 85* of blessing, as on the episcopal seals: and a large, staring head of Christ on a blue background. They have been usually attributed to a St. Albans artist, and Prof. Lindblom thinks them the work of Matthew Paris himself.

The activity of the St. Albans school of illumination does not seem to have long survived the death of Matthew Paris, although in a document of 1351 the monks of that Abbey are still enjoined, as one of their activities, to illuminate books. At any rate, before the 14th century the outline style had completely died out, and it is probable that any books produced at St. Albans after this date would have been merely examples of the East Anglian style, which was then paramount.

LATER THIRTEENTH CENTURY ILLUMINATION

THERE are a few manuscripts belonging to the period between 1280 and 1300 which shew the trend of illumination at the Court and elsewhere, before all the output of the country became merged in East Anglian work.

Plates 86 & 87 The most important of these, the Psalter of Alphonso, (B. M. Add. 24686) sometimes called the Tenison Psalter, because of its having formed part of the collection of Archbp. Tenison, is an example of work executed to the order of Edward I, and shews how strongly French influence had invaded the taste of the Court by this time. All the French affectation is evident in the expression of the face and pose of the hands of the figure of David harping, which forms the initial of the first page of the Psalter. Several new details occur in the border, which were to become characteristic features of later, and especially of East Anglian work. These are the exquisite natural paintings of birds already mentioned, the use of coats of arms as part of the decoration, and the practice of introducing more or less humorously conceived scenes, the figures of which stand on the bottom border. On the first page, David and Goliath are represented; on several other pages there are hunting scenes. The use of a continuous bar border round the whole page is also an innovation, and paves the way for the elaborate border decoration of East Anglian MSS. In the pages containing each four figures of saints, which form a prefix to the same MS., the typically French curve of the body and tall slender proportions are evident at once; and yet the English qualities of the MS. are no less clear. Compared with French work, these figures are strikingly simple in treatment and rather rough; the handling of the drapery, in particular, is broad, and shews that the tradition of the Court School of Henry III was not altogether lost.

As is well-known, this Psalter was destined for Prince Alphonso, the son of Edward I, at his marriage, but it was unfinished at the time of the young prince's premature death in 1284, and was completed in a rougher manner by an inferior artist. The examples reproduced are from the earlier and more finely finished part of the book.

A series of portraits of English kings and scenes from their lives, in another British Museum MS. of the end of the century, (Vitellius A XIII) has been associated by Vitzthum with the Psalter of Alphonso. The drawing of the faces, with their curled locks, small mouths and eyebrows going up to a point above the nose, is characteristic of Anglo-French work. The MS. begins with an account of the foundation of the Abbey of Chertsey, and as this Abbey during Henry III's reign had been in close touch with Westminster, producing, probably, the tiles which were used for the flooring in Westminster Abbey, it is only natural that this MS. should be allied to the Court work of the close of the century.

Another MS. produced after 1280, and shewing the invasion of French mannerism into English art, is the Psalter, (Add. 38116) purchased by the British Museum from the Huth Collection. Several pages of miniatures at the beginning are arranged under arcades in the manner common to French MSS. The last page, representing the Last Judgement, is arranged differently, in *Plate 88a* three tiers, recalling the usual arrangement of the subject over French Gothic doorways, with the souls of the blessed being led away by an angel and rowed in a boat to Paradise, while the damned are thrust by demons into a boiling cauldron. A Jesse tree forms the main decorative motive on the Beatus page, as it continued to do almost uniformly in East Anglian art. The initial page *Plate 88b* before the last division of the psalms contains representations of the Trinity, the Coronation of the Virgin, and the Church and Synagogue, the latter being represented in the usual way, with blindfolded eyes and crown falling off. The MS. is probably connected with Lincoln, which afterwards became one of the centres of East Anglian work.

The Grandison Psalter is another provincial work of the latter years of *Plate 89* the century, which shews strong French influence, but little French charm. It is interesting to see in the miniature of the Baptism the traditional iconography, derived from early Syrian sources, surviving even in this sophisticated age, — the waters rising in a heap and the angel standing beside, holding Christ's garment, while the Baptist pours water on his head.

Although the work of the different schools of Gothic illumination has been as far as possible distinguished and considered separately, it must not be forgotten that there was very close intercourse between monasteries during the whole mediaeval period, and a constant passing to and fro, both of artistic products, and also of artists when these were needed for the execution of any particular piece of work. Thus Henry III ordered the shrine of St. Thomas for Canterbury Cathedral from the monks of St. Albans, and Master William came up from Winchester to work at Westminster. It is not, therefore, surprising that there should be confusing cross-influences in the different styles, but rather that they should be as distinguishable from each other as they actually are.

The thirteenth century had been a time of seething activity in English illumination. It had seen the rough but sincere work of the transitional period gradually give way to the accomplished local styles of Peterborough, Salisbury, St. Albans and of the Court School. Now at the close of the century all styles were merging again into one current, to issue in the last great outburst of English illumination, the East Anglian style.

CHAPTER VII

APOCALYPSES

APART from the illustrated Bibles, there are perhaps no more characteristic works of the *Channel School* of painting in the 13th and 14th centuries than the illustrated editions of the Apocalypse, which were produced in considerable numbers both in England and in Northern France, but even more in this country than on the other side of the Channel. Indeed, these may be claimed with some justice as constituting not only the most beautiful, but also the most essentially national expression of English art in the Middle Ages. For although Apocalypse illustrations were no new thing, they took on a fresh and well-defined form in England in the 13th century, which became the accepted version throughout Western art, and was copied in Flanders, Germany, Italy and elsewhere. (see M. R. James. *The Trinity College Apocalypse*).

In these Apocalypses the illustration was not an adjunct to the text, as in the Bibles, but formed the principal part of the book, the text being considered merely as an explanation of the pictures. Indeed, in one of the earliest extant Apocalypses there is no text at all, and in several other early examples the explanatory writing is all contained in the picture itself, on scrolls or la- *see Plate 91*
bels, or filling spaces in the background. A little later on, it became the usual custom to fill half the page with a picture and leave the other half for the corresponding verses of Revelation, while a commentary explaining the symbolism was frequently added. In the great majority of Apocalypses the illustrations are of uniform oblong shape, measuring some 6 x 4 ins. They are enclosed in ruled borders, tinted with a plain colour; details of the picture, such as angels' wings, feet of men and horses, and roofs of buildings frequently extend over this border; indeed, a margin to a mediaeval artist never formed an inexorable limit, but could always be ignored if exigencies of space or composition required. In some of these MSS. a quaint and original use is made of this border. It is treated as though it were a partition, the wall of a house or of Heaven, and a small window is cut in it, through which St. John, standing outside, looks in at the scene represented in the picture.

The number of pictures in one of these Apocalypses varies from about 65 to 90. Delisle has made a list of 98 different subjects treated in the various

Apocalypses, but no one MS. contains them all. In addition to the illustrations to the Book of Revelation itself, there are frequently, especially in the English examples, a series of scenes from the legendary life of St. John, (as contained in the *Acts of John*, a 2nd century work alleged to be by one of his disciples) some of which are placed before the main body of illustrations, and the rest at the end. One MS., (No. 55 in Mr. Yates Thompson's collection) contains 153 pictures, but half of these refer, not to the text itself, but to the commentary.

The pictures in all the principal Apocalypse MSS. of the 13th and early 14th centuries represent the same scenes more or less in the same way. Clearly they are based ultimately on some common prototype. A comparison of Plates 93, 95a and 97a, all representing the Woman on the Beast, or of Plates 94b and 100, representing the Rider on the White Horse, will illustrate the essential similarity of treatment and composition in the different versions as well as the divergencies which were introduced by the various illuminators.

In judging of the principal English Apocalypses purely by the artistic style of their illustrations, apart from the question of their matter or text, they would seem to fall into the following grouping: —

Plate 90	Paris B. N. fr. 403	tinted	early	13th cent.	St. Albans?
Plate 91	Bodl. Auct. D. 4 17	,,	,,	13th ,,	
	J. P. Morgan (not seen)	,,	,,	13th ,,	
Plates 92 & 93	Trin. Coll. Camb. R. 16 2	coloured		c. 1230	St. Albans?
Plate 95b	D. Perrins 10	tinted	middle	13th cent.	St. Albans
Plates 94, 95a	Br. Mus. Add. 35166	,,	late?	13th ,,	St. Albans
Plate 97b	Bodl. Douce 180	coloured (unfin.)		c. 1270	Court?
Plates 96, 97a	Paris B. N. lat. 10474	,,	,,	13th cent.	Court?
Plate 98	Lambeth 209	coloured	late	13 cent.	Canterbury
	H. Yates Thompson 55	(not seen)	coloured	c. 1290	Canterbury
Plate 99	B. M. Roy 19 B. XV.	tinted (on col'd ground)	early	14th cent.	E. Anglian
Plate 100	B. M. Roy 15 D. II	coloured (in washes)	early	14th cent.	E. Anglian

The MSS. which are bracketed together shew such a close resemblance in their style that they must either have been executed by the same person, or, at least, in the same school and at the same period. The dates given are according to various authorities: — the Palaeographical Soc., Sir G. Warner, Dr. James, Mr. Cockerell and M. Delisle.

This grouping agrees in general with the classification of French and English Apocalypses which Delisle made, (see Delisle et Meyer *L'Apocalypse en français au XIIIe siècle)* on the basis of the subject matter of the illustrations contained in the different examples, and the relative importance of the written text. The first three, the examples in Paris, Oxford and New York, with two later French MSS. which Delisle includes in the same group, are probably the nearest to the original prototype or prototypes of the whole series, whatever these may have been. Delisle speaks of the common type having been established in England or the North of France in the 12th century. In this connection it is interesting to note that these three earliest Apocalypses are all now considered English, and that their illustrations are in each case outline drawings which are merely tinted with a few light, bright colours, the whole of the background and considerable parts of the picture being left white. Now tinting was a practice apparently confined during the 13th century to the St. Albans School, with which school the general style of these illustrations would also connect them, in particular on account of the elaborate folds of the draperies and the delicate gradations of the line-drawing.

It seems therefore that the prototype of these MSS. must have been in the St. Albans scriptorium early in the 13th century, but whether it was produced at St. Albans itself, or imported from some other monastery, has not been established. Certainly this original must have been a very remarkable work of art for the time at which it was produced; for these early 13th century copies shew nothing of the awkwardness of the transitional period, but rather a fully-developed Gothic grace of line and ease of pose, which are considerably in advance of their period. If they are rightly assigned to so early a date, they are the earliest existing examples of the tinted drawings produced at St. Albans. Haseloff has assigned them, however, to the middle rather than the early part of the century.

Certain of the illustrations are practically identical in the two copies: for instance, the picture of St. Michael piercing the dragon in the Oxford MS.

Plate 90 b is an almost exact replica of the one in the Paris Apocalypse, even to the folds of the draperies, the shields carried by the angels and St. Michael's halo and wings; but the artist's individual style comes out in the type of face, which *Plate 90 a* is less attractive in the copy at Oxford. On the other hand, the warrior scene occurs in a modified form in the Bodleian MS., with less figures introduced, and faces which are not quite so humorously ugly.

In general, the copy in the Bibliothèque Nationale has a shorter and sturdier type of figure than the MS. in the Bodleian, and it shews considerable characterisation in the faces. In all Apocalypse MSS. there is a greater or smaller element of the grotesque, and in this one it bears a considerable part; on the other hand, serious and refined types are sometimes represented, and the women's faces are often charming. The colouring is chosen merely to enliven the effect, with no regard for verisimilitude, horses being coloured blue, brown and red promiscuously. The dragon in Plate 90b is very decorative in colour, the main portion of its body being red, and the wings shaded green, yellow and blue.

Plate 91 The artist who executed the Oxford MS. is rather more idealistic in his style; his angels are tall and thin, with long, curving necks and finely-drawn attractive features, not at all unlike the type seen in Matthew Paris' own work, e.g. the portraits of kings (Plate 80): the bottom line of the drapery has a noted tendency to droop to a point at each side, and there are many tipped-up corners, such as that of the angel's cloak. Another characteristic of this illuminator is his love of nature, which is shewn in the birds and animals perched on every available branch of the customary conventional trees.

The Apocalypse in Mr. Pierpont Morgan's collection is reported by Delisle to be very close to the Oxford one, and obviously copied from the same model.

Plates 92, 93 The Trinity College Apocalypse is in some ways an example which stands by itself. It is of larger form than the others (17 x 12 ins.), and the pictures do not fill uniformly the top half of the page, but are inserted in different places in the text. But the chief difference from the average 13th century apocalypse lies in the richness and completeness of its colouring; the backgrounds are of the panelled variety, coloured in different shades of deep blue and lake, and powdered with stars, crosses and other patterns; a number of vivid as well as soft shades are used for the clothes, including much blue, and a good deal of scarlet, and occasionally two tints are used together, giving an attractive shot effect, as in the woman's dress in Plate 93, where alternating grey and pink combine to produce a soft mauve. Gold, highly burnished, is used freely for haloes, crowns, cups and other details, as well as for the outer margin of the pictures. Three or four artists appear to have taken part in the execution of the book, and the one who did the scenes from the life of St. John uses a heavier and less varied range of colours than the others, leaf-brown and a dull blue being his favourite tints. The drawing of the figures is beautifully executed, but the types are not pleasing, with their large, round heads and prominent eye-balls. Similar types appear, as we have said, in the marginal sketches in Matthew Paris' Chronica Maiora and also in the St. Albans Psalter, (Roy. 2 B. VI); and this, as well as the technique of the drawing, would bear out the suggested attribution of the MS. to St. Albans' Abbey, in spite of the fact that the colouring is unusually elaborate for that school. Westminster is another possible source for these paintings, but the drawing of the draperies is very much more like those in St. Albans MSS. than anything produced by the Court School. *Plate 92*

The next couple of MSS., one in the British Museum and one in Mr. Dyson Perrins' collection, are perhaps the most charming of all the Apocalypses. The illustrations are again tinted outline drawings, and their resemblance to the drawings in the Life of St. Edward and other lives of saints by the school of M. Paris is so noticeable that there seems little doubt that they were executed at St. Albans about the middle of the century, when that school was at its height. The artist who gave such a dainty and serious grace to his figures, and such childlike freshness to the colouring, might well be called the Fra Angelico of English painting.

The pages representing Christ in Majesty adored by the heavenly choirs, shew a reverence of attitude in the worshippers and a sweetness of expression, combined with a varied characterisation, which are worthy of the Italian monk-artist of two centuries later, although the technical knowledge at the disposal of the English illuminator was no doubt much less than his. These pages are the only ones which have a coloured background, and the tinting of some of the figures is unfinished. The picture of the Rider on the White Horse gives an idea of the grace of line and attitude, and skill in composition which characterize the artist. The blurs round the angel's halo and the *Plate 94 a* *Plate 94 b* head of the arrow are due to the perishing of the silver with which they *Plate 95a* were painted. In the illustration of the Woman on the Beast, the birds perched on the trees recall those in the Oxford manuscript already mentioned.

Mr. Dyson Perrins' Apocalypse has also great beauty of line and gentle charm: it is perhaps by a pupil of the other artist, who at times almost if not *Plate 95b* quite equals his master. The illustration of the dragon fighting on the sand of the sea shews him in a more lively vein than usual, but at the same time betrays a certain weakness of drawing. St. John, as often in this manuscript, is represented outside the picture: in some other cases he is peeping through a window at the scene.

So far, all the Apocalypses mentioned have been connected, with more or less probability, with St. Albans' Abbey, which seems to have been the cradle of apocalypse illustration in England. We now come to a couple of slightly later MSS. which differ in some respects from any of the foregoing, and may probably be assigned to painters connected with the Court during the last years of Henry III's reign and the first years of Edward I's. One of these, *Plate 97b* which is in the Bodleian, (Douce 180) is sometimes known as the Douce Apocalypse. It was intended to be fully coloured, but with the background left plain. It is, however, incomplete, and many of the pictures are in outline merely. Curiously enough, its sister MS. at Paris, in the Bibliothèque Nation- *Plates 96, 97a* ale, (lat. 10474) in also unfinished, only the first ten pictures being fully painted, and a number of others having the gold and silver touches filled in, but no other colour applied. The outline drawings in the two cases are remarkably similar; the same light, clear line is used: the conventional trees are identical in foliage and structure, (cf. Plates 96b and 97b): the grass is in each case indicated with sketchy, upright strokes: and the same type of figures appears, in particular an angel with a large, round head, a somewhat roguish expression and a mass of close radiating curls. The arrangement of the subjects is often different in the two MSS., so that they would seem to be the work of artists in the same scriptorium, but copying different models. The colouring in each case, though carefully applied, lacks freshness and charm, and tends to a somewhat murky hue; a good deal of grey and dark brown are used, with crimson and deep blue, but hardly any light or pale colours. Some instructive half-finished pictures at the end of the Oxford example shew that pale, flat washes were put on first, and these were gradually covered up with others until the required depth and shading were attained. This is contrary to the usual directness of manuscript painting, and accounts for the rather muddled effect produced. A notable feature of these two MSS. are the grassy foregrounds dotted with flowers and leaves; in these a light turquoise blue is applied first, which shews through in the flowers and leaves, while the rest is painted over until it becomes a dark grey colour.

There are documentary reasons as well as reasons of style to connect the Douce Apocalypse with the Court School; for the kneeling figures of Edward I, not yet king, and of Eleanor of Castile, identifiable by their coats of arms, appear in the first initial in the book. Much discussion has been provoked as to whether the MS. was actually produced in England or in France, but there seems no need to assign a foreign origin for the book, for the style of the figure-painting with its careful shading and rather severe folds of drapery, is characteristic of later 13th century work executed for royal patrons at Court, such as, for instance, the Tenison and Arundel Psalters. The MS. might possibly, of course, have been ordered from Canterbury, but no works known to come from that scriptorium reach so high a standard as these, and it seems more reasonable to suppose that they were executed by Court artists, for there were still at this period a number of painters engaged in decorating the Painted Chamber at Westminster, and executing other commissions for Henry III and his successor. Sir E. Maunde Thompson has suggested that the reason for the unfinished condition of the Oxford MS. may be found in the fact that it was destined, like the Tenison Psalter, as a marriage gift for that prince or his bride, and left incomplete at his death in 1284.

An example of the work of Canterbury is afforded by the Apocalypse in the Archbishop of Canterbury's library at Lambeth, (No. 209) which was *Plate 98* probably written and decorated at Canterbury towards the end of the 13th century. It contains the arms and effigy of a Lady de Quincey, and may therefore perhaps be called the De Quincey Apocalypse. The pictures fill the upper half of each page, and are on panelled grounds of gold, terracotta-pink and very deep blue. In this respect they resemble the Trinity Coll: Apocalypse, but they do not otherwise shew any special stylistic analogies with that MS.; the colouring, in particular, is duller; the shading on faces and elsewhere is often effected by smudging the brown ink used for outlines, a practice which was frequent at this period. Although the actual figure-drawing is well and carefully done on the whole, there are signs of haste which suggest that the pictures may have been finished and painted by an inferior artist; the lines of the backround are often not straight, and the edges of the colouring and gilding not exact. Possibly the same artist who did these Apocalypse scenes did also the full-page miniature of St. Christopher at the end of the MS., and the few others which have coloured backgrounds (see Chap. 6). *Plate 72*

These Canterbury illustrations are only second-rate when compared with the best examples of the type, and shew a style modelled on that of the Court painters, but inferior to the work which was produced immediately under royal patronage.

The Apocalypse belonging to Mr. Yates Thompson, (No. 55, a few pages are reproduced in the plates of Delisle et Meyer, *op. cit.*), shews similar characteristics: the draperies are broad and rather angular in the folds, the heads small and either daintily pretty or grotesquely ugly. The Virgin in the Pentecost picture is, however, of quite an original type. The workmanship of the diaper backgrounds and the borders is again somewhat rough. Its close resemblance to the Lambeth Apocalypse has led to its being considered also a product of Canterbury.

Plates 99, 100 The two remaining Apocalypses in the list, (B. M. Roy. 19 B. XV and Roy. 15 D. II) belong to the early 14th century, and are products of a different artistic era from the rest. While carrying on the general tradition of subject-matter, the 14th century illuminators introduce innovations in the mode of representing the scenes, and have more regard for abstract symmetry and decorative composition than had their predecessors of the 13th century. Complete coloured backgrounds are used in both these MSS.: in the first, flat surfaces of red and blue are arranged in panels, stripes, or arches, behind the figures, which themselves are only tinted, the flesh-parts being left white, and therefore stand out in strong relief against the background. The picture of St. John kneeling before the risen Christ, with a conventional oak-tree, lily and rose filling the interstices between the figures, illustrates the charm of the artist's style and his feeling for decorative composition. The horseman issuing from Hell, shews the movement and life which he is capable of imparting to his figures, and especially to his animals, which are everywhere very well-drawn. The picture is also interesting as one of the last in the long series of representations of the jaws of Hell, that favourite subject of English illuminators; they are here depicted in a truly gruesome manner, with teeth and tusks, and issuing flames, from which an agonised human head emerges. Although the artist has been spoken of as a single person, the work is in reality the product of a school or workshop, and several hands have taken part in the decoration; the school is certainly the same which produced that early 13th century masterpiece, Queen Mary's Psalter, and one of the illuminators appears to be actually the creator of that work. The soft and rather blurred tinting of the draperies is characteristic of the school, and so is the indication of the curling hair by a few bold strokes, rather than by shading, or by a multitude of fine lines. *see Plate 101, 102*

The second Apocalypse (Roy. 15. D. ii) is still more decorative and abstract in its treatment. It is East Anglian work, and was probably illuminated at the Nunnery of Greenfield in Leicestershire. The technique of the pictures is the same as that of the bar borders and initials with which they are connected, i. e. the colouring is applied in absolutely flat washes, outlined with ink lines; the indication of folds is reduced to the minimum, and consists merely of a few penstrokes. The backgrounds are in plain colours, diapered; gold is added for details, but more sparingly than in most East Anglian manuscripts: the colour scheme consists principally of blue and a purplish lake, with vermilion and green as subsidiary tints. In spite of faulty anatomy and affectation of pose and expression, this manuscript has a peculiar charm of quaintness and decorative fitness, with its elimination of the unessential and its emphasis on design, Some very fine dragons occur in the miniatures, as well as in the borders and initials. *Plate 100*

Artistically, it may be said that the Apocalypses of the 13th centuries form a class by themselves. They partake to some extent of the style of the place and period in which they were produced, but they have more affinities with each other than they have with contemporary manuscripts of a different kind. The characteristics of the general *Apocalypse style* may be summed up as follows, allowing for variations in particular examples: —

1 drawing of great delicacy and charm, usually superior to the painting,
2 bright, light colouring, frequently applied as tinting only,
3 plain backgrounds, varied by a few conventional trees or buildings,
4 tall, thin figures of a graceful ideal type to represent St. John and the angels, contrasted with grotesquely ugly forms for the powers of evil.

Perhaps the comparative unity of style may arise from the fact that they all originated from manuscripts produced in one particular workshop: or possibly it is to be sought still further back, in the supposed Roman MS. of the 4th or 5th century from which Dr. James traces all apocalypse illustrations. But although a few Continental examples exist dating from the 8th to 9th centuries, the succession is broken after that, and the English manuscripts as we have them appear practically unheralded at the beginning of the 13th century, and present an interesting problem for investigation.

CHAPTER VIII

EAST ANGLIAN ILLUMINATION

THE early 14th century is the period of East Anglian illumination. More than had ever been the case since Anglo-Saxon illumination centred in Winchester, one part of the country seems to have dictated the style of book decoration for the whole of England. But in this case it was the Eastern counties which were artistically active, while the Southern counties had now sunk into insignificance.

Peterborough, Ely and Bury St. Edmunds had already been for a century or more notable monastic centres in which much artistic work was produced. During the 13th century a number of new priories were founded in Norfolk and Suffolk, and richly endowed by the surrounding gentry, and these rapidly became great centres of religious zeal and artistic activity, so that in the early 14th century they were at least as important as those older foundations in the Eastern counties, which like them were included in the general district of *East Anglia*.

The county of Norfolk, with Norwich as its centre, was, indeed, entering in the late 13th century on a period of artistic prominence which continued until the 16th century (see G. E. Fox in *Victoria County History of Norfolk*). Paintings were executed in the Cathedral in the late 13th and early 14th centuries. Entries in the Court rolls of Norwich between 1285 and 1298 give nine painters resident there, of whom several at least are local Norfolk men, and only one, *Giles le Fleming of Bruges*, a foreigner. Few wall-paintings of this period have been discovered, and it is permissible to wonder whether some of these painters were not employed on book illumination. In the later 14th and 15th centuries many wall-paintings were executed in Norfolk churches, and even a few panel pictures of that period have survived destruction; while from the 15th century date the series of painted rood-screens for which Norfolk is famous.

But in the early 14th century it is by the decoration of manuscripts that the quality of East Anglian artists can best be judged. They evolved an elaborate style of ornamentation which was distinctive, and unlike any contemporary Continental work; and their products constitute practically the whole of the output of the country during the first half of the century. The manuscripts in which ornament is predominant, and figure painting takes quite a secondary place, are the most typically East Anglian. Such, for example, are the Douai, Gorleston and St. Omer Psalters and the Tiptoft Missal, besides many others. But there are also a few manuscripts produced at this period which do not altogether conform to this type, and in which the figure-subjects form the main element in the decoration, and the borders, initials and line-endings are of less importance. It will be convenient to consider these before the East Anglian manuscripts proper, and in order to throw light on them it will be necessary to say a few words about illumination in Paris in the late 13th century. For although the East Anglian style of *decoration* was essentially national, the figure-painting of the period has certain analogies with contemporary French work.

Towards the close of the thirteenth century the secularisation of art had been progressing rapidly, both in France and England. In France, where even many of the principal cathedrals, such as Chartres and Amiens, were built as civic rather than as monastic enterprises, the process advanced even more rapidly than in England. Whereas in England there were comparatively few secular books illuminated in the 13th century or indeed during the whole history of the art, in France numerous romances, fables, and other secular works were produced from the 13th century onwards, and illuminated by lay artists who belonged to workshops or guilds, but were not attached to any religious house. The University of Paris, founded in 1200, which attracted students from all the countries of Europe, became also a centre for art work, and the records of Paris of 1292 shew 17 *enlumineurs* living and working in the neighbourhood of the University, among whom is one Englishman, *Jehan Lengloys.* We may well imagine that this Englishman, as well as some of the English students studying at the University, would bring back to this country accounts of the technical methods in vogue in French illumination, and specimens of the work done in Paris, and thus Parisian influence would again affect English work. One of the most important illuminators in Paris at this time was a master called Honoré, and his style can be seen from certain manuscripts which are known to be his work — the principal being the Breviary of Philip the Fair, made for the King in 1296 (reproduction in G. Vitzthum, *Die Pariser Miniaturmalerei*). Certain peculiarities of his figure drawing are distinctly to be traced in such English work of the early 14th century as Queen Mary's Psalter and the manuscripts allied with it: the peculiar snaky locks of hair curling over the ears and forehead are especially characteristic, and so are the rather thick eyebrows going up to a sharp point.

The figures in French manuscripts at this time generally have a pronounced *Gothic bend*, swinging back at the shoulders and forward at the hips. This is reproduced also in English manuscripts, such as the Peterborough Psalter at Corpus Christi College, Cambridge, Queen Mary's Psalter and the Stowe *Plates 101-104* Breviary, (British Museum, Stowe 12). Again, some of the mincing gestures *Plate 112* of the French figures, the gesticulating from the wrist with the hand turned back and the cocking outwards of the elbow, appear from time to time in English early 14th century manuscripts, although they are not nearly so universal or so prominent in English as in French work. The architectural settings of cusped and crocketted arches are also ultimately French in origin. It must therefore be conceded that the figure work of the early 14th century was strongly influenced from Paris.

The group of English manuscripts to which we have referred as especially under French influence, are contemporary with the East Anglian School, but seem to be only rather loosely connected with it. One of them, the Psalter (combined with a Bestiary) belonging to Corpus Christi College, Cambridge, *Plates 103, 104* was produced, it is true, at Peterborough, but it is too much of a picture-book and too little of a decorative whole to be at all typical of East Anglian work. Another is the famous and extraordinary collection of pictures which forms *Queen Mary's Psalter,* which again has little decorative work and nothing spe- *Plates 101, 102* cifically East Anglian. A third is a compatively simple Psalter written for the monk Richard of Canterbury, (now in Mr. Dyson Perrins' collection) and decorated in the East Anglian style, but with figures in the initials which are probably by the artist of Queen Mary's Psalter: and a fourth is the Apocalypse (Roy. 19 B. XV) mentioned in the last chapter, some of the illustrations in *Plate 99* which again seem to be by this prolific artist. In all these the figure drawing takes an unusually important part for English work of the period, and is much under French influence. On the other hand, the technique of the painting is in several instances of the *water colour* type which is not found in French work nor in the strictly East Anglian manuscripts. The majority of the pictures in Queen Mary's Psalter, including all the Old Testament scenes at the beginning and the small scenes at the bottom of the pages, and a number of the large figures in the Peterborough Psalter, are lightly tinted with a few colours in a soft and sketchy manner, similar to that used for many of the 13th century apocalypses: others in the Peterborough Psalter and in the Apocalypse are washed all over with colours, but in a flat manner, with little or no shading, and are therefore quite unlike the carefully graded paintings of the East Anglian and Parisian workshops.

The large size, also, of some the figure subjects in this group of manu-
Plate 106 scripts as well as in the rare full-page miniatures of East Anglian psalters, is opposed to the French practice, and might point to a connection with wall-painting. The church at Gorleston itself, which was a famous centre of East Anglian illumination, had a painting of the legend of the Three Living and Three Dead Kings, a subject which forms a full page decoration to one of the psalters in Arundel 83. So that it is quite likely that the two forms of painting were practised by the same artists.

Queen Mary's Psalter is unrivalled among the manuscripts of the period for the high quality of its figure paintings, which are apparently all by one artist, and uniformly excellent, a fact which is all the more astonishing considering the immense number of miniatures it contains. It is thought by Sir G. Warner that it may have been executed to the order of Edward I or Edward II; he points out that the secular character of many of the illustrations, and the mistake made by the scribe in the transcription of names of saints in the Calendar, render it unlikely that it was made for a religious house, and the sumptuous way in which it is decorated points to some exceedingly wealthy and important personage as its recipient. There is, however, no definite information as to its place of origin, and its date can only be given as the early 14th century. The association with Queen Mary merely refers to an episode more than two hundred years after the book was written; it was seized by a customs officer in 1553 when being shipped to France, and presented to Queen Mary, since which date it has been incorporated in the Royal collection of manuscripts.

The psalter opens with 118 pages of Old Testament pictures, beginning with the Creation and ending with the death of Solomon. The softness of touch displayed in these drawings is remarkable: they are full of life, although so slightly sketched in, and modelling is suggested by faint tinting with green,
Plate 102 violet, red and brown. A similar type of drawing appears in the 464 small

scenes which decorate the bottom of the pages of the text. Some of these are genre scenes, representing hunting and other sports, others are subjects taken from bestiaries, grotesque scenes with animals and monsters, and representations of the Miracles of the Virgin, a theme which later became a popular one for illustration. The series is closed by a number of scenes from the lives of saints: the one reproduced shews St. Edward being stabbed while drinking, at the command of his stepmother. The stories are interesting, and may be studied in detail in Sir G. F. Warner's introduction to the facsimile edition of the Psalter.

Besides these tinted drawings, there are many fully coloured miniatures on gold or diapered grounds in the main part of the Psalter; these include a full-page Jesse tree with a graceful design of curling vine branches; calendar illustrations consisting of scenes founded on the signs of the zodiac and the occupations of the months, some figures of saints, and a large number of scenes from the life of Christ, mostly contained in medallions, four on a page, although a few are larger and take up the greater part of the page. In these miniatures the painting is still comparatively light, and is washed on flatly, with only slight shading, in a method which is more akin to water-colour technique than to the usual elaborate processes of illumination. *Plate 101*

This free *water-colour technique* appears again on a large scale in the scenes from the Nativity and Passion which are prefixed to the Psalter from Peterborough, now at Corpus Christi College, Cambridge. A comparison of the figure of Christ in the Coronation of the Virgin from this Psalter with that of the High Priest in the Presentation scene in Queen Mary's Psalter will shew the strong resemblance in the drawing of the face in the two manuscripts, although the style is hardly similar enough to shew the hand of the same artist. These fully coloured pictures on a gold background alternate with pages by another hand, containing each a figure of an Old Testament and a New Testament character, on a plain ground, executed as tinted drawings, like the more sketchy pictures in Queen Mary's Psalter, although the figure drawing is considerably more mannered and less skilful than in that masterpiece; the pointed eyebrows and mincing gestures being exaggerated in some of the figures to the point of absurdity. This manuscript, therefore, reproduces both the unusual types of painting which are found in Queen Mary's Psalter, and must emanate from the same school or workshop. The pages of *Plate 104* *Plate 103*

the text are decorated with bar borders of late 13th century type, with a few innovations, such as the use of daisy buds; and the decoration of the
Plate 55 bestiary which is bound up in the same volume (see Chap. 4) is more definitely East Anglian, introducing a variety of foliage and grotesques, as well as human heads in some of the initials.

Plate 99 The remaining two manuscripts mentioned above, the Apocalypse and the Psalter of Richard of Canterbury, must be assigned to the same group of artists. The Psalter of Richard of Canterbury, in Mr. Dyson Perrins' collection, has comparatively simple decoration of the East Anglian type, and the figures only appear in the historiated initials: it was apparently executed for a monk of St. Augustine's Abbey at Canterbury.

It is instructive to find such a varied group of manuscripts containing figure-subjects which are unmistakably related in style. One book is connected with Canterbury, another with Peterborough, a third possibly with the Court: two have decoration of a simple East Anglian type, one is an apocalypse, and another a picture-book with but little decorative ornament. Evidently a circle of lay painters existed, of whom the master who illustrated Queen Mary's Psalter was the chief: they must have been familiar with the work of Honoré and the Paris School, for its influence on their style is clear; apparently they went from place to place, supplying figure paintings wherever they were wanted, either as the whole decoration of a manuscript or in conjunction with decorative work carried out by other artists. This was quite in accord with the usual practice of the day, and although most of the purely East Anglian manuscripts appear to have been produced in or for monasteries, it is quite likely that in them also much of the work was carried out by lay artists who were sent for when a special piece of work was in hand. Individual patrons also employed artists for book illumination; for instance, Bishop Richard de Bury of Durham (1281-1345) is said to have kept *no small multitude of scribes and illuminators* in his different manors.

One interesting manuscript may be cited as a last output of the Court School before it became swallowed up in the universal prevalence of the East Anglian type of illumination. This is the Psalter of Queen Isabella, now at Munich (Cod. gall. 16, a page reproduced in colour in Leidinger, *Meisterwerke der Buchmalerei*). It was probably illuminated as a wedding gift for Isabella, the daughter of Philip the Fair of France, on the occasion of her marriage to Edward II in 1308. The figure painting is distinctly influenced by the Parisian style of Honoré and his school, though the stiff gestures and large hands betray a less accomplished artist than those who decorated Queen Mary's Psalter or the Peterborough manuscripts. The ornament is tasteful in design and definitely English; it continues the type of decoration of Court manuscripts of the late 13th century, such as the Tenison Psalter, but with some further development towards the East Anglian style. The bar borders have still but little foliage springing from them, but they are decorated with a few grotesques, natural birds and shields; and a whole scene, such as David playing to Saul, is sometimes representd on the bottom bar, as was frequently the case in East Anglian works.

THE EAST ANGLIAN STYLE OF DECORATION

BEFORE describing the characteristics of the East Anglian School of illumination, it will be as well to give a list of the most important manuscripts which are connected with it in style, with their approximate dates and provenance where known. The facts are principally taken from Mr. S. C. Cockerell's monograph on the Gorleston Psalter.

		Present Location	*Date*	*Provenance*	
1	Arundel Psalter Part II	British Museum (Arundel 83)	before 1300	—	*Plates 105-107*
2	Peterborough Psalter	Brussels	c. 1300	Peterborough	
3	Ramsay Psalter	Abbey of St. Paul, Carinthia	1285-1300	Ramsay	
4	Windmill Psalter	Pierpont Morgan collection, New York	late 13th or early 14th century	—	
5	Tiptoft Missal	" "	between 1278 and 1332	—	
6	Arundel Psalter Part I	British Museum	1300-1306	—	*Plate 108*
7	Ormesby Psalter	Bodleian (Douce 366)	early 14th century	Gorleston or Norwich?	*Plates 109, 110*

Plate	No.	Manuscript	*Present Location*	*Date*	*Provenance*
	8	Gregorii Moralia	Emanuel College, Cambridge	early 14th century	Norwich?
Plate 111	9	Gorleston Psalter	Dyson Perrins collection, Malvern	1299-1306	Gorleston
	10	Douai Psalter	Douai (now almost destroyed)	1322-25	Gorleston or Norwich?
Plate 112	11	Stowe Breviary	British Museum (Stowe 12)	1322-25	Norwich?
Plates 113, 114	12	St. Omer Psalter	British Museum (Add. 39810)	c. 1325 finished in 15th century	Gorleston?
	13	Luttrell Psalter	Lulworth Castle	c. 1340	—

Plates 115, 116 Besides these there are a number of simpler manuscripts, such as the Psalter at All Souls' College, Oxford (from Ely?) which shew the same type of illumination on a less ambitious scale.

The School did not flourish for a long period; the dates 1300-1325 cover the main examples, and later manuscripts such as the Luttrel Psalter only shew the style in a very debased form. The majority of the principal manuscripts are psalters. One of the most important centres of production seems to have been Gorleston, a village on the coast of Suffolk, near Yarmouth, which possessed in the 14th century two priories and two churches. But considering the mobility of both monks and lay artists at this period, resemblances of style do not form a very safe basis for deciding the particular monastery at which a manuscript was produced, and the artists who are known to have worked at Gorleston may also have executed commissions at other centres, such as Norwich, Ely, Bury and even Peterborough. The Ormesby Psalter had already found its way by 1325 to Norwich Priory, and might even have been produced there.

The style of decoration evolved by the East Anglian artists, although developed to some extent out of elements which were present in 13th century manuscripts, such as bar borders and drolleries, became in their hands something new and distinctive and highly elaborate. While the decoration in French manuscripts was tending to become more and more stereotyped, and resolve itself gradually into a monotonous repetition of the *ivy-leaf* motive, the English artists were continually introducing fresh leaves and flowers into their designs. The five-lobed vine-leaf (in some cases looking more like a maple-leaf) forms the basis of the designs in several of the earlier manuscripts, such as the Tiptoft Missal and the Windmill Psalter: in later work no one form of foliage is predominant, but a large number of different leaves and flowers are combined to form the borders. Among the leaves may be enumerated the ivy-leaf, oak-leaf (often with acorns), a heartshaped leaf (lime?) and a long serrated leaf which often decorates the solid part of a bar border, and which has been called the cabbage-leaf, although it bears little resemblance to that vegetable. In the St. Omer Psalter, which is particularly rich and varied in its decorative motives, a number of other species are used, such as rose-leaves, holly with berries, trefoil and kidney-shaped leaves. These leaves in East Anglian manuscripts are coloured green, red, blue or mauve as fancy dictates, and the veins are picked out with white, which is also frequently used on the highlights of the larger leaves, to give the effect of modelling. The flowers introduced include the daisy-bud, a particular favourite, the pimpernel, pea, corn-flower and marigold: these, unlike the leaves, are generally distinguished by their natural colours.

Shields with armorial bearings are a favourite motive in the borders, as they had been already in the work of the later Court school, such as the Tenison Psalter. The coats of arms used were not confined to those of the donors or recipients of the particular manuscript, but included those of any of the leading noblemen of the day, as well as the arms of monastic houses.

Another new element which the East Anglian illuminators introduced into their borders consisted of medallions containing human heads, sometimes stylised and sometimes more or less of a portrait character. Heads of the former description occur in the later part of the Arundel Psalter, in the Peterborough Psalter in Brussels, and in the Calendar of the Gorleston Psalter. Heads of a more realistic type, but with certain well-marked peculiarities — small features, eyes close together, and fluffy hair, either black, brown or quite white — occur in the St. Omer Psalter, the Douai Psalter, and also in the *Plate 113* frame of the Crucifixion in the Gorleston Psalter: this type of head would seem to be the distinguishing mark of a single artist.

Natural paintings of birds continued to be a usual feature of decoration, as they had been in late 13th century work both in France and England. Paintings of animals and insects also frequently appear; for instance, a snail and a butterfly occur in one of the borders of the Ormesby Psalter, an eel, a hare *Plate 113* and an elephant in the Windmill Psalter, and the Beatus page of the St. Omer Psalter contains finely shaded drawings of a stag, a dappled horse, rabbits and numerous other animals.

But by far the most striking and characteristic feature of East Anglian illumination is the wealth of grotesque figures and of humorous and genre scenes which abound on every page of these manuscripts. They include all the repertoire which had already become common in the 13th century, the human-headed animals, and birds dressed like human beings in the fashion of the day, grotesque musicians and acrobats: but to these they add an almost endless series of scenes in which men and animals take part. Some are simply genre scenes: — men cutting down a tree, an old man rocking a cradle, a woman making a garland, hunting scenes, a thief caught redhanded by a soldier, and so on. Others are humorous and satirical, and among these are many in which the jest is at the expense of the clergy and monks; a fox dressed as a bishop is shewn preaching to a congregation of ducks, and a funeral procession is represented, in which priest, candle-bearers and bellringer are all rabbits, and the bier is carried by two dogs (see reprodctions in S. C. Cockerell, *The Gorleston Psalter*).

The basis of the border, to which all this elaborate decoration is applied, remains in the earlier manuscripts, such as the Peterborough Psalter and the Psalter in Carinthia, as well as in less richly ornamented manuscripts, such as the All Souls' Psalter, of the same type as the bar borders of the preceding century, namely irregularly shaped bands of gold, blue and lake, decorated with dots and patterns in white, and tailing off at the ends into sprays of foliage. But they are frequently extended so as to enclose the whole of the page, and are treated with great freedom; and in such flowing designs as those in the Ormesby Psalter, there is little left of the rigidity of the original bar borders. In the principal examples of a slightly later date, when the style may be said to have reached its perfection, the border has quite lost its original form, and become a more or less regular straight band of gold and colours surrounding the whole page, as with a frame. Into this frame are set medallions at intervals, and over and around it are grouped all the other decorations. A favourite element which appears both in the borders and also to form large initials such as the B of the Beatus page, is a plaitwork of thin stems. The large initials are usually set on a square background of diaper-work, as in the 13th century.

No description can give an adequate idea of the richness of the ornamentation of these manuscripts: each of them generally contains more than 100 illuminated pages, all glowing with gold and colours. Probably no manuscript was completed by one single artist, and in several of them a number of different hands can clearly be traced.

A few points of interest in connection with the individual manuscripts may be noted.

Two psalters at the British Museum (Arundel 83) are bound together and are usually known collectively as the Arundel Psalter. The second of them is the earlier in date, and is incomplete, containing indeed nothing of the text, but only a large number of whole page miniatures which preceded it. But its style shews that it emanates from the same centre as the other psalter with which it is bound, which has the East Anglian type of decoration, and it is probable that the text of this one was decorated in the same manner. There is also evidence to connect it with Robert de Lisle, whose family was associated with Norfolk. Both psalters are peculiar for the large number of allegorical pages which they contain — representations of the *wheel of opposites*, the ten ages of man, the *mirror of theology*, the trees of virtues and of vices, the twelve articles of faith, and so on. Among those in the earlier Psalter is, as has been already said, a picture of the Three Living and Three Dead Kings, a subject which became frequent in English wall-paintings in the 14th and 15th centuries and which was also popular on the Continent (cf. the fresco commonly called *The Triumph of Death* in the Campo Santo at Pisa).

Plates 105-108

Plate 105

This Psalter (Arundel 83 II) contains also some figure subjects on a large scale which are the finest examples of English figure painting of the period. There is a breadth and monumental quality about the design of some of them which suggests an artist familiar with wall or panel painting, while the technique is that of the Parisian illuminators' workshops. The paint is applied in a dry, almost stippled manner, working up to white in the high-lights. There is still a distinct trace of the English Court School of the 13th century in the figures, especially the Virgin in the Crucifixion (reproduced S. C. Cockerell, *The Gorleston Psalter*), who has the traditional short arms and waving hair, and a simply-draped cloak with *vair* lining, such as that of the West-

Plate 106

minster Abbey St. Faith. The architectural settings of several of the subjects, e.g. the well-known Madonna and Child (reproduced in colour in *Schools of Illumination, Part III*) are in the newer Parisian taste, but French influence is much less apparent in these paintings than in those of the group connected with Queen Mary's Psalter. The figures have a greater dignity and weight, and the faces a more serious cast of expression than those in contemporary French manuscripts. This may be seen by comparing the Christ in Glory with a similar treatment of the subject in the Châlons Missal (Paris, Arsenal 595, reproduced Vitzthum, Pl. 13) which has greater suavity and flow of line, but far less solemnity.

Plate 107 The groups of smaller Biblical scenes in the same manuscript are less impressive, but are serious in feeling, and well designed in their architectural niches. It is interesting to note how closely the Harrowing of Hell keeps to the traditional treatment of the subject current in England since the 10th century.

The Peterborough Psalter at Brussels is written entirely in blue and gold, and is magnificent in its decoration: it is the earliest example of East Anglian work to shew this typical richness of ornamental work. At the same time it still contains a large picture-book element, and Dr. James has shewn that its numerous miniatures from the Old and New Testaments were copied in subject and arrangement from 12th century paintings which were formerly on the choirstalls of Peterborough Cathedral. The figure drawing is derived from the Parisian: the hair is of the curly type seen in Queen Mary's Psalter and the other Peterborough Psalter, but the gestures are affected and the expressions strained, and the whole work is inferior to those manuscripts: the rather flat treatment of the drapery, in which the folds are marked by sudden gradations, again recalls the other Psalter of the same origin, but in the elaboration of its decorative borders, which are full of grotesques and varied foliage and flowers, it is in an altogether different class and is the first of the definitely East Anglian manuscripts.

The Windmill Psalter (reproductions in James: Catalogue of Pierpont Morgan Collection) is very original, and not particularly typical of East Anglian work, either in its figure style or decorative borders: but here we have the Jesse tree filling the B of the Beatus, as it does in all the important East Anglian psalters; it is freely treated and combined with Creation scenes, a Virgin and Child, and a number of grotesque figures made of vine-leaves.

The opposite page is still more unusual: the design of the large initial E contains the Judgment of Solomon, and an angel swooping down, shewing the soles of his feet as he flies forward; above is the windmill from which the manuscript takes its name; but the whole background of the page is filled in with an elaborate pattern formed of red and blue *flourished work,* like that so often used for small initials and borders, in this case leaving spaces to form a vine-leaf design, which has been touched with green. Nothing at all analogous to this occurs in any other manuscript.

The Tiptoft Missal (reproductions as above) is noticeable especially for the fact that it has 615 borders, all of a uniform style. They surround the whole page and are based on a plain gold ground between coloured bars, varied by medallions of plaitwork patterns at intervals. The ornamentation applied to the borders is very varied, and contains all the East Anglian elements, heraldic, grotesque and natural, as well as some full-length figures of saints under canopies. It would seem to indicate a date towards the end rather than the beginning of the East Anglian period.

The Ormesby Psalter at Oxford is one of the few manuscripts which is *Plates 109, 110* still bound in its original wooden boards, enclosed in a loose chamois leather cover with flapping ends like those seen on mass-books in early Flemish pictures, such as Jan Van Eyck's Van de Paele Madonna. Its decoration is by several different hands, and varies considerably; some parts are unfinished. The best of the borders are firstrate works of art, freely and well designed, and exquisitely carried out. The little scene of the hunting of the unicorn in the lower margin of our illustration is a dainty gem, beautifully shaded in pale colours; the maiden is dressed in pink lined with green, the knight in grey lined with pink. The scene of Christ before Pilate is an instance of the intrusion even into serious subjects of the humorous element, for the face of Pilate is strongly akin, whether deliberately or not, to the grotesque dog-lady in the margin, who raises the hand on the end of her tail in blessing. The large figure of David as harpist is one of the additions made to the manuscript by a slightly later artist, who seems to have been the same one who was responsible for the decoration of the St. Omer Psalter and one page of the Gorleston Psalter. The crossed leg is an attitude which appears very frequently in pictures of kings and other important people, and was evidently considered in those days particularly dignified.

The Gorleston, Douai, and St. Omer Psalters, and the Stowe Breviary, form a group by themselves: these three psalters are (or were, in one case) the most beautiful of the East Anglian manuscripts, and seem to have emanated from Gorleston. The Douai Psalter, which has been considered the most beautiful of all, was unfortunately ruined during the late war by the caving in of the airtight box in which it had been buried for safety. It can therefore now only be judged from reproductions (see the publication of the New Palaeographical Society, Part I, and S. C. Cockerell, *The Gorleston Psalter*).

Plate 111 The Gorleston Psalter, belonging to Mr. Dyson Perrins, is decorated on every page with ornament of a high, though not uniform standard of excellence. It was probably written for Roger le Bigod, Earl of Norfolk, who died in 1306. Its Beatus page, which contains several scenes besides the Jesse tree, is remarkable for the daintiness and fluency of line and movement in its figures and decoration. The colouring, as usual, consists chiefly of soft pinks, blues and greens, and the shading is very finely graded, with the slightly stippled effect seen in many other East Anglian manuscripts. The fullpage Crucifixion is a separate leaf added by a later artist (see above). There is less variety of foliage in this manuscript than is usual. Grotesque scenes and heraldic decorations are very numerous.

Plates 113, 114 The St. Omer Psalter, presented to the British Museum in 1918 by Mr. H. Yates Thompson, has some pages which are probably the most marvellous, if not the most beautiful, production of English miniature artists. The fertility of invention shewn in their decoration, and the fineness of execution on a minute scale, have never been surpassed. It would be difficult to count the number of human figures, not to speak of the birds and animals, human heads and foliage, contained in the decoration of the Beatus page, the whole on a surface measuring $13^{1}/_{4}$ x 9 inches. Even less important pages may contain as many as 10 complete Biblical scenes. The figures are full of life and expression, even on so small a scale, and the colour-scheme is restrained and attractive: violet is a favourite colour: the grounds of the medallions are gold. The manuscript was not finished during the East Anglian period, and a large number of its pages were ornamented in the 15th century with borders in the feathery style then current. But in the best of its 14th century ornament this manuscript has never been surpassed for intricacy and charm.

Plate 112 The Stowe Breviary is a less ambitious production, but its decoration, including the flourishing of the smaller initials, is very fine and minute, and uniform all through. It may formerly have contained large miniatures as well, for some pages have been cut out.

The picture-book which had commonly preceded the Psalter was suppressed in most East Anglian manuscripts, some of its features being, as it were, absorbed in the decoration of the Psalter itself, especially of the Beatus page. Both the Gorleston Psalter and Douai Psalter contain, however, full-page Crucifixions, treated in the same abstract manner as in the Arundel Psalter, but less true in sentiment and monumental in drawing. The Virgin and St. John are tall figures standing in histrionic attitudes of grief. The Douai Psalter has (or had) also a standing Madonna, the Child holding a goldfinch as in the Arundel Psalter. The St. Omer and Ormesby Psalters have no miniatures at all apart from the text. On the other hand, the Beatus pages of all these manuscripts are very elaborate, and often include a large number of scenes. The B is nearly always filled in with a Jesse tree, and a series of prophets or kings is frequently introduced in the border as well. Biblical scenes are also included either as part of the Jesse tree, or in the border: for instance, the Gorleston Psalter contains a Virgin and Child, a Crucifixion, and Christ in Glory as part of the Jesse tree, and five Nativity scenes in the lower border; and the St. Omer Psalter includes nine medallions of scenes from *Plate 113* Genesis in the decoration of the border. Thus the Beatus page by itself has become a picture-book of Biblical history.

To resume, the general characteristics of East Anglian illumination may be summed up as follows:

1 Great profusion of decoration, principally in the form of elaborate borders.

2 Greater emphasis on ornament than on figure-subjects; few full-page miniatures.

3 Much use of gold; a scheme of colouring tending to lightness and softness rather than depth, (violet, not used in the preceding century, is a favourite colour).

4 Exaggeration of the grotesque element, and a secular spirit in the whole decoration.

5 A large variety of leaves and flowers used in the ornamentation of borders.

6 The use of human heads in medallions, and of coats of arms, as decorative elements.
7 Elaborate Beatus pages containing Jesse trees and other scenes.
8 A development from the bar-borders of the previous century towards more or less uniform frames enclosing the pages.

In the history of English illumination, the East Anglian period occupies a position corresponding to the Late Renaissance in Italian art. It is a period of sophisticated art, when the long process of learning and experiment had resulted in perfect mastery of the medium and great freedom of invention and design; when richness and intricacy were esteemed above simplicity and breadth; and when, in spite of great technical perfection, something of the inner spirit which had animated the earlier works had already been lost. In some of the more elaborate manuscripts we feel that the artist has overreached himself, and shewn less taste and moderation than his colleagues of an earlier and less sophisticated age. Art had become a matter for the display of skill, rather than for the expression of ideas. The seeds of growth were lacking, and it was inevitable that a period of decadence should follow.

There was, however, still sufficient vitality in this phase of English art for it to have a notable influence on the Continent. The school of Honoré was succeeded in Paris by the school of Jean Pucelle, his pupil, who signed the Breviary of Belleville, executed at some date prior to 1343. In the productions of this school we see a number of the elements of East Anglian illumination: the Breviary of Belleville has natural flowers as well as realistic animals and birds in the borders, and hunting, animal and other scenes at the bottom of the pages. Shields and human heads are used as ornament in the borders of other French manuscripts, while grotesques grow more numerous than they had ever been before. These are, however, only scattered manifestations in a style which had developed in general in a different direction from the English. The free exuberance of fancy displayed in the East Anglian style did not appeal to the more logical and formalistic temperament of the French. But the Belgian school of illumination, which flourished from 1300 onwards, took much of its inspiration from East Anglian and other English work, and became a channel, as Vitzthum has shewn, through which English influence helped to mould the Cologne School of painting in the early 14th century.

CHAPTER IX

THE LAST PHASE

In the late phase of English illumination all distinction of local schools is lost. The best work is done for notable individuals, — the King and his relatives, the leading nobles, an alderman of London, and so on. Each patron employs the best illuminator he can find, be he monk or layman, Englishman or foreigner, native of London or of a distant county. There are, however, guilds of artists in the principal centres: for instance, the Guild of *Peyntres de Loundres* is mentioned in 1389 as holding its meetings in St. Giles' Church.

The result is that the manuscripts of the late 14th and early 15th centuries shew considerable diversity and are not easily classified, apart from one small group which hangs together. It is a period of dispersion rather than of development, and the chief interest lies in tracing, as far as may be, the currents of foreign influence which successively flowed into the country.

There is no lack of examples of the work of this period, but very few are of the first quality. A host of inferior Books of Hours were produced for the multitude: one in the British Museum, (Egerton 2781), shews the kind of rough *Plate 117* paintings which satisfied all but the most exacting patrons. These Books of Hours are often interesting for the surprising number and range of subjects they contain. This particular example has many Biblical scenes from both the Old and New Testaments, others from the Apocryphal Gospels, from the life of the Virgin and from the lives of the saints, and a series of eleven pictures representing miracles of the Virgin. These latter are favourite subjects for illumination in the 14th century. The Carew-Poyntz Horae in the Fitzwilliam Museum at Cambridge contains an exceptional number of them. In this respect again manuscript painting seems to have given the lead to more monumental art, for it is in the later 15th century that the subject is used for the wall-paintings by William Baker in Eton College Chapel and for those in Winchester Cathedral.

The Presentation of the Virgin is represented in this manuscript in the same way as in Italian art from Giotto to Titian: — the child walking up the steps of the Temple to the High Priest, while her parents and friends wait below, — and we are reminded again of the part manuscripts played in establishing the iconography of religious scenes over the whole of Europe, and providing ready-made subject-matter for the painter and the sculptor.

THE LATEST PHASE OF THE ENGLISH BORDER

In a period when the English had lost confidence in their own power of figure - drawing, and sought help and inspiration in that domain from foreign artists, the style of decorative ornament enters on a new phase which is as distinctly national as any that have gone before. The borders become much lighter than the East Anglian ones had been, and consist mainly of feathery sprays of flowers and foliage. Narrow bars of gold and a colour (pink or blue) form a framework, as they did in the 13th century bar borders. The decoration generally surrounds the whole page, and medallions are formed at the corners and elsewhere by plaitwork or clumps of leaves. The natural species of leaves and flowers in use early in the 14th century give place gradually to types which have no resemblance to nature: *spoon-shaped* and diamond-shaped leaves are much used, as well as serrated leaves of the acanthus type, curling gracefully round the bars, and forming designs in medallions; in a stiff corkscrew pattern these acanthus leaves, coloured pink or blue, form the most usual filling for the framework of the initials. Various types of bell-
Plate 124 shaped flowers are often used, and in the 15th century large, highly-coloured and entirely conventional fruits make their appearance. But what distinguishes these borders especially from earlier work are the feathery sprays, indicated by pen-work lightly touched with green and ending in flourishes like the tendrils of a vine, which everywhere fill up the interstices of the more solid ornament. Little gold bosses are strewn among them like fruit, and the whole effect is light and attractive. In colouring, blue and a lake pink predominate, both for leaves and flowers, but vermilion, yellow and green are used as subsidiary tints.

Plate 118 The large Wycliffe Bible in the British Museum, (Egerton 617 and 618) shews a stiff and transitional stage of border, with the daisy-buds and holly-leaves familiar in East Anglian work still appearing. The initial with its filling of conventional foliage, is the precursor of the beautiful ones in Richard II's Bible. Characteristic and beautiful examples of the 15th century border are seen in the two Books of Hours in Mr. Dyson Perrins' collection. Coloured penwork flourishes were still sometimes used to ornament lesser initials, as may be seen in the Chichele Breviary. *Plates 125, 126*

A number of manuscripts, such as the Hours of Elisabeth ye Quene, the Grandison Hours (Roy. 2 A xviii) and the earlier Psalters of John of Gaunt and Humphrey de Bohun, have some of their borders formed of architectural canopies decorated with pinnacles, in the ornate style then in vogue. These were introduced also as incidental elements in the borders of John Siferwas: *Plate 127* Architectural work in the details and backgrounds of miniatures is also very frequent at this period, and wherever it is found, whether in miniatures or borders, it is coloured with no regard for nature, pink, pale blue and lilac being favourite tints.

BACKGROUNDS AND FOREGROUNDS OF MINIATURES

MORE or less natural landscape foregrounds had already been used in the St. Omer Psalter and a few other East Anglian manuscripts, and by some of the Apocalypse artists, but they become the rule instead of the exception in the later 14th and 15th centuries. The grass in Richard II's Bible and a number of other manuscripts is coloured such a dark green as to be nearly black, and strewn all over with flowers; water and trees are represented more in accordance with nature than they had been before, but it cannot be said that the English school of manuscript painting rises to any great heights in its landscape work, compared with the contemporary Franco-Flemish school. Such naturalism as there is, seldom extends to the background, which is almost always of a plain colour, covered with a diaper pattern or a gold arabesque. A few exceptions occur, however, as in the Crucifixion miniature in the Hours of Elysabeth, where the sky is filled with gold cherubim among clouds.

In the same way the backgrounds of interior scenes are filled in with gold patterns on a plain colour, while the foregrounds generally have designs of squares in doubtful perspective, to represent tiles. The numerous figures of St. Jerome in Richard II's Bible introduce us to a variety of mediaeval seats, *Plate 121* book-presses and beds, but there is nothing in English illumination to rival the detailed painting of interiors in the French manuscripts of the early 15th century.

PORTRAITS

MANY manuscripts of this period contain individual portraits of the patron, the illuminator, and occasionally other persons as well. Sometimes the patron or his wife are kneeling as worshippers in a sacred scene, after the manner of donors in early Flemish pictures: sometimes the portraits are tiny figures in a border; and sometimes a full-page miniature shews the illuminator or author presenting his book to the patron. There is a beautiful miniature in a volume of Occleve, (Brit. Mus. Arundel 38), shewing Prince Henry, later Henry V, as a pensive boy, receiving the book from its author (reproduced in *Schools of Illumination, Pt. IV*). Portraits of Richard II and other Kings of England are found in Mr. Dyson Perrins' manuscript of the Statutes of England, 1413.

FIGURE PAINTING IN ENGLAND, AND ITS RELATION WITH OTHER COUNTRIES

IN THE art of the later 14th and early 15th centuries the cross-currents of international influence become more important than ever, and at the same time more obscure and confusing. The Lower Rhine, Flanders and France were all in intimate artistic relationship with England, and to understand the development of English illumination it is necessary to have some idea of the artistic movements of the time in those countries.

Painting in the Rhine district centred in Cologne, and flourished greatly in the latter half of the 14th century. Under Edward III, (1327-1377) there had been much commercial and political intercourse between England and that part of Germany. The King had financial dealings with Cologne merchants, and even pawned his crown to them for some years. He himself visited Cologne in 1338. It is, then, not surprising that Rhenish artists of the later 14th century should have been familiar with English work, as appears to have been the case.

The question of the inter-relations between the English and Cologne schools of painting in the 14th and 15th centuries is still somewhat obscure. German writers, such as Vitzthum and Clemen have drawn attention to the fact that, at any rate in its beginnings, Rhenish art owed much to England.

Two early Cologne manuscripts, the Graduals of Valkenburg, derived elements from East Anglian illumination by way of Belgian manuscripts. The 14th century paintings in the choir of Cologne Cathedral have been compared with those formerly in St. Stephen's Chapel at Westminster, which were probably executed a few years before them, and with the still earlier English altar-piece in the Cluny Museum, (reproduced in Borenius and Tristram. *English Mediaeval Painting*).

Illumination was, however, practically in abeyance in England in the middle of the 14th century, so that this branch of art can afford no clue to the interaction of the two schools at this period. When it appears again in the reign of Richard II, it shews affinity, in its soft modelling and indefiniteness of line, with the earlier phase of Cologne art, represented by Meister Wilhelm (d. about 1380), or the group of painters whose works go under his name. In fact, the presence of Low German inscriptions in the paintings of Richard II's Bible, in the British Museum, would seem to shew that it was actually an artist of the Rhenish school who executed the figure-paintings in this manuscript, (Roy. 1 E ix) and its companion Missal, of which only the initials *Plates 119-121* are now preserved. (Add. 29704) These two volumes are such exceptionally beautiful examples of the illuminator's art that it is tempting to claim them for an English painter, and there is indeed a realistic side to them, which is little in harmony with the mysticism of Rhenish art. Some scenes introduce crowds of typical yokels, and the accessories and clothing throughout are closely copied from contemporary life. Nebuchadnezzar's siege of Jerusalem *Plate 120* shews us a mediaeval town, with its beamed houses, cruciform church, turreted walls and moat, while the king might be Richard II himself, issuing from his tent, surrounded by his armed knights. In another picture, the Feast of Ahasuerus, the table manners of the day are shewn, the guests being provided each with a knife, but helping themselves from the dish with their fingers, while flute-players provide an entertainment. All this detail is in keeping with the new movement which was stirring throughout Europe, and issued at the beginning of the 15th century in the courtly pageants of the Limbourgs and of Gentile da Fabriano.

The extraordinarily glowing colour of these miniatures constitutes their particular charm. At the same time, a good many soft intermediate shades are used, especially of pinks and browns. In the initial representing Abishag *Plate 119a* being brought before David, the king wears an apple-green mantle and rests on an ochre-coloured couch. Abishag is dressed in scarlet, and wears a wreath of pink roses on her bushy hair, while the duller colours of the courtiers' clothes serve to throw the main figures into relief. A very rich and brilliant blue is used in many of the miniatures.

It has been thought that the style of figure-painting in these and other allied manuscripts was due to Bohemian artists who came to England in the train of the new queen, Anne of Bohemia, in 1382. But several considerations militate against this theory. Firstly, the Low German inscriptions in the Bible of Richard II point to an artist from the north rather than the south of the German-speaking territories. Secondly, the school of Prague, which represents Bohemian art at this period, was really a cosmopolitan collection of artists brought together by Anne's father, Charles IV, to decorate his palaces and churches, and had as yet no distinctive and unified style. The famous paintings in the palace at Karlstein, near Prague, executed for this monarch, are of various different styles. (See Neuwirth, *Wand-und Tafelmalerei der Burg Karlstein*). Thomas of Modena, Theodoric of Prague and Nicholas Wurmser of Strassburg all worked there. It is true that some pictures in the palace, notably the beautiful Crucifixion in St. Catherine's Chapel, have a certain analogy in their soft technique, serious feeling, and dignity, as well as in the humorous realism of some of their portrait types, to the English illuminations. But it may well be that these pictures were the work of German artists, and in any case, there seems no need to turn to Bohemia for the type of influence which was coming more directly to England from the Rhine district.

The slight similarities in figure painting between English manuscripts and the *Wenzel Bible* in Vienna, illuminated at Prague under Charles IV's successor, Wenceslas, may be explained by the fact that the Bohemian miniature-painters had by that time assimilated many of the qualities of the Rhenish artists who had worked in Prague in the preceding reign.

A still later manuscript of the Bohemian school, the Hours of 1465 in Mr. Dyson Perrins' collection, has figures which are nearer to the type, — rounded faces with small eyes and flowing hair — which appears in the English miniature paintings, but in this case the influence, if it exists, must be in the opposite direction.

Another Rhenish painter, to judge by his name Herman, signed the illu-

Plates 122, 123a

minations of the Chichele Breviary at Lambeth, (no. 69), a very fine manuscript of the early 15th century. It is possible that he also executed at least one of the miniatures in the Grandison Hours, (Brit. Mus. Roy. 2 A xviii), for a picture of the Annunciation in that manuscript, (Brit. Mus. Reproductions, Series I) bears the same motto as one of the initials in the Chichele Breviary: — *Si quis amat non laborat.*

The work of the Chichele Breviary is characterised by dainty finish and careful shading on a small scale, and by very great richness of colour, but the figures are of a heavy type and have neither the charm of those in the great Bible, nor the refinement of those in the Annunciation of the Grandison Hours. The Breviary is linked on to Richard II's Bible and Missal by its decorative work, which is very similar to that of those manuscripts; (cf. the initial A and leafwork decoration in Plates 121 and 122) and by the fact that it bears the royal arms on the first page, and appears to have been presented by Henry V or VI to Archbishop Chichele. It may therefore be taken as a further example of work done for the Court by Rhenish painters. The Grandison Hours is a composite book of the same school, but finished by inferior artists. In the latter part of the book the borders and initials are far superior to the miniatures.

Illumination was not, however, entirely in the hands of foreign artists at this period, for the famous Sherborne Missal, belonging to the Duke of Northumberland, (reproductions in Roxburghe Club edition) and Lord Lovel's Lectionary at the British Museum, (Harley 7026) are examples of first-rate *Plate 127* work done by an English Benedictine monk, John Siferwas, working between 1396 and 1407. He gives us a number of portraits of himself, as well as of his patrons, and of the scribe John Was, who collaborated with him. One of these portraits, (B. M. Reproductions, Series 2) in the Lectionary, is a tinted drawing on a large scale, (in no sense a miniature), shewing a monk with a sensitive artist's face presenting his book to Lord Lovel, who had ordered it for the Cathedral at Salisbury. As the other book was made for Sherborne Abbey, it seems likely that Siferwas came from some monastery in the West of England. His ornamental borders are quite distinctive, although containing medallions, leaf-work and feathery sprays, like other manuscripts of the time. For one thing, the framework of bars is much more evident than is usual, and the light sprays of foliage are only incidental adjuncts, and do not conceal it; many of the medallions contain very lifelike heads, probably portraits of his friends and acquaintances: he continually introduces angels with flying draperies and red or black wings, climbing about the bars of the framework: and he is fond of filling one side of the border with a figure in an architectural niche resting on a slender column. In the Lectionary his colouring has a certain heaviness; much black, grey and deep red are used, and comparatively little gold is introduced. A special feature of the Missal are the beautifully finished pictures of English birds which are introduced into the borders, each with its name: a stork, a jay, a sparrow hen, and so on. Very few grotesque figures occur; as a decoration for borders they fell altogether out of fashion after the East Anglian period.

The figure-work in Siferwas' manuscripts gives us interesting light upon the style current in England at the time, especially when it is compared with some panel-paintings of the same period. Analogies to German work are apparent, but the figures are of a different build to those in Richard II's Bible and the other kindred manuscripts: slighter and taller, with something more severe and stately in the sweep of their long garments, something akin to the rich dignity of the early Flemish painters. Some of the heads appear to be English portrait types, but there is not much life or expression in their faces.

The full-page miniature of the Crucifixion in the Sherborne Missal, (reproduced in the Roxburghe Club edition of the Missal, 1920), has been discussed in connection with the contemporary panel-painting of the same subject belonging to Lord Lee of Fareham; (see Borenius and Tristram: *English Mediaeval Painting* and the Burlington Magazine, Dec. 1914). It has a strong element of realism, as indeed have all the Crucifixion pictures of this period, but it is of a much more dignified type than the coarse, homely realism of the panel-painting: the blood-marks on the body of Christ are accentuated, the arms are abnormally thin: the Virgin is fainting, the women's faces are sweet but sad, with heavy lids and straight mouths; the thieves are writhing in agony. Around these main figures are a crowd of soldiers and spectators, some on horse-back and some on foot, with jewelled headdresses, patterned robes and gay trappings. In these we see again plainly the revival of interest in the details of contemporary life, and especially the rich life of courts, which characterised the paintings of the early 15th century in all countries, and intruded even into the most sacred scenes.

An analagous Crucifixion scene in Mr. Dyson Perrins' *Hours of Elysabeth ye Quene* shews less of the elaborate accessories and more of realistic portraiture in the faces of the bystanders, but here, too, the centurion is a courtly 15th century figure, with his ermine-lined mantle and jewelled collar. The body of Christ shews a curious convention current at the time, being evenly dotted all over with blood-marks. Some of the women's faces have a certain French daintiness, and the sky-background is sprinkled with cherubs' heads in gold. *Plate 125*

This manuscript takes its name from Henry VII's queen, who at one time owned it, and whose signature can be seen at the foot of the page which contains the Crucifixion miniature. But the book was made in the first quarter of the 15th century for Cecily, Duchess of Warwick. All the pictures which it contains are of the very finest quality; the faces are exquisitely modelled, and the figures well-drawn and proportioned: great technical skill is shown in the painting of details, such as the transparent veil hanging over the tomb in the entombment scene. Indeed, these pictures shew the highest point attained by English illumination in the 15th century, and are worthy to be compared with the works of the Franco-Flemish school of the French court, with which they have more affinity than with Rhenish art. In some details, such as the coloured cherubim filling the background in the Mass of souls, and the occasional use of lines of gold or a contrasting colour to pick out the highlights on draperies, they forestall the work of Fouquet.

A more everyday realism breathes in the volume, also in Mr. Dyson Perrins' collection, which was decorated about the same time for Henry Beauchamp, Duke of Warwick, the husband of Cecily. Perspective and the proportions of figures are not the strong points of the artist who executed most of the pictures, but he is an adept at facial characterisation. The colours are gay and varied, but there is a certain lack of depth in shading. Altogether, these pictures are distinctly inferior to those of the other Book of Hours, and the types represented are sometimes coarse and heavy. The decoration also is not quite so dainty; the style of its foliage work shews a slightly later date. A complete landscape background of sky and flowery meadow appears in the miniature of the Betrayal, but in interior scenes there is the usual gold arabesque on a coloured ground. *Plate 126*

These two manuscripts, with those decorated by Siferwas, are the most characteristic and interesting English examples of this period, before the introduction of printing, which was brought from Flanders by Caxton about the year 1474, put a stop to the development of the art. The fact that they are so varied in style shews that there was no predominant strain in English miniature painting at this period, but that it was played on by influences from several directions.

The Wingfield Book of Hours, in Mr. Yates Thompson's collection, seems again to shew influence from France, especially in its borders, but the figures are of a heavy build not found in French manuscripts. The book was decorated in 1450, and is thus one of the latest good examples of English miniature painting. The conventional background has been discarded here in favour of sky and natural landscape.

Plate 129 An interesting and original miniature of Chaucer speaking to a company of lords and ladies grouped round him in a meadow outside the walls of a castle forms the frontispiece of a manuscript copy of Chaucer's Troilus of the first half of the 15th century, now in the library of Corpus Christi College, Cambridge. It is unique of its kind. With its *all-over* composition and rich, gay colour, it reminds us of nothing so much as a Persian miniature, but it is probable that its inspiration comes from the courtly scenes in some of the French manuscripts, such as those executed for the Duc de Berri and John, Duke of Burgundy in the early 15th century. In the latter's Breviary at the British Museum we find similar castles perched on equally impossible rocks and surrounded by mushroom trees of a like growth. (See f. 188 b, reproduced in B. M. Reproductions, series III). This miniature from the Chaucer manuscript is a strikingly beautiful work of art, executed with the utmost taste and delicacy, and forms a refreshing oasis in a period of general decadence. It connects English miniature-painting definitely with the gay and courtly *international style,* of which Pisanello and Gentile da Fabriano were the principal representatives in Italy, and the Duc de Berri's miniature-painters in France.

At this period, the first half of the 15th century, it was not unusual for wealthy patrons in England to order their manuscripts actually from France, where there were more highly-skilled painters than in this country. The British Museum contains fine French manuscripts executed for Henry VI and for John, Duke of Bedford.

A good many French manuscripts of the 15th century shew strong Italian influence, but little of this seems to have penetrated to England, although a few motives in borders may be of Italian origin.

Nor was direct Flemish influence a strong factor in English painting of the early 15th century, as it was in France, where the Limbourgs and other artists from the Low Countries were employed by the great patrons of art. By the middle of the century, when Flemish art was known and appreciated in England, little manuscript painting of the first rank was being produced: but the inferior Books of Hours which were turned out in such quantities during the century have often a Flemish appearance in their figure-painting. A number of the large, roughly painted manuscripts of the Ghent and Bruges workshops found their way to this country towards the end of the century, some being actually ordered by Edward IV and Henry VII.

It is not right to attribute all the realism in late English illumination to Flemish influence. In much of the inferior work of the 15th century, the painful elements in the scenes are accentuated, and ugly types of people are represented, so that the result verges on the grotesque. But the grotesque and ugly had always had a certain appeal to the English mind, and it was only natural that the new spirit of realism which was abroad in all countries, even France, should sometimes take that form in England.

In the early 15th century, grisaille painting, which was used by Jacquemart de Hesdin and other painters in France, had found its way also to England. A grisaille picture of the Crucifixion, which looks Flemish in its style, appears in a manuscript of Michael de Massa, now at the Bodleian, which was written in Norfolk by Ralph de Medylton in 1405, and it is possible that it is to Flanders that we owe this new type of painting, of which several examples exist from the 15th century. In a sense it carries on the old English tradition of outline drawing, but in a new guise. Some classical stories are illustrated in this way in a copy of the rhymed *Epistle of Othea to Hector,* which is now *Plate 128*
in St. John's College, Cambridge. Percyvalle (Perseus) is charging on Pegasus to the rescue of a thoroughly contemporary Andromeda, in tight bodice and flowing skirt, from the gaping jaws of the sea-monster. The sky is washed with blue, the horse's wings are pink and the sea is expressed by undulating greenish lines, but the main figures are merely drawn and shaded in black and white.

Some fine grisaille drawings of a slightly later date, (1457-61) occur in

Thomas Chaundler's manuscript copy of his own works in Trinity College, Cambridge (reproduced in the Burlington Fine Arts Club catalogue of illuminated manuscripts). This whole series of 15th century monochrome illustrations may perhaps shew some of the early work of a regular school of English painting in grisaille, under Flemish influence, which finally bore fruit in the magnificent wall-paintings by Baker at Eton (1479-88). Indeed the pictures by Chaundler are not at all far removed in style from the work of Baker. The clothes fall in firm, thick folds, often resting on the ground, the types, even of angels, are ugly and realistic, and the shading gives the effect of rather streaky brushwork, as in the paintings at Eton.

The same qualities are found in a series of excellent drawings in the British Museum (Add. 24189) illustrating the Buke of John Maundevill (reproduced in the Roxburghe Club edition of the Book). They are commonly attributed to Flemish artists, but since the discovery of the work of William Baker it may well be that these and other similar works may be allotted to English artists of the middle and late 15th century, working in the Flemish style.

This sketch of English illumination will, I hope, have shewn how considerable were the achievements of the English artists throughout all the very varied phases of the art. Vitality and originality, combined with a strong decorative sense, rather than finish or ease of manner, were the principal qualities of their work. It never remained long enough in one groove to become stereotyped, but was constantly breaking out in fresh directions. If there is nothing in later years quite comparable to the famous Très Riches Heures of the Duc de Berri at Chantilly, neither did any other country produce early works as fine as the Lindisfarne Gospels and the Benedictional of St. Aethelwold. And the average level throughout the whole period was perhaps higher than that of any other country.

BIBLIOGRAPHY

GENERAL WORKS

BIRCH, W. DE G. and JENNER, F. *Early Drawings and Illuminations.* London, 1879.

BORENIUS, T. and TRISTRAM, E. W. *English Mediaeval Painting.* (101 plates) Paris, The Pegasus Press, 1928.

DELISLE, L. *Livres d'images*, in Histoire littéraire de France t.xxxi. Paris, 1890.

HASELOFF, A. *Sections on English illumination* in Michel, Histoire de l'art, t.i et ii. 2nd ed. Paris, A. Colin, 1922.

HERBERT, J. A. *Illuminated Manuscripts.* London, Methuen, 1911.

LAURIE, A. P. *The Pigments and Mediums of the Old Masters.* London, 1914.

MADAN, F. *Books in Manuscript.* London, Kegan Paul, 1920.

MILLAR, E. G. *English Manuscript Illumination* from the 10th to the 13th centuries. Brussels, Van Oest, 1926.

MIDDLETON, J. H. *Illuminated Manuscripts in Classical and Mediaeval Times.* Cambridge, Univ. Press, 1892.

THEOPHILUS (Rugerus). *An Essay upon Various Arts,* by Theophilus, trans. R. Hendrie. London, 1847.

MAUNDE THOMPSON, E. *English Illuminated Manuscripts.* London, Kegan Paul, 1895.

TYMMS, W. R. and WYATT, M. D. *The Art of Illuminating.* (coloured plates). London, 1860.

VITZTHUM, G. *Die Pariser Miniaturmalerei von der Zeit des heiligen Ludwig bis zu Philipp von Valois.* Leipzig, 1907.

CATALOGUES

British Museum. *Catalogue of Western MSS. in the Old Royal and Kings' Collections.* G. F. Warner and J. Gilson. 1921.

British Museum. *Guide to the Exhibited MSS.* 1923.

Burlington Fine Arts Club. *Exhibition of Illuminated MSS., Illustrated Catalogue.* S. C. Cockerell. 1909.

Cambridge, Fitzwilliam Museum. *Catalogue of MSS.* M. R. James. 1895.

Cambridge, Fitzwilliam Museum. *Catalogue of MSS.* McLean Collection. M. R. James.

Cambridge, Corpus Christi College. *Catalogue of MSS.* M. R. James. 1912.

Cambridge, St. John's College. *Catalogue of MSS.* M. R. James. 1913.

Cambridge, Trinity College. *Catalogue of MSS.* M. R. James. 1900-1904.

Cambridge, University Library. *Catalogue of MSS.* Various authors. 1857.

Chantilly, Musée Condé. *Cabinet des livres, les manuscrits.* Duc d'Aumale. 1900.

Glasgow. *Catalogue of MSS. in the Hunterian Museum.* J. Young and P. H. Aitken, 1908.

Manchester, *John Rylands Library. Catalogue of an Exhibition of MSS. etc.* H. Guppy. 1924.

Oxford, Bodleian Library. *Western MSS. in the Bodleian Library.* Additional volume by F. Madan and H. H. E. Craster. 1922.

Oxford, All Souls' College. *Catalogue of MSS.* H. O. Coxe. 1842.

Private Collections:

MSS. of J. Pierpont Morgan. M. R. James. 1906. (some plates in colour).

MSS. of C. W. Dyson Perrins. G. F. Warner. 1920.

MSS. of H. Yates Thompson. M. R. James and others. 1896-1907.

Earl of Leicester's Collection. Les MSS. à peintures à Holkham Hall. Dorez. Paris, 1908.

COLLECTIONS OF REPRODUCTIONS

British Museum. *Reproductions from Illuminated MSS.*, 3rd ed. 1923.

British Museum. *Schools of Illumination.* 4 pts. 1914 etc. (some plates in colour).

British Museum. *Illuminated MSS. in the British Museum.* (colour) G. F. Warner. 1899-1903.

Palaeographical Society. *Facsimiles of MSS. and Inscriptions.* 1873-1894.

New Palaeographical Society. *Facsimiles of ancient MSS.* 1903 etc.

HUMPHREYS, A. N. and OWEN JONES. *Illuminated MSS. of the Middle Ages.* (colour) London, 1844.

LEIDINGER, G. *Meisterwerke der Buchmalerei.* (Munich MSS. in colour). Munich, 1920.

THOMPSON, H. Y. *Illustrations from* 100 *MSS.* in the library of H. Yates Thompson. London, 4th series, 1914.

WESTWOOD, J. O. *Facsimiles of the Miniatures and Ornaments of Anglo-Saxon and Irish MSS.* (colour). London, 1868.

WESTWOOD, J. O. *Palaeographia Sacra Pictoria* (colour). London, 1845.

WORKS ON PARTICULAR PERIODS AND SPECIAL MANUSCRIPS

CELTIC

ROMILLY ALLEN, J. *Early Christian Symbolism in Great Britain.* London, Whiting. 1887.

BALDWIN BROWN, G. *The Arts in Early England.* London, J. Murray, 1903 etc.

BRUUN, J. A. *Celtic Illuminated MSS.* Edinburgh, 1897.

DALTON, O. M. *Byzantine Art and Archaeology.* Oxford, Clarendon Press, 1911.

DALTON, O. M. *East Christian Art.* Oxford, Clarendon Press, 1925.

GILBERT, J. T. *National MSS. of Ireland.* London, 1874.

LEPRIEUR, P. Article in *Michel, Histoire de l'art,* t. l. 1905.

MILLAR, E. G. *The Lindisfarne Gospels.* 1923. London, British Museum (coloured plates).

STOKES, M. *Early Christian Art in Ireland.* London, South Kensington Museum, 1887.

SULLIVAN, E. *The Book of Kells.* London, The Studio, 1920 (coloured plates).

ZIMMERMANN, E. H. *Vorkarolingische Miniaturen.* Deutscher Verein für Kunstwissenschaft, 1914.

ANGLO-SAXON

BIRCH, W. DE G. *The Utrecht Psalter.* London, 1876.

DURRIEU, P. *L'origine du manuscrit célèbre dit le psautier d'Utrecht.* Paris, 1895.

FORBES-LEITH. W. *The Gospel-book of St. Margaret.* Privately printed, 1896. (coloured plates).

HOMBURGER, O. *Die Anfänge der Malschule von Winchester im zehnten Jahrhundert* in J. Ficker, *Studien über christliche Denkmäler.* Leipzig, 1912.

MITCHELL, H. P. *Flotsam of later Anglo-Saxon art.* Burlington Magazine, 1923.

MOREY, C. R. Chapter in C. W. Kennedy, *The Caedmon Poems.* London, Routledge, 1916.

SPRINGER, A. H. *Die Psalterillustrationen im frühen Mittelalter.* Leipzig, Königliche sächsische Gesellschaft der Wissenschaften. 1883.

STETTINER, R. *Die illustrierten Prudentius-Handschriften.* Berlin, 1895 and 1905.

TIKKANEN, J. J. *Die Psalterillustration im Mittelalter.* Helsingfors, 1895.

WARNER, G. F. and WILSON, H. B. *The Benedictional of St. Aethelwold.* Roxburghe Club, 1910 (coloured plates).

WILSON, H. B. *The Benedictional of Archbishop Robert.* Henry Bradshaw Society, 1903.

WILSON, H. B. *The Missal of Robert of Jumièges.* Henry Bradshaw Society, 1896. (coloured plates).

Utrecht Psalter. Facsimile edition. Palaeographical Soc., 1874.

ROMANESQUE AND TRANSITIONAL

BIRCH, W. DE G. *Memorials of St. Guthlac.* Wisbech, Leach & Son (only 100 copies), 1881.

DELISLE, L. *Le psautier de St. Louis â Leyde.* 1902.

FORBES-LEITH, W. *Life of St. Cuthbert.* Privately printed, 1888 (coloured plates).

GOLDSCHMIDT, A. *Der Albanipsalter in Hildesheim.* Berlin, 1895.

HERBERT, J. A. *Article on Psalter,* Roy. l. D. x., in Walpole Soc. Annual, 1914. (coloured plates).

BESTIARIES

ROMILLY ALLEN, J. *Early Christian Symbolism in Great Britain.* London, Whiting, 1887.

CAHIER ET MARTIN. *Le Bestiaire,* in Mélanges d'archéologie. Paris, 1851.

DRUCE, G. F. *Mediaeval Bestiaries,* in Journal of British Archeological Association, 1919 and 1920.

DRUCE, G. F. Articles in the Archaeological Journal, 1910-1923.

JAMES, M. R. Introduction to *A Peterborough Psalter and Bestiary,* Roxburghe Club, 1921.

LAND, J. P. N. *Physiologus,* in Encyclopaedia Britannica, 9th edition, 1875.

GOTHIC

JAMES, M. R. *La Estoire de Saint Aedward.* Roxburghe Club, 1920.

JAMES, M. R. *The Life of St. Alban* in Trinity College, Dublin. Oxford, 1924.

LETHABY, W. R. Articles on the St. Albans and Westminster (Court) schools in the Burlington Magazine, 1916, 17, 18, 24.

PAGE, W. *The St. Albans School of Painting, Mural and Miniature,* in Archaeologia, 1902.

APOCALYPSES

COXE, H. O. *The Apocalypse of St. John the Divine* (Bodleian Auct. D. 4.17.) Roxburghe Club, 1876 (coloured plates).

DELISLE, L. and MEYER, P. *L'Apocalypse en français.* Paris, 1901. (with autotype facsimile of Apoc. B. N. fr. 403).

DIDOT, A. F. *Les apocalypses figurées,* in Catalogue raisonné des livres de la bibliothèque de A. Firmin Didot, Paris, 1867.

JAMES, M. R. *The Trinity College Apocalypse.* Roxburghe Club, 1909.

JAMES, M. R. *The Apocalypse in Latin and French* (Bodleian Douce 180). Roxburghe Club, 1922.

EAST ANGLIAN AND LATER MANUSCRIPTS

COCKERELL, S. C. *The Gorleston Psalter.* London, Chiswick Press 1907 (coloured plates).

EISLER, R. *Die illuminierten Handschriften in Kärnten,* in Wickhoff, Beschreibendes Verzeichnis der illuminierten MSS.. in Oesterreich. Vienna 1905.

HERBERT, J. A. *The Sherborne Missal.* Roxburghe Club, 1920.

JAMES, M. R. *A Peterborough Psalter and Bestiary.* Roxburghe Club, 1921 (coloured plates).

JAMES, M. R. *The Holkham Picture Bible,* in Walpole Soc. Annual 1923.

VAN DEN GHEYN, J. *Le psautier de Peterborough,* in Le Musée des Enluminures, ed. P. de Mont, Haarlem. 1905.

WARNER, G. F. *Queen Mary's Psalter.* London, British Museum. 1912 (coloured plates).

WARNER, G. F. *The Buke of John Maundevill.* Roxburghe Club, 1889.

INDEX OF MANUSCRIPTS

GENERAL INDEX

PLATES 1-50

I

LINDISFARNE GOSPELS

Cruciform page, *British Museum*

c. 700

2

LINDISFARNE GOSPELS

Initial page of Preface to St. Matthew's Gospel

British Museum

c. 700

ihs xps · Matheus homo
incipit euangelii
genelogia mathei

3

LINDISFARNE GOSPELS

Canon Tables, *British Museum*

c. 700

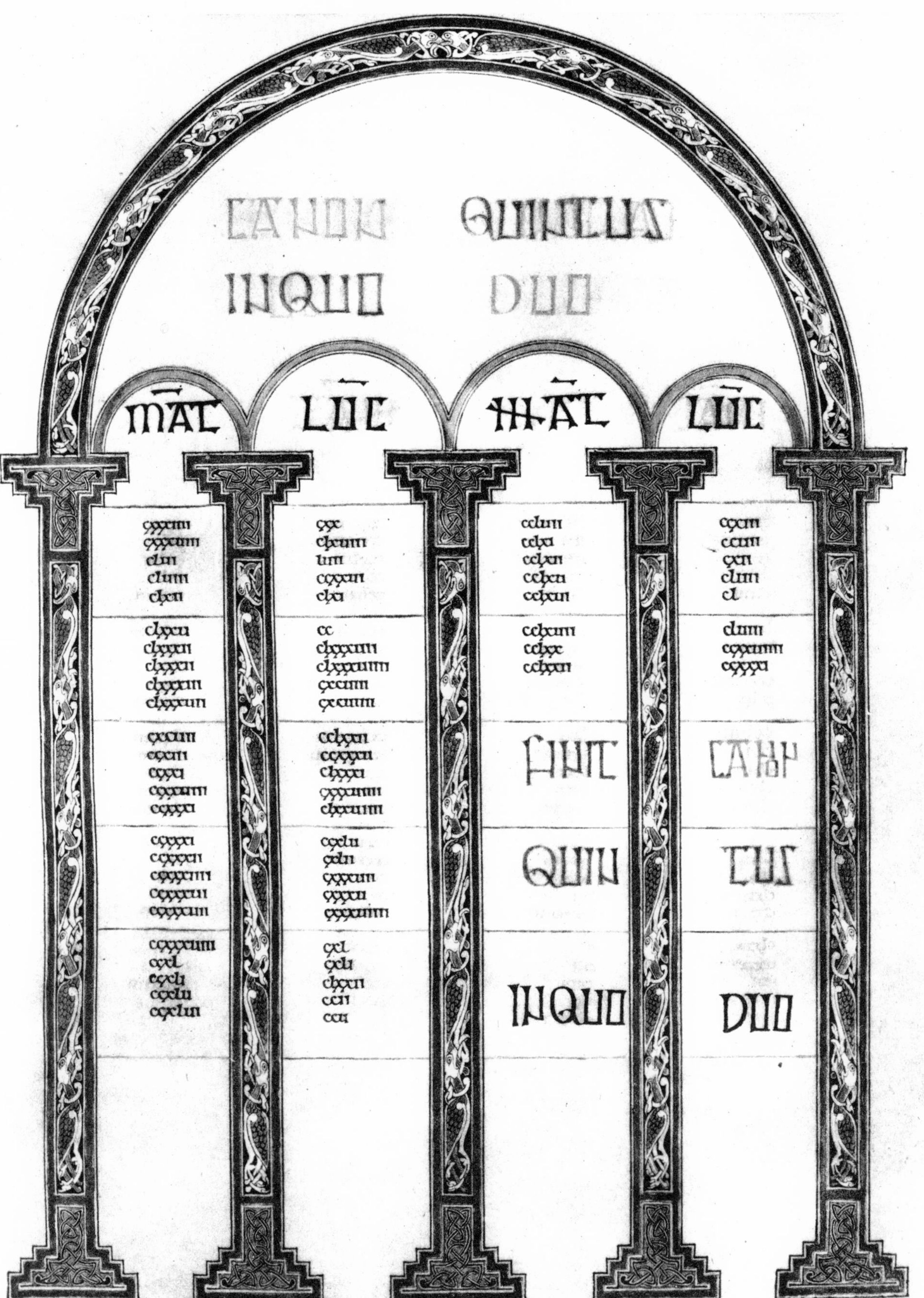
CANON QUINTUS
IN QUO DUO
MAT
LUC
MAT
LUC
FINIT CANON
QUIN TUS
IN QUO DUO

4

THE BOOK OF KELLS

Initial page of St. Matthew's Gospel

Trinity College, Dublin

c. 700

h generatio

5

THE BOOK OF KELLS

Evangelist Symbols

Trinity College, Dublin

c. 700

6

THE BOOK OF KELLS

The Temptation

Trinity College, Dublin

c. 700

7

THE BOOK OF KELLS

St. Luke III, Page of text

Trinity College, Dublin

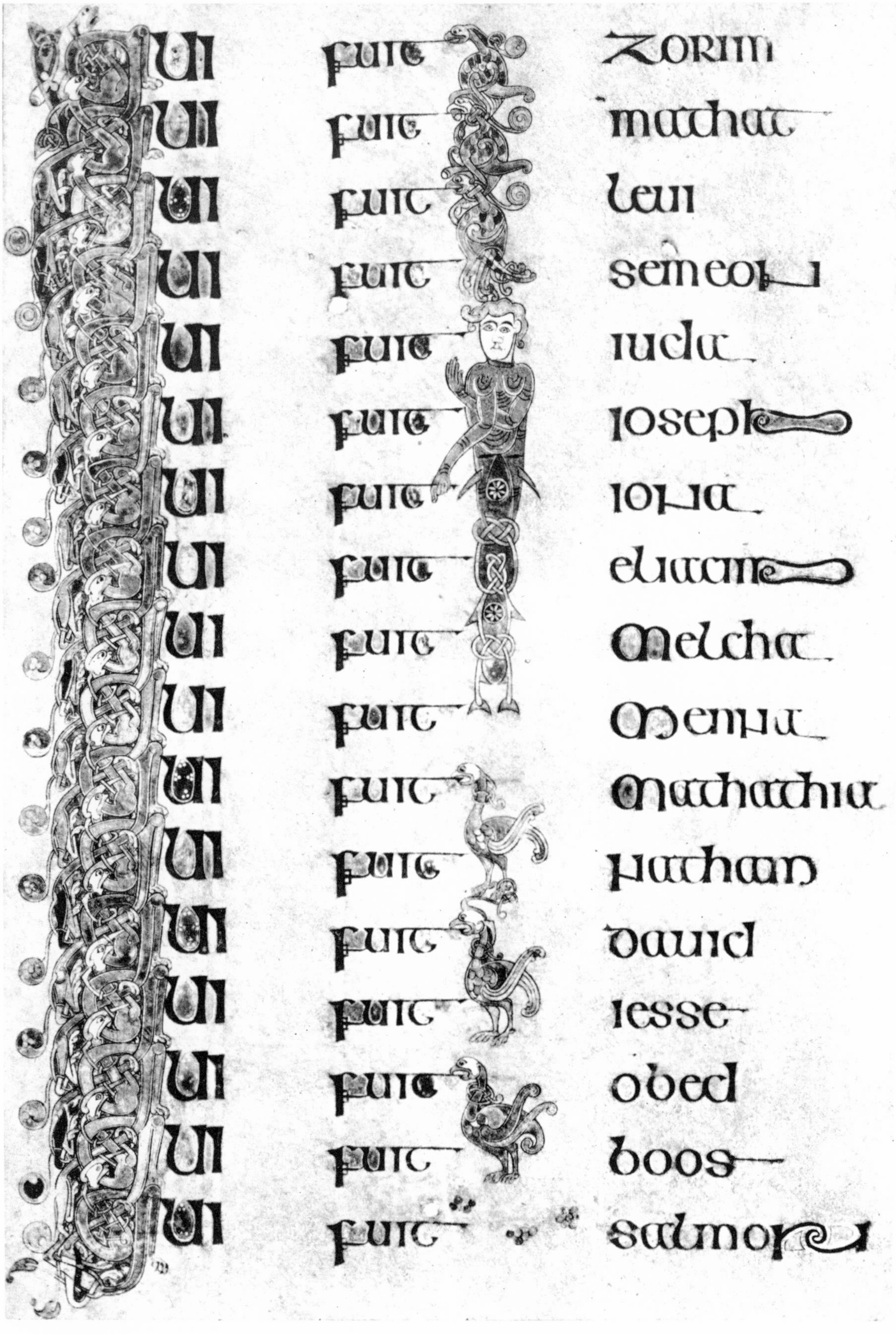

Qui fuit Zorim
Qui fuit Matthat
Qui fuit Levi
Qui fuit Semeon
Qui fuit Iuda
Qui fuit Ioseph
Qui fuit Iona
Qui fuit Eliacim
Qui fuit Melcha
Qui fuit Menna
Qui fuit Mathathia
Qui fuit Nathan
Qui fuit David
Qui fuit Iesse
Qui fuit Obed
Qui fuit Boos
Qui fuit Salmon

8

ST. CHAD'S GOSPELS

Cruciform page, *Lichfield Cathedral Library*

Early 8th century

9

ST. CHAD'S GOSPELS

Corner of Cruciform page (enlarged)

Lichfield Cathedral Library

Early 8th century

10

MACREGOL (RUSHWORTH) GOSPELS

Initial page of St. Luke's Gospel

Bodleian Library Oxford

c. 820

II

MACREGOL (RUSHWORTH) GOSPELS

St. John, *Bodleian Library, Oxford*

c. 820

Io
han
nis

12 a

MACDURNAN GOSPELS

Initial page of St. Luke's Gospel

Lambeth Palace Library

Late 9th or early 10th century

12 b

MACDURNAN GOSPELS

St. Luke, *Lambeth Palace Library*

Late 9th or early 10th century

MQUIDEM
multi conati sunt ordi
nare narrationem quae
in nobis completae sunt re
rum sic[ut] tradiderunt no
bis qui ab initio ipsi uiderunt
et ministri fuerunt sermo
nis. Visum est et mihi adse
cuto a principio omnibus di
ligenter ex ordine tibi scribere optime
theophile ut cognoscas eorum uerborum
de quibus eruditus es ueritatem :—:—
Fuit in diebus herodis regis iudaeae sacerdos
quidam nomine zacharias de uice abiae et
uxor illi de filiabus aaron et nomen eius
elizabeth. Erant autem iusti ambo ante deum
incedentes in omnibus mandatis et iustifica
tionibus domini sine querella. Et non erat illis
filius eo quod esset helizabeth sterilis. Et
ambo processissent in diebus suis. Factum est
autem cum sacerdotio fungeretur in or
dine uicis suae ante deum secundum

13

IRISH PSALTER FROM DOVER

Crucifixion, *St. John's College, Cambridge*

10th century

14

IRISH PSALTER FROM DOVER

Psalm CI (CII) *St. John's College, Cambridge*

10th century

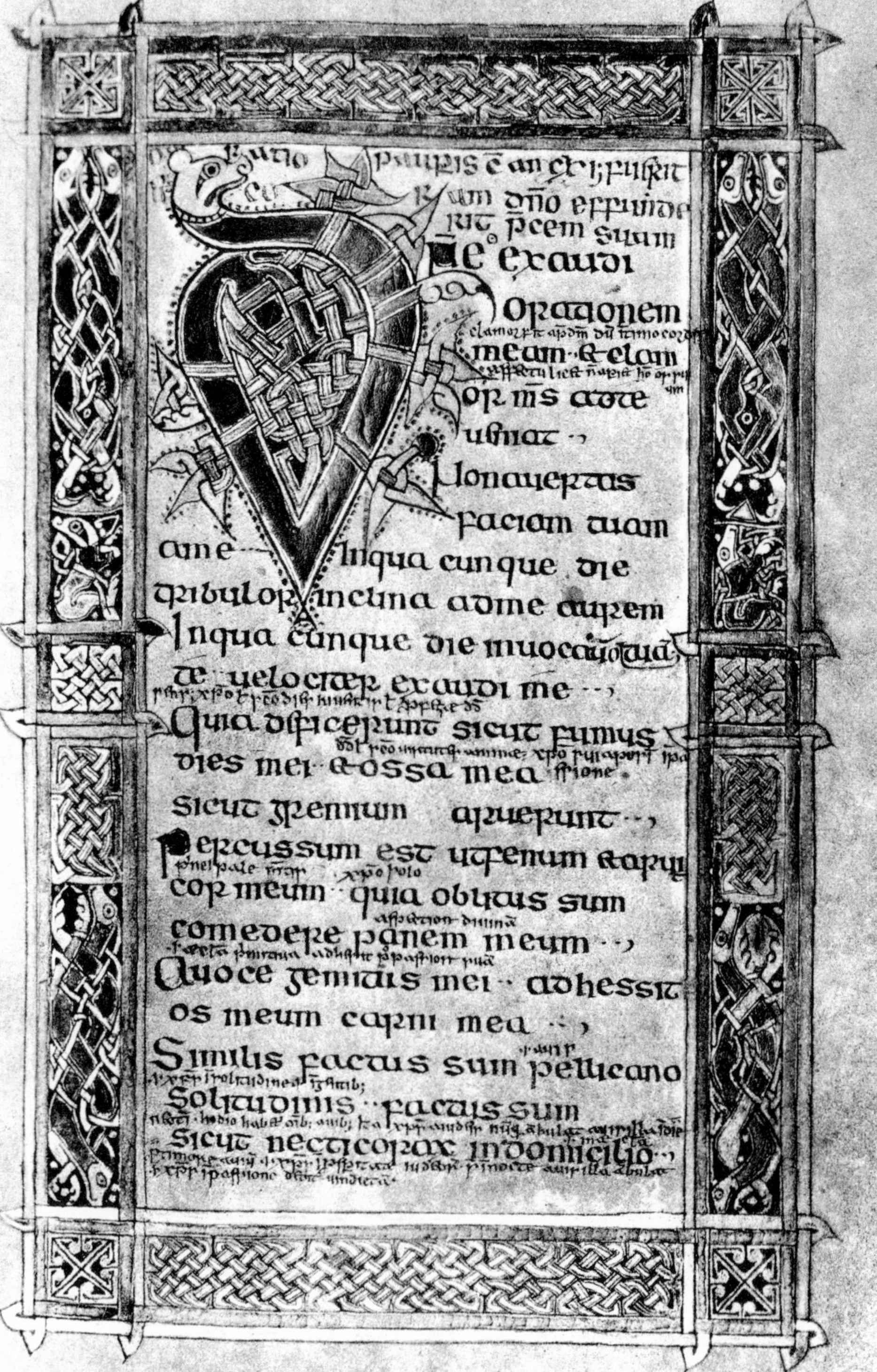
Oratio pauperis cum anxius fuerit et coram dño effuderit precem suam
Domine exaudi orationem meam et clamor meus ad te ueniat
Non auertas faciem tuam a me in qua cunque die tribulor inclina ad me aurem
In qua cunque die inuocauero te uelociter exaudi me
Quia defecerunt sicut fumus dies mei et ossa mea sicut gremium aruerunt
Percussum est ut fenum et aruit cor meum quia oblitus sum comedere panem meum
A uoce gemitus mei adhesit os meum carni meæ
Similis factus sum pellicano solitudinis factus sum sicut necticorax in domicilio

15

CANTERBURY GOSPELS

St. Mark, *British Museum*

Late 8th century

16

BEDE'S ECCLESIASTICAL HISTORY

Initial B, *British Museum*

9th century

17 a

KING ATHELSTAN'S PSALTER

Christ in glory with Virgins

Martyrs and Confessors

British Museum

925-940

17 b

RAMSEY BENEDICTIONAL

Initial page with border, *Paris*

Late 10th century

OMNIS CHORUS
MARTYRUM
CONFESSORUM
OMNIS CHO
VIRGINUM
OMNIS CHORU

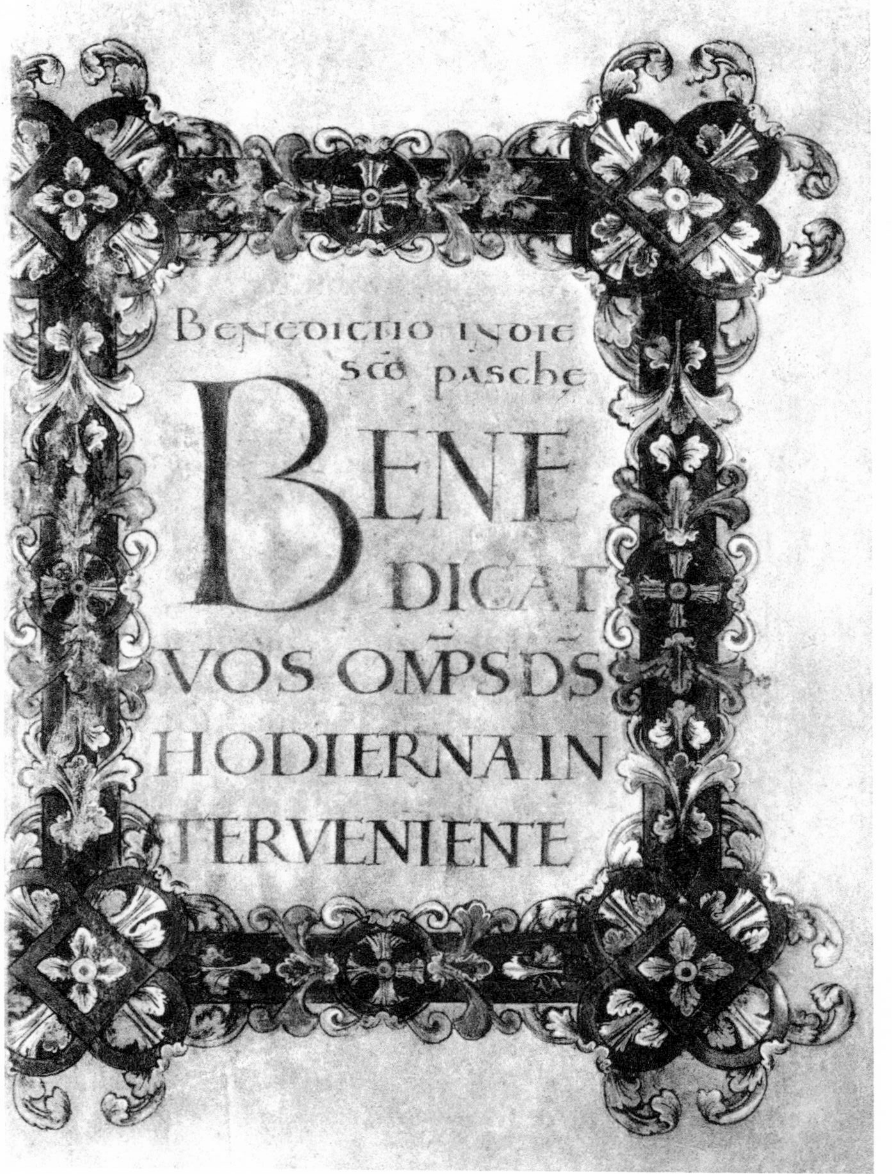
Benedictio in die
sco pasche
BENE
DICAT
VOS OMPS DS
HODIERNA IN
TERVENIENTE

18

BENEDICTIONAL OF ST. AETHELWOLD

St. John, *Chatsworth, Derbyshire*

c. 980

19

BENEDICTIONAL OF ST. AETHELWOLD

Baptism, *Chatsworth, Derbyshire*

c. 980

20

BENEDICTIONAL OF ST. AETHELWOLD

Entry into Jerusalem

Chatsworth, Derbyshire

c. 980

21

BENEDICTIONAL OF ST. AETHELWOLD

Ascension, *Chatsworth, Derbyshire*

c. 980

22 a

BEDE'S CASSIODORUS

Initial B, *Durham Cathedral Library*

8th century

22 b

ALDHELM: "DE VIRGINITATE"

Initial H, *Lambeth Palace Library*

9th century

22 c

ALDHELM: "DE VIRGINITATE"

Initial P, *Lambeth Palace Library*

9th century

22 d

CODEX VOSSIANUS

Initial N, *Bodleian Library, Oxford*

Early 10th century

22 e

CODEX VOSSIANUS

Initial A, *Bodleian Library, Oxford*

Early 10th century

23

GOSPELS

Canon-tables, *British Museum*

11th century

CANON DUO IN QUO TRES
MATH.
MARC.
LUCAS.
cclviiii
cclxiiii
cclxviiii
cclxxi
cclxxviii
cclxxxi
cclxxxv
cclxxxv
ccxcvi
ccxcv
ccci
cccviii
cccxii
cccxvi
cccxvii
cccxxii
cccxxxviii
cccxxxix
cccxl
cccxlii
cccxliii
cccxlvi
cccliii
cccliiii
cli
clv
cliiii
clii
clx
clxiii
clxvi
clxvi
clxxvii
clxxvii
clxxii
clxxxix
cxciii
cxcvii
cxcviii
cci
ccxviii
ccxviiii
ccxx
ccxxii
ccxxiii
ccxxv
ccxxxiii
ccxxxiii
MATH.
MARC.
LUCAS.

24

PSALTER FROM WINCHESTER

Calendar for October, *British Museum*

c. 1060

Hebraice KL Tesri. Grece. Hyperbercheos. Aegiptii. faoni.

TERTIUS OCTOBRIS GLADIUS X ORDINE NECTIT

October habet dies xxxi. luna xxx.

xvi	S	A		KL	OCTS Scorum germani. remigii. uedasti.
v	T	B	vi	NO	Sci leodegari mar. In attica corona
xiii	V O	C	v	NO	mane oritur.
ii	A	D	iiii	NO	
	B	E	iii	NO	
x	C V	F	ii	NO	
	D	G		NON	Sci marci pape.
xviii	E	A	viii	ID	Sci ipigii con.
vii	F A	B	vii	ID	Scorum dionisii. rustici. & eleutherii.
	G	C	vi	ID	Sci paulini epi.
xv	H	D	v	ID	
iiii	I E	F	iiii	ID	Sci uuilfridi epi.
	K	F	iii	ID	Transl. sci Eadwardi reg. confessor
xii	L	G	ii	ID	Sci kalesti pp.
i	M I	A		IDUS	
	N	B	xvii	KL	NOV
ix	O	C	xvi	KL	Sce æðeldriþe uir.
	P O	D	xv	KL	Sci luce euan. & iusti mar. Sol in scorpionem.
xvii	Q	E	xiiii	KL	
vi	R	F	xiii	KL	
	S V	G	xii	KL	Sci hilarionis con.
xiiii	T	A	xi	KL	
iii	A A	B	x	KL	
	B	C	ix	KL	
xi	C	D	viii	KL	Scorum crispini & crispiniani.
	D E	E	vii	KL	
xix	E	F	vi	KL	vigilia.
viii	F	G	v	KL	Apostolorum Simonis et iude. ✝
	G I	A	iiii	KL	
xvi	H	B	iii	KL	
v	I	C	ii	KL	Sci quintini mar. Uigilia.

OCTOBER hora iii et ix pedes xiii.

25

PSALTER FROM WINCHESTER

Beginning of Psalm CI (CII)

British Museum

c. 1060

[D]NE EAUDI
ORATIONEM
MEĀ ET CLA
MOR MS AD
E VENIAT

26 a

GOSPEL BOOK OF ST. MARGARET

St. John, *Bodleian Library*, *Oxford*

Early 11th century

26 b

Offices of the Holy Cross

Crucifixion, *British Museum*

11th century

SCS IOHANNES
EVANGELISTA

HECCRUX
CONSIGNET
CORPORE
MENTE
LUNA
SOL
INQUA
SUS
DSOM
HIA
PENDENS
SE
CUM
SCA
MARIA
SCS IO
HANNES

27

PSALTER FROM PETERBOROUGH

Christ triumphant, *Bodleian Library, Oxford*

Late 10th or early 11th century

28

PSALTER

The Harrowing of Hell, *British Museum*

11th century

XPS INFERNU DESPOLIAT
114

29

PSALTER

Beatus page, *British Museum*

11th century

INCIPIT LIBER
PSALMORV̄ SCOM̄
TRADITIONĒ SCI
HIERONIMI· PR̄SBĪ
A
VS
ABIIT IN CON
SILIO IMPI
ORVM

30

PSALTER (COPY OF UTRECHT PSALTER)

Illustration to Psalm XI (XII)

British Museum

9th century

IN FINEM PRO OCTAVA PSALMUS · DAVID · XI ·

SALUUM ME FAC
dn̄e qm̄ defecit sc̄s .
quo diminutę sunt ueri
tates a filiis hominum ;
Vana locuti sunt unusquis
que ad proximum suum
labio doloso . in corde &
corde locuti sunt mala ;
Disperdat dn̄s uniuersa
labia dolosa . & linguam
mali loquam ;
Qui dixerunt linguá nr̄am
magnificabimus . labia
nr̄a a nobis sunt . quis nr̄
est dn̄s .
Propter miseriam inopum
& gemitum pauperum .
nunc exurgam dicit dn̄s ;
Ponam super salutare
meum . fiducialiter agá
in eo ;
Eloquia dn̄i eloquia casta :
argentum igne examina
tum . terrę purgatum
septuplum ;
Tu dn̄e seruabis nos . & custo
dies nos . a generatione hac
in ęternum ;
In cir cuitu impii
ambulant . sc̄dm̄ altitudi
nem tuam multiplicasti
filios hominum ;

31

MALMESBURY PRUDENTIUS

Lot taken prisoner by the kings

Corpus Christi College, Cambridge

c. 1040-1050

+ hier dar rit kunigar berwarpoden loch dz hur ahcon

32

MALMESBURY PRUDENTIUS

Avarice binds her victims

Corpus Christi College, Cambridge

c. 1040-1050

33 [a]

PRUDENTIUS

Pride riding forth, *British Museum*

Early 11th century

33 [b]

PRUDENTIUS

Wisdom enthroned, *British Museum*

Early 11th century

sublevans elevatas culmina.
nmensas rapiens alta ad fastigia gemmas

34 [a]

ST. ALBAN'S PRUDENTIUS

The virtues slay discord, *British Museum*

1119-1146

34 [b]

PSALTER

Initial C, *British Museum*

Late 12th century

34 [c]

PSALTER

Initial D, *British Museum*

Late 12th century

Virtutes scindunt discordiam

CANTATE
dño canticum
quia mirabilia
Saluauit sibi

35

PSALTER

Beatus page, *British Museum*

Late 12th century

EATVS ∴ VIR ∴ QVI ∴ NON ∴
ABIIT : IN : CONSILIO

36

WINCHESTER BIBLE

Initial F, II Samuel

Winchester Cathedral Library

Late 12th century

E L R I.

INCIPIT CAPITULA LIBRI REGUM II:

e planctu dauid quomodo lxerit Saul & Jonathan.
D e reditu dauid in hebron ubi secundo unctus est.
& de abner & isboseth & Joab. & de preglio ubi luserunt pueri
& Asael occubuit. filii Saul.
e filiis dauid in hebron natis. & quomodo cepit recepit
Michol. & de Abner a Joab interfecto. & de morte isboseth
D e cunctis tribubus secutis dauid. & quomodo
ingressus est Syon & de hiram artificibus & lignis. & de uxorib.
& filiis qui nati sunt ei. uerit Nationes.
e duobus preliis quibus dauid percussit philisteos.
& de Arca adducta in Jerusalem. secuta.
D e Nathan propheta ubi prohibuit dauid edificare templum.
& prophetat de xpo. & quomodo dauid omnis in centuum humilia
e mifiboseth filio Jonathe. & de Anon rege
Amon quomodo illuserit pueris dauid & de uindicta in
D e bethsabee uxore urie parabola per Nathan.
& de morte pueri de stupro nati. & de natiuitate Salomonis.
e urbe Rabbath a dauid capta. & que de Ammon
& thamar memorantur. & de Absalon quomodo interfec
D e fuga Absalon ad holmai. Amnon.
regem syrie ingressur. & de muliere thecuite que pro da
uid locuta est. modo patre expulit regno.
e Absalon pulchritudine. & quos habuerit filios. & quo
D e consilio Actofel & chusai dato Absalon.
& de Achimaa & Jonathan exploratoribus dauid.
e bello ubi Absalon periit. & quomodo cum dauid luxerit. XIII
D e reditu dauid in ierlm & recuperatione regni. XIIII
e Siba qui cum parte populi rebellauit contra dauid
& de Amasa quem interfecit Joab. & de fame que accidit
per gabaonitis. quos ultus est dauid in septem crucifixis
de stirpe Saul. uiris tribus.
D e preglio philistinorum in quo dauid patuit discrimini.
& de reliquis bellis. & de Cantico. & de prophetia de xpo.
e uiris fortissimis in preliis Cum dauid. & de cor
D e indignatione diuina cur dauid populum
iusserit numerari. & de optione per Gad tribus modis obla
ta. & de interfectione in septuaginta milium per angelum
illata. & de sacrificio oblato a dauid in Area Areuna ie
busei.

EXPLICIUNT CAPITULA:

INCIPIT LIBER

FAC

TUM EST

AUTEM POSTQUAM
MORTUUS EST SAUL. UT DAUID RE
uerteretur a cede amalech. & ma
neret in siceleg dies duos. In die au
tem tertia apparuit homo ueniens
de castris saul ueste conscissa. &
puluere aspersus caput. Et ut ue
nit ad dauid. cecidit super faciem
suam & adorauit. Dixitque ad eum
Vnde uenis? Qui ait ad eum. De
castris israel fugi. Et dixit ad eum
dauid. Quod est uerbum quod fac
tum est? Indica michi. Qui ait.
Fugit populus e preglio. & multi
corruentes e populo mortui sunt.
sed & saul & ionathan filius eius
interierunt. Dixitque dauid ad ad
olescentem. qui nuntiabat ei. Vn
de scis quia mortuus est saul & io
nathan filius eius? Ait adolescens
qui narrabat ei. Casu ueni in mon
tem gelboe. & saul incumbebat
super hastam suam. porro currus &
equites appropinquabant ei. Et
conuersus post tergum suum. uidens
que me uocauit. Cui cum respondis
sem assum. dixit michi. Quis nam
es tu? Et aio ad eum. Amalechites
sum. Et locutus est michi. Sta
super me & interfice me. quoniam tenent
me angustie. & adhuc tota anima
mea in me est. Stansque super eum. occidi illum.
Sciebam enim. quod uiuere non poterat post
ruinam. Et tuli diadema quod erat in capite
eius. & armillam de brachio illius. & attuli
ad te dominum meum huc. Apprehendens autem da
uid uestimenta sua scidit. omnesque uiri qui erant
cum eo. & planxerunt & fleuerunt & ieiuna
uerunt usque ad uesperam super saul & super iona
than filium eius. & super populum domini & super do
mum israel. quod corruissent gladio. Dixitque

37

WINCHESTER BIBLE

Joel preaching. *Winchester Cathedral Library*

12th century

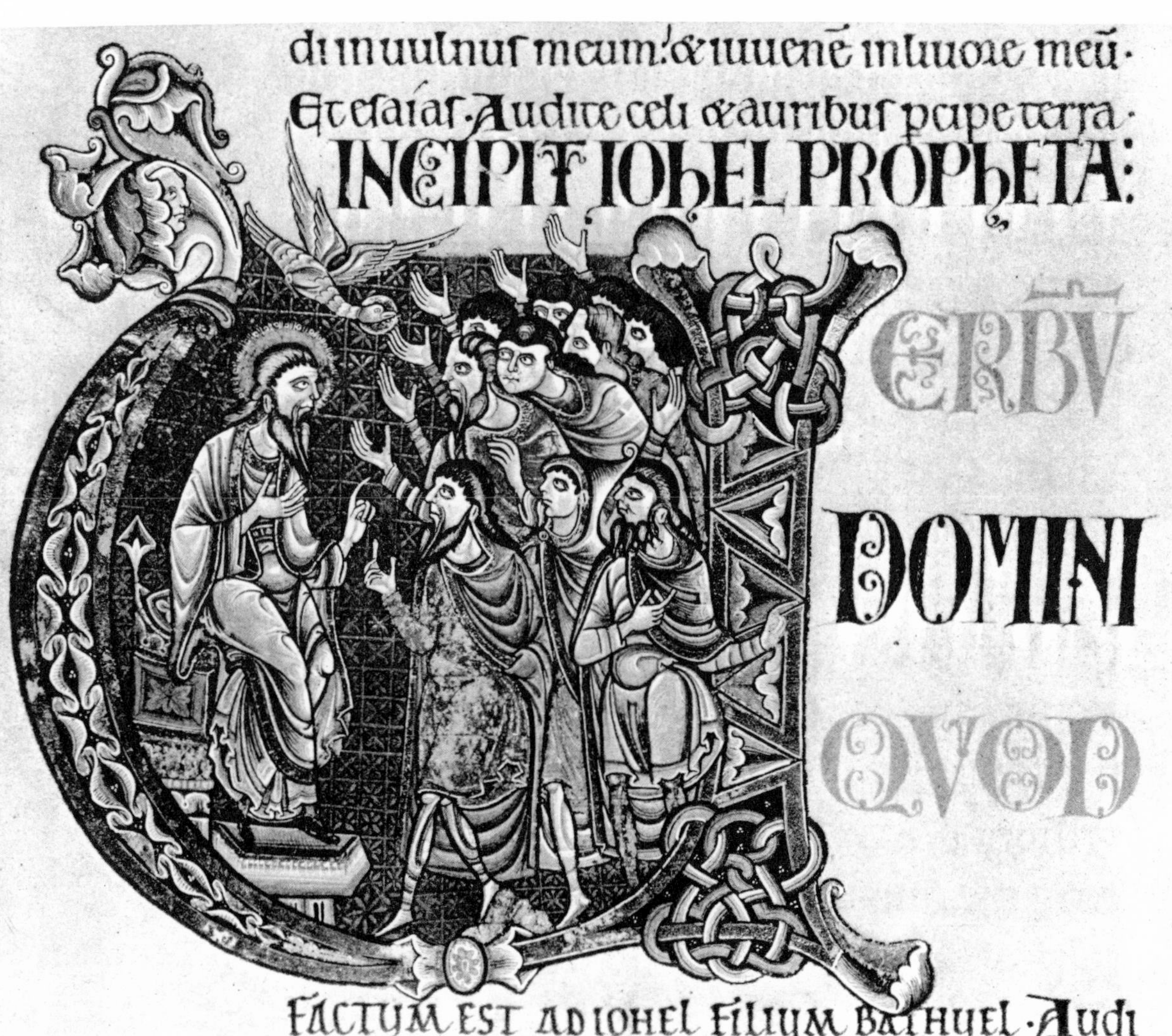

di in uulnus meum: & iuuenē in liuore meū·
Et esaias. Audite celi & auribus pcipe terra·

INCIPIT IOHEL PROPHETA:

VERBV
DOMINI
QVOD
FACTVM EST AD IOHEL FILIVM BATHVEL· Audi

38

PSALTER OF HENRY OF BLOIS

Kiss of Judas, the Scourging

British Museum

1129-1171

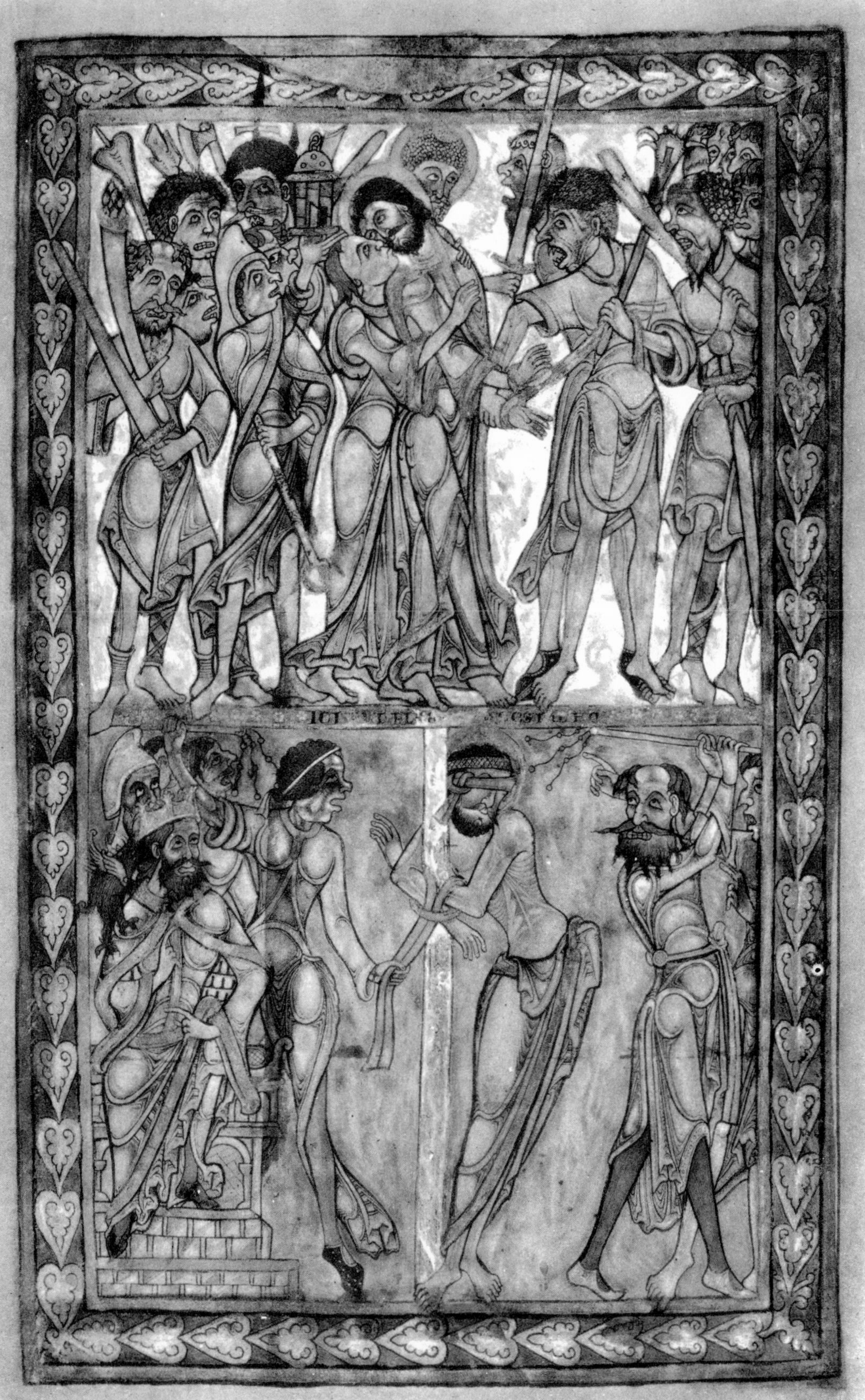

39

BIBLE

Abraham entertains angels unawares.

Sacrifice of Isaac. Jacob's dream (reduced).

Lambeth Palace Library

12th century

EGO · SUM · DEUS · BETHEL · UBI · UNXISTI · LAPIDE

40

BIBLE

Jesse Tree (reduced)

Lambeth Palace Library

12th century

41

BURY BIBLE

Initial page, Epistle of St. Jerome (reduced)

Corpus Christi College, Cambridge

12th century

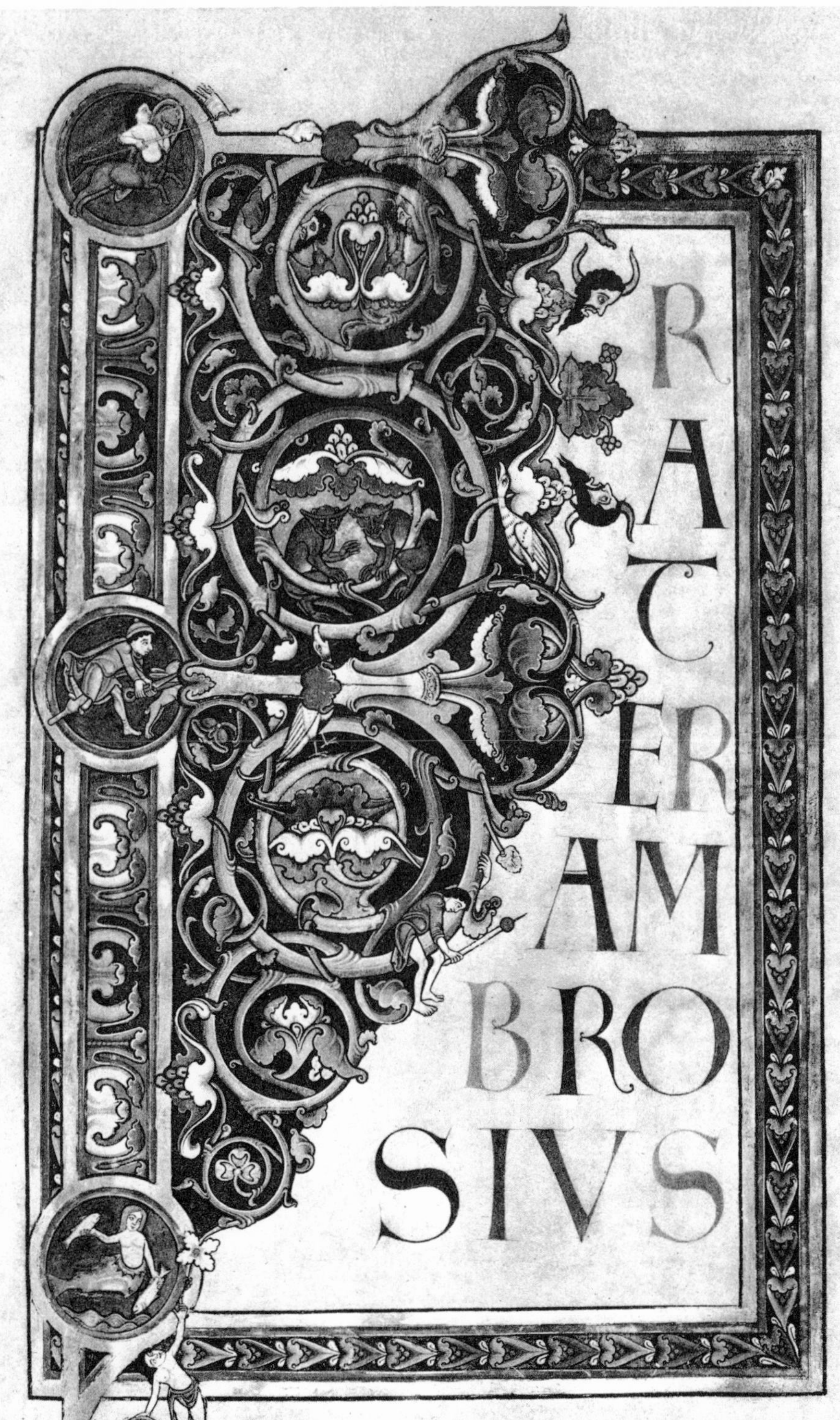

Frater ambrosius tua michi munuscula perferens detulit
simul et suavissimas litteras que in principio amiciciarum
fidem probate iam fidei et veteris amicicie [illegible]

42 a

BURY BIBLE

Initial V. (Isaiah)

Corpus Christi College, Cambridge

12th century

42 b

PSALTER FROM SHAFTESBURY ABBEY

God sends forth the Angel Gabriel

British Museum

Latter half of 12th century

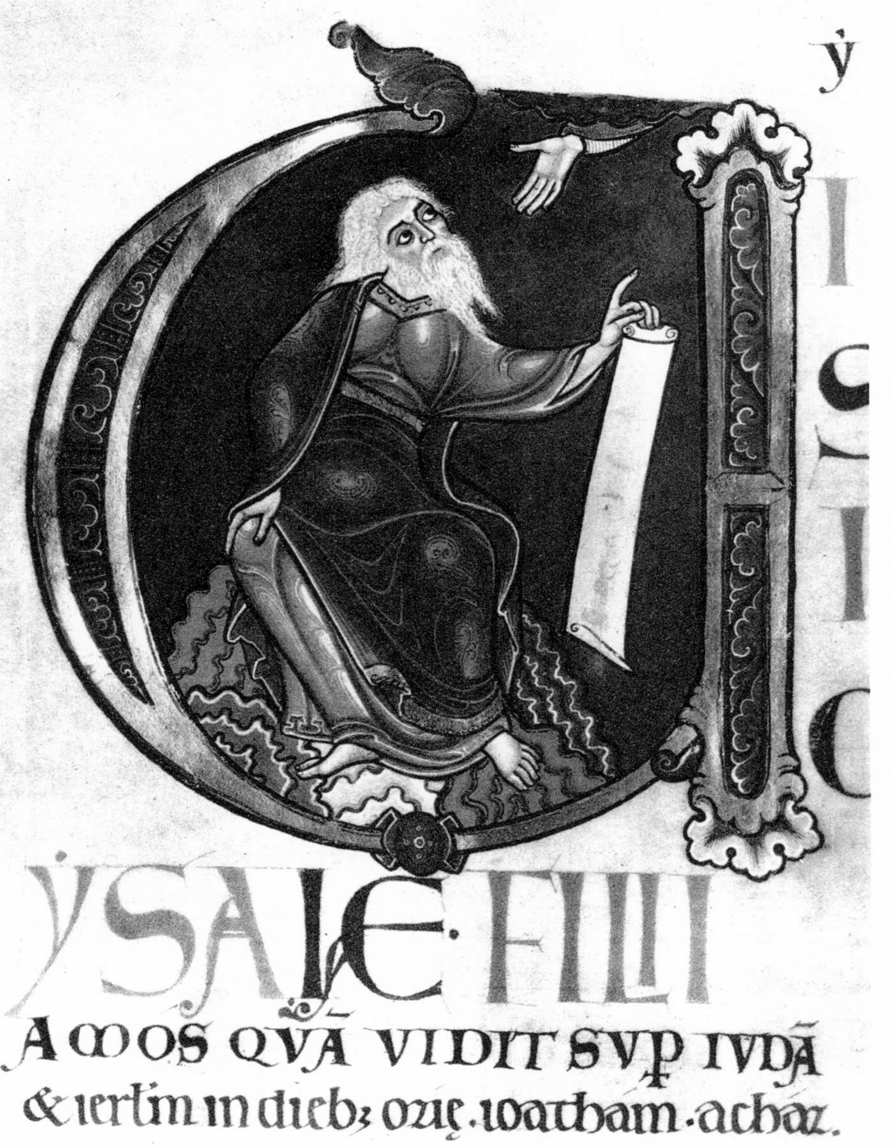
YSAIE FILII
AMOS QVĀ VIDIT SVP̄ IVDĀ
& ierlm in dieb; ozie. ioatham. achaz.

43

PSALTER FROM YORK

Pentecost

Hunterian Museum, Glasgow

c. 1170

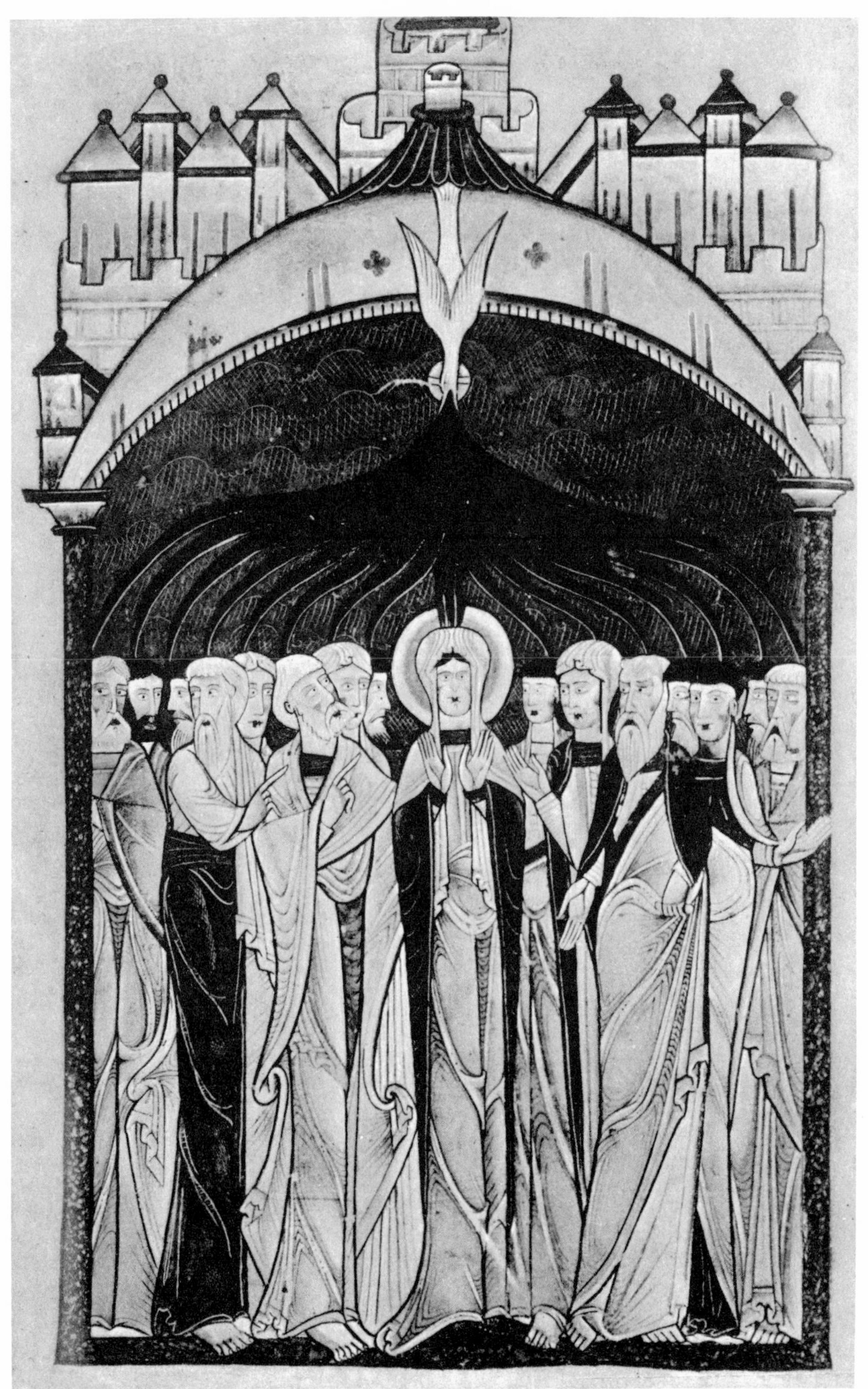

44

PSALTER FROM YORK

Temptation, Raising of Lazarus

Hunterian Museum, Glasgow

c. 1170

ua de ret
satha
na c o
Hec omnia tibi dabo si cadens adoraue

45

PSALTER FROM YORK

Supper at Emmaus and Appearance to Disciples

Hunterian Museum, Glasgow

c1. 170

46

BEDE ON THE APOCALYPSE

Christ of the Apocalypse

St. John's College, Cambridge

Latter half of 12th century

47 [a]

ST. JEROME ON ISAIAH

Portrait of Hugo, the illuminator

Bodleian Library, Oxford

12th century

47 [b]

LIFE OF ST. CUTHBERT

St. Cuthbert at play

University College, Oxford

Latter half of 12th century

48

ST. JEROME ON ISAIAH

Initial E, Death and Assumption of the Virgin

Bodleian Library, Oxford

12th century

49 [a]

BESTIARY

The creation of trees

Bodleian Library, Oxford

Late 12th century

49 [b]

BESTIARY

Hunting of the Unicorn

Bodleian Library, Oxford

Late 12th century

50

BESTIARY

Perindens tree

Bodleian Library, Oxford

Late 12th century

perindens s arbor indie

ENGLISH ILLUMINATION

BY

O. ELFRIDA SAUNDERS

Volume II

PLATES 51-129

51 a

BESTIARY

Caladrius, *British Museum*

End of 12th century

51 b

BESTIARY

Phoenix, *British Museum*

Late 12th century

52 a

BESTIARY

Salamander, *British Museum*

End of 12th century

52 b

BESTIARY

Manticora, *British Museum*

End of 12th century

53

BESTIARY

Elephant, *British Museum*

12th century

54

BESTIARY

Whale, *University Library, Cambridge*

13th century

habeant. Anphi enī grece utrumq; dr̄. i. q̄a in aq̄s ⁊ t̄ris uiuunt.
ut phoce. cocodrilli. ẏpotami. hoc est equi fluctuales.

55

BESTIARY FROM PETERBOROUGH

Leucrocotta etc.

Corpus Christi College, Cambridge

Early 14th century

remi· nec aliud q̃m cornua· aut nares pe
tiit· Cornua: ut pondere desinat· Nares:
ut acrior dolor sit in loco teneriore·

In india nascit bestia nõie leu
crota· que uelo
citate precedit

feras uniũsas.
Ipsa asini fit magnitudine· ceruinis clunis
bus· pectore ac cruribus leonis· capite equi
bisulca ũgula· ore usq; ad aures. Dentiũ
locus osse ppetuo. Hec quidẽ ad formã· nã uo
ces loquentium sonos emulatur.

Cocodrillus a croceo colore dictus
Gignit in nilo flumĩe· aĩal qua
drupes· in terra et in aqua ualẽs.
Longitudine plerumq; xx· cubitorum. Denci
um et unguium imanitate armat. Tan
taq; cutis duricia: ut q̃mus fortiũ ictu
lapidum tergo repulcat: nõ nocet ei· Nocte
in aq̃s· die ĩ humo quiescit· Oua ĩ tra
fouet· Masculas et uices femina seruat·
Hunc pisces quidã serratã hñtes cristam:
tenera uentrium desecantes: interimunt:
Solus aut ẽ omnibus aĩalibus superiora oris
mouet· inferiora uero ĩmota tenet· Stercꝰ
eius fit unguentum· unde uetule et rugose
meretrices facies suas pungunt· fiuntq;
pulcre donec sudor defluens lauet· Cui
Sp̃ualiter· figurã portant ypocrite· siue luxuriosi
atq; auari· qui q̃mus uicio superbie
inflent: tabe luxurie maculent: auari
cie morbo obsideant: tñ rigidi ac uelut
sãnissimi ĩ iustificacõibus legis corã hõibus
sese ostendũt mcede· Nocte in aq̃s. die ĩ
humo quiescit· qr ypocrite q̃mus luxuriose uiuãt
tñ sẽ et iuste uiuere dici delectant· Conscii sũ
e malicie corda plangũt· licet usu semp tra
hãt assuetudo eos ad peccatã. Superiora oris
mouet: qr hñ scõrum patrum exempla· uiborumq; co
piam aliis ĩ uerbo ostendũt· cũ minime cor
que dicũt in se ostendũt. De stercore eiũ
guentum fit: qr plerumq; mali ab imperitis
laudant de perpetrato malo. aut uelut un
guento huĩ mundi fauoribus extolluntur. Se
cũ iudex districtus peccatis malis iram
suã ad feriendũ pmouebit· tũc omnis
ille decor laudis uelo fumi euanescet·

In india nasci
tur bestia que
manticora dr.
triplici dentiũ
ordine coeun
te uicibus alter

nis facie hõis. glaucis oculis. sanguineo co
lore· corpore leonino. cauda uelut scorpio
nis aculeo spiculata· uoce tam q̃m sibila
ut imitetur modulos fistularũ. Humanas
carnes auidissime affectat· pedibus sic
uiget· saltibus sic potest ut morari eã nec
extentissima spacia possint· nec obsta
cula latissima.

Ethiopia
mittit
bestiã pa
randrũ nomine
bou magnitudĩe·

bisulco uestigio. ramosis cornibus· capite cer
uino. ursi colore· et pari uillo profundo.
Hunc parandrũ affirmãt habitũ metu
uertere et cũ delitescit: fieri ad similitudinẽ
cuiuscumq; rei proximauit. siue illa saxo al
ba sit. seu frutecto uirens. siue quẽ aliũ
modũ pferat.

Vulpis
dr̃ q̃si
uolupis

56

WESTMINSTER PSALTER

Psalm LI, *British Museum*

Late 12th century

holocaustis non delectaberis.
Sacrificium deo spiritus contribulatus: cor con
tritum et humiliatum deus non despicies.
Benigne fac in bona voluntate tua syon:
et edificentur muri ierusalem.
Tunc acceptabis sacrificium iusticie obla
tiones et holocausta: tunc imponent
super altare tuum vitulos.

QUID GLORIA
RIS IN MALI
CIA: QUI PO
TENS ES
IN INIQUITATE

Tota die iniusticiam cogitavit lingua
tua: sicut novacula acuta fecisti dolum.
Dilexisti maliciam super benignitatem:
iniquitatem magis quam loqui
equitatem.
Dilexisti omnia verba precipitationis:

57

WESTMINSTER PSALTER

Annunciation, *British Museum*

Late 12th century

Aue maria gratia plena.

58 a

MANERIUS BIBLE

Initial page from Genesis, *Paris*

Late 12th century

58 b

PSALTER

Initial Q to Psalm LI, *British Museum*

Late 12th century

58 c

PSALTER

Initial S of Psalm LII, *British Museum*

Early 13th century

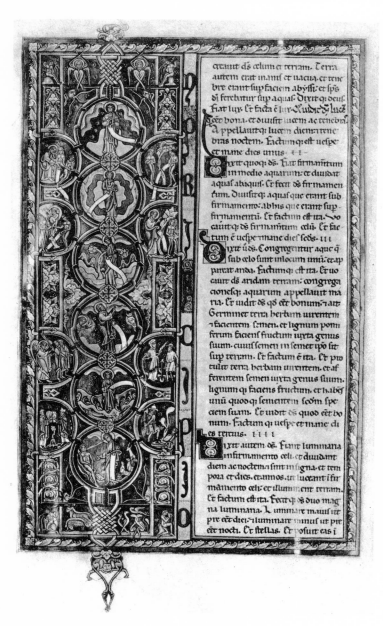

59 [a]

LIFE OF ST. CUTHBERT

An eagle provides food, *British Museum*

C. 1200

59 [b]

LIFE OF ST. CUTHBERT

St. Cuthbert heals a child, *British Museum*

C. 1200

xxxiii·cap· Quom epr mortalitatis morientē
puerum matri sanum restituerit.

60

LIFE OF ST. GUTHLAC

St. Guthlac carried off by demons

British Museum

Late 12th century

Demones fert Guthl in aere
cedentes eum.
Guth
lac.
Beccelin.

61

PSALTER

Feast in Simon's house, Entry into Jerusalem

British Museum

Early 13th century

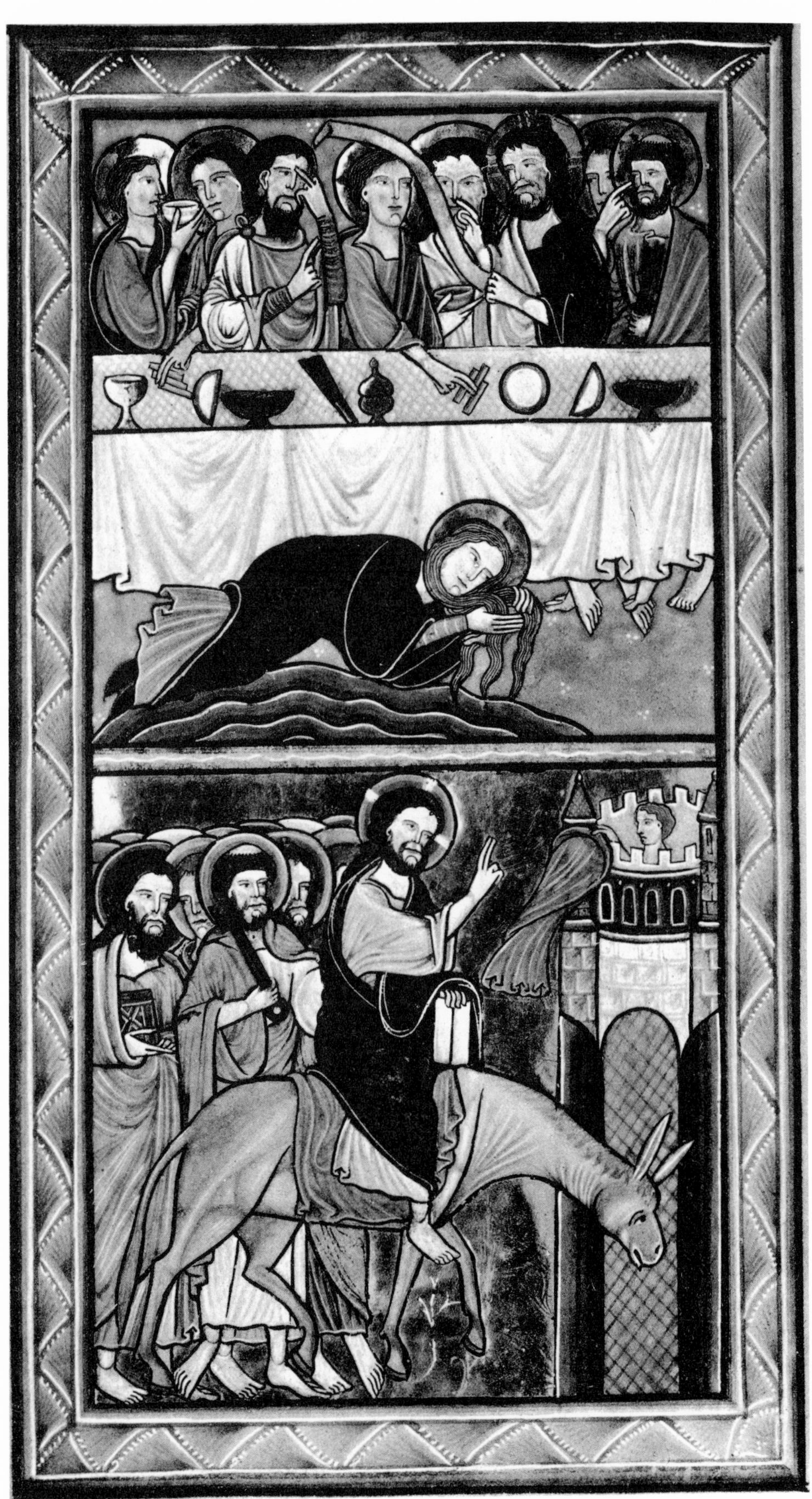

62

PSALTER

Calendar for February, *British Museum*

Early 13th century

Quarta [K] subit mortem, prosternit tercia fortem.
Februarius habet dies xxviii luna xxix.

D
xi E iiii non. Purificatio sce Marie
xix F iii non. Sce werburge uirginis
viii G ii non.
A Nonas Sce agathe uirg. et mris.
xvi B viii id. Scor. Vedasti et amandi
v C vii id.
D vi id.
xiii E v id.
ii F iiii id. Scar. virginum Scolastice et Austroberte
G iii id.
x A ii id. Translatio sce frideswide uirg.
B Idus
xviii C xvi kl. Marcii. Sci valentini mris.
vii D xv kl.
E xiiii kl. Sce Iuliane uirg.
xv F xiii kl. Sci ... epi. et confess.
iiii G xii kl.
A xi kl.
xii B x kl.
i C ix kl.
D viii kl. Cathedra sci petri.
ix E vii kl.
F vi kl. SCI MATHIE APOSTOLI
xvii G v kl.
vi A iiii kl.
B iii kl.
xiiii C ii kl. Sci Oswaldi archiepi.

Memento quod anno bisextili lune februarii mensis xxx dies computes et tamen luna marcii mensis xxx dies habeat sicut semper habet ne paschalis lune uacillet.

63

PSALTER

Crucifixion (slightly reduced)

Fitzwilliam Museum, Cambridge

1260-1270

64

PSALTER

Beatus page, Christ in glory

Fitzwilliam Museum, Cambridge

1260-1270

EATVS VIR

65 a

HOURS BY WILLIAM DE BRAILES

Passion Scenes

Dyson Perrins Collection

1220-1240

65 b

PSALTER

Initial D of Psalm XXVI

All Souls' College, Oxford

c. 1250

omine labia mea aperies:
et os meum annunciabit

es meus stetit in directo: in ecclesiis bene
dicam te domine.

66

PSALTER

Crucifixion

All Souls' College, Oxford

c. 1250

IHC NAZARENUS:
REX IVDEORVM:

67

MISSAL OF HENRY OF CHICHESTER

Nativity, *Rylands Library*, *Manchester*

13th century

68

MISSAL OF HENRY OF CHICHESTER

Virgin and Child

Rylands Library, Manchester

13th century

FILI·DEI·MISERERE·MEI

69

GLOSSED PSALTER AND HOURS OF ROBERT DE LINDESEY

Angels appearing to shepherds, Three kings before Herod

St. John's College, Cambridge

C. 1220

70

OSCOTT PSALTER

Apostle, *Dyson Perrins Collection*

Latter half of 13th century

71

DE QUINCEY APOCALYPSE

St. Catherine, *Lambeth Palace Library*

Late 13th century

72

DE QUINCEY APOCALYPSE

St. Christopher, *Lambeth Palace Library*

Late 13th century

73

DE QUINCEY APOCALYPSE

Allegory of the penitent

Lambeth Palace Library

Late 13th century

74

DE QUINCEY APOCALYPSE

Crucifixion, *Lambeth Palace Library*

Late 13th century

75 a

BIBLE OF ROBERT DE BELLO

Initial F before II Macabees

British Museum

1224-1253

75 b

BIBLE OF ROBERT DE BELLO

Initial V before Isaiah

British Museum

1224-1253

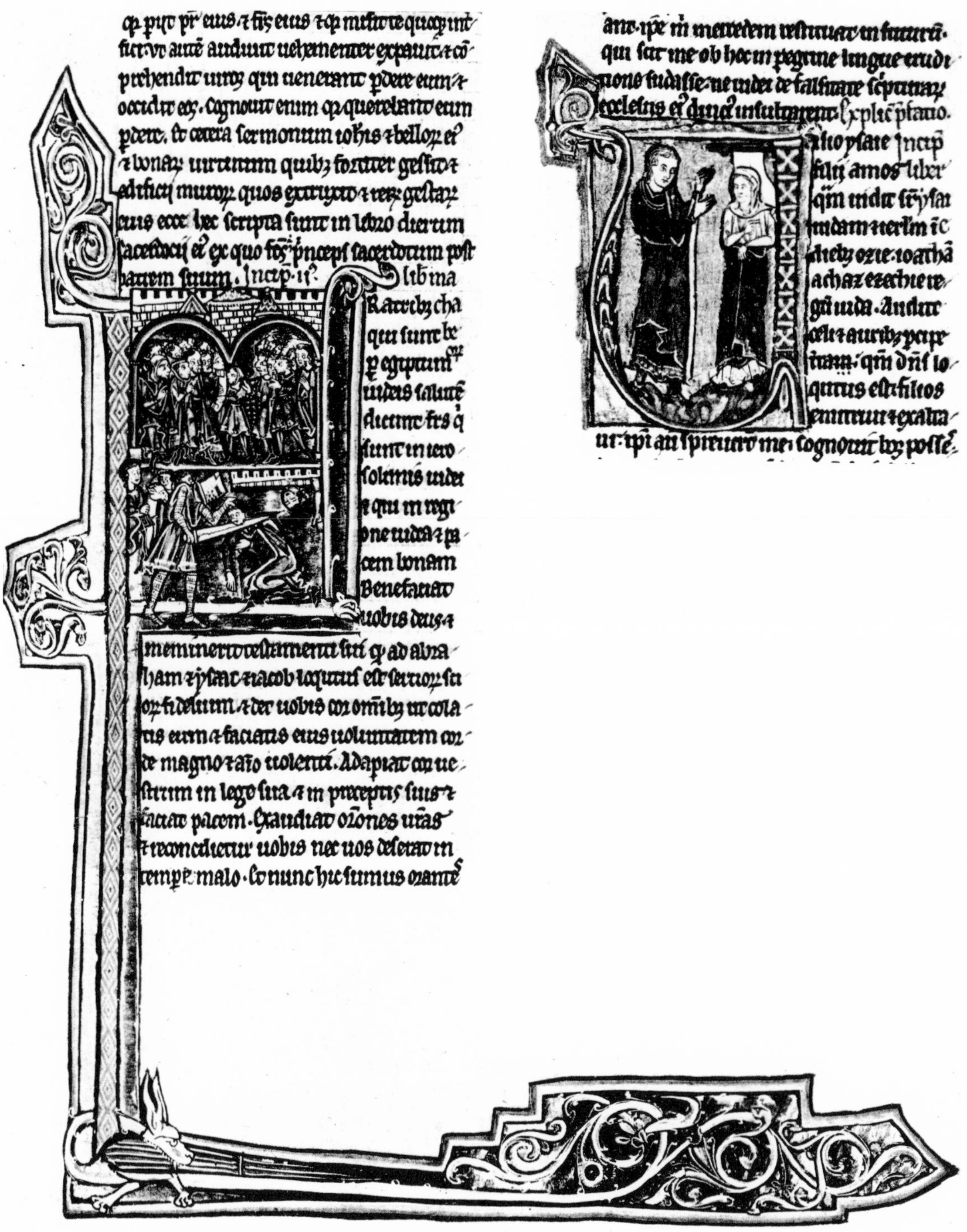

quod prius pater eius et filii eius et quod misisset quoque interfecit. Ut autem audivit vehementer expavit et con-
prehendit viros qui venerant perdere eum et
occidit eos. Cognovit enim quod querebant eum
perdere. Et cetera sermonum Iohannis et bellorum eius
et bonarum virtutum quibus fortiter gessit et
edificii murorum quos extruxit et rerum gestarum
eius ecce hec scripta sunt in libro dierum
sacerdotii eius ex quo factus est princeps sacerdotum post
patrem suum. Incipit II liber Ma-
chabeorum.

Fratribus qui sunt per Egyptum Iudeis salutem dicunt fratres qui sunt in Ierosolimis Iudei et qui in regione Iudee et pacem bonam. Benefaciat vobis Deus et meminerit testamenti sui quod ad Abraham et Ysaac et Iacob locutus est servorum suorum fidelium. Et det vobis cor omnibus ut colatis eum et faciatis eius voluntatem corde magno et animo volenti. Adaperiat cor vestrum in lege sua et in preceptis suis et faciat pacem. Exaudiat orationes vestras et reconcilietur vobis nec vos deserat in tempore malo. Et nunc hic sumus orantes

ant. Ipse in mercedem restituat in futurum qui scit me ob hoc in peregrine lingue eruditione sudasse ne Iudei de falsitate scripturarum ecclesiis eius diutius insultarent. Explicit prefatio. Incipit Ysaie prophete.

Visio Ysaie filii Amos quam vidit super Iudam et Ierusalem in diebus Ozie, Ioatham, Achaz, Ezechie regum Iuda. Audite celi et auribus percipe terra quoniam Dominus locutus est. Filios enutrivi et exaltavi, ipsi autem spreverunt me. Cognovit bos possessorem

76

BIBLE BY WILLIAM OF DEVON

Initial A before Judith (slightly reduced)

British Museum

1251-1274

doctum· ius q; sacerdotale ⁊ leuiticum.
Igr̄ mundaui eos ab omnibȝ alieni
genis· ⁊ ɔstitui ordines sacerdotū ⁊ le
uitaꝝ uniūqȝ in ministerio suo ⁊ in ob
li. latōe lignoꝝ· in temporibȝ ɔstitutis
⁊ in primitiuis. Memento mei d̄s meus
in bonum: am̄. prologus iudith·

A pud hebreos liber
iudith inter agiog
pha legr̄: cui aucto
ritas ad roboran
da illa que in ɔten
tiōem ueniunt mi
nus ydonea iudica
tur· chaldeo tn̄ sermone ɔscriptus: in
ter historias computatur· s; qr hunc
librum synodus nicena in nūo scrip
turaꝝ scāꝝ legitur computasse.
adquieui postulatōi ur̄e immo exac
tioni· ⁊ sepositis occupatōibȝ quibus
uehem̄ter artabar: huic unam lucu
braciunculā dedi: magis sensum ex
sensu q̄m ex ūbo ūbum transferens.
Multoꝝ codicum uarietatē uiciosissi
mā amputaui· sola ea que intelligē
cia integra in ūbis chaldeis inuenire
potui: latinis expressi· Accipite iu
dith uiduam castitatis exemplum
⁊ triumphali laude preconiis perpe
tuis eam declarate· hanc enim nō so
lum feminis s; ⁊ uiris imitabilē de
dit: qr castitatis eius remunerator
uirtutem ei talem tribuit: ut inuic
tum omnibȝ hominibȝ uinceret: et
insup̄abilem superaret·
Incipit liber iudith·

A rphaxat ita; rex
medorum subiu
gauerat multas
gentes imperio
suo· ⁊ ipse edifica
uit ciuitatem po
tentissimā q̄m ap
pellauit egbatanis· Ex lapidibus
quadratis ⁊ sectis fecit muros eius
in altitudine cubitoꝝ· lxx· ⁊ in lati
tudine cubitoꝝ· xxx· turres ūo eius
posuit in altitudine cubitoꝝ centū·
per q̄drum ūo earum latus utrumq;
uicenoꝝ pedum spatio tendebatur·
posuitq; portas eius in altitudinē tur
rium· Et gl'abatur q̄i potens in poten
cia exercitus sui· ⁊ in gl'a q̄drigaꝝ sua
rum· Anno igitur· xii· regni sui· na
bugodonosor rex assirioꝝ qui regna
bat in niniue ciuitate magna· pug
nauit contra arphaxat· ⁊ optinuit e
um in campo magno qui appellatur
ragau circa eufraten ⁊ tigrim ⁊ iado
dam in campo erioch regis elicorum.
Tūc exaltatum ē regnum nabugod.
⁊ cor eius eleuatum ē· ⁊ misit ad om
nes qui hītabant in cilicia ⁊ damas
co ⁊ libano· ⁊ ad gentes que ī carme
lo sunt ⁊ cedar ⁊ inhītantes galileā
⁊ in campo magno esdrelon· ⁊ ad oēs
qui erant in samaria ⁊ t'ns flumē ior
danē usq; ad ierl'm ⁊ omnē terram
iesse: quousq; perueniatur ad mon
tes ethiopie· Ad hos omnes misit
nuntios nabugodon· rex assirioꝝ· q
omnes uno animo ɔtradixerunt· ⁊ re
miserunt eos uacuos· ac sine honore
abierunt· Tunc indignatus nabu
god· rex ad omnē t'ram illam: iura
uit per tronum suum ⁊ regnum q se
de omnibȝ defenderet·

A nno· xiii· nabug· regis uicesima
⁊ secunda die mensis primi: fcm̄
est ūbum in domo nabug· regis assi
rioꝝ: ut defenderet se· Vocauitq; om̄s
maiores natu· omnesq; duces bella
tores suos· ⁊ hūit cum eis misterium
consilii sui· Dixitq; cogitatōem su
am in eo ēē ut omnē t'ram suo subiu
garet imperio· Qd̄ dictū cū placuis
set omnibȝ: uocauit nabug· rex ho
lofernem principem milicie sue: ⁊ dix
it ei· Egredere aduersus omne regnū occi
dentis· ⁊ contra eos precipue qui con
tempserunt imperiū meum· n̄ parcet
oculus tuus ulli regno· omnemq; urbē
munitā subiugabis m̄· Tunc holo
fernes uocauit duces ⁊ magistratus uir
tutis assirioꝝ ⁊ dinumerauit uiros in
expeditōem· sicut preceperat ei rex· cen
tum· xx· m̄· peditum pugnatorū· ⁊ e
quites ⁊ sagittarios· xii· m̄· omnesq;
expeditōem suam fecit preire in mul
titudine innumerabiliū cameloꝝ cū

77

PETRUS COMESTOR FROM ASHRIDGE COLLEGE

Initials R and I before Genesis (reduced)

British Museum

1283-1300

Reue
rendo pa
tri et do
mino su
o Willel
mo dei
gracia
Senonen
si archiepiscopo petrus seruus xpi
presbiter trecensis uitam bonam
et exitum beatum. Causa suscepti
laboris: fuit instans peticio soci
orum. Qui cum hystoriam sacre
scripture in serie et glosis diffusa
lectitarent: breuem nimis et inex
positam: opus aggredi me compu
lerunt. Ad quod pro ueritate hys
torie consequenda: recurrerent. In
quo sic animus stilo temperauit.
ut a dictis patrum non recederem.
Licet nouitas fauorabilis sit et mul
ceat aures. Porro a cosmographi
a moysi inchoans: riuulum hys
toricum deduxi: usque ad ascensionem
saluatoris. Pelagus misteriorum
peritioribus relinquens. in quibus et
uetera prosequi: et noua cudere li
cet. De hystoriis quoque ethnicorum
quedam pro ratione temporum
inserui. instar riuuli. qui secus
alueum diuerticula que inue
nerit repellens: preterfluere tamen
non cessat. Verumptamen quia
stilo rudi opus est lima: uobis
pater inclite limam reseruaui. ut
huic operi deo uolente et correctio
uestra splendorem: et auctoritas
prebeat perhennitatem. per omni
a benedictus deus amen. Incipit

Imperatoris maiestatis est: in pa
latio tres habere mansiones. au
ditorium. uel consistorium. in
quo iura decernit. Cenaculum in
quo cybaria distribuit. thalamum:
in quo quiescit. Ad hunc modum
imperator noster qui imperat uen
tis et mari: mundum habet pro au
ditorio. ubi ad nutum eius om
nia disponuntur. Unde illud celum
et terram ego impleo. Secundum hunc
dicitur dominus. Unde domini est ter
ra et cetera. animam iusti pro tha
lamo quia delicie sunt eius esse cum
filiis hominum. et secundum hunc dici
tur sponsus. et anima cuiusque ui
ri sponsa. Sanctam scripturam
pro cenaculo. in qua sic suos in
ebriat: ut sobrios reddat. Unde am
bulauimus in domo domini cum
consensu. idest in sacra scriptura
idipsum sapientes. Secundum hunc
dicitur paterfamilias: huius ce
naculi sunt tres partes. funda
mentum. paries. tectum. Hystori
a est fundamentum. cuius sunt
tres species annalis. kalendaria.
effimera. Allegoria paries superi
nitens que per factum: aliud fac
tum figurat. Tropologia doma
culminis. superpositum. que per
id quod factum est: quid a nobis
sit faciendum insinuat. prima:
planior. secunda: acutior. tercia:
suauior. A fundamento: sumemus
principium: loquendi. immo ab
ipsius fundamenti principio. co
operante qui omnium princeps
est et principium.

78

PETRUS COMESTOR FROM ASHRIDGE COLLEGE

Initial Q before Numbers (reduced)

British Museum

1283-1300

Hystoria numeri uel numerorum.

Quarta huius hystorie distinctio hebraice dicitur ua... edaber quod sonat et locutus est. Apud nos tamen et non habetur nomen grecum arithmoth: latinum est liber numeri uel numerorum. uel dicitur quandoque numeri pluraliter. Unde et dici solet legitur hoc in numeris. Merito autem hoc nomine censetur: quia quatuor hic principaliter numerantur. scilicet de omni populo: uiri apti ad arma ferenda. primogeniti. leuite qui etiam bis numerantur. mansiones per quas profecti sunt. Sed nec mulieres nec minores uiginti annorum. nec uulgus permixtum. nec debiles ad bella numerantur. Ad hanc partem hystorie transit sic Iosephus.

Moyses predictam constitutionem legum dum sub syna moraretur a deo cognouit. et hebreis scriptam tradidit. Cumque circa legis lationem hec sufficere putaret: ad exercitium militaris uite conuersus est. et numerari iussit populorum capita pugnare ualentium. Moyses dicit super hec dominum sibi locutum fuisse dicens.

Locutus est dominus ad moysen in deserto syna in tabernaculo federis. prima die mensis secundi anno secundo egressionis ex egypto. Et nota quia pretermittit hic quedam que facta sunt in primo mense anni secundi. scilicet oblationem principum duodecim quam fecerunt singuli singulis diebus in dedicatione tabernaculi. et sollempnitatem phase. que proprio nomine dicitur pascha in deserto celebratum. et sortem de sanctificatione leuitarum. De his tamen infra aget per recapitulationem. Prosequentes ergo ordinem libri dicimus quia moyses et aaron. et duodecim principes tribuum ex precepto domini anno secundo mense secundo die prima mensis numerauerunt uiros preter tribum leui a uicesimo anno et supra. Iosephus certum terminum ponit. scilicet usque ad quinquagesimum annum. et numerati sunt per generationes et familias et domos. et nomina et capita singulorum. Hec autem quinque ad inculcationem tantum quidam posita tradunt. et hic et in iosue. sed congrue distingui possunt. Generationes et cognationes uocat hic tribus ipsas duodecim familias: que ex ipsis filiis patriar

79

CHRONICA MAIORA OF MATTHEW PARIS

Heads of Christ and Virgin

Corpus Christi College, Cambridge

Middle of 13th century

80

CHRONICA MINORA OF MATTHEW PARIS

Norman Kings (slightly reduced)

British Museum

Middle of 13th century

81

COLLECTIONS OF MATTHEW PARIS

The knighting of Offa

British Museum

Middle of 13th century

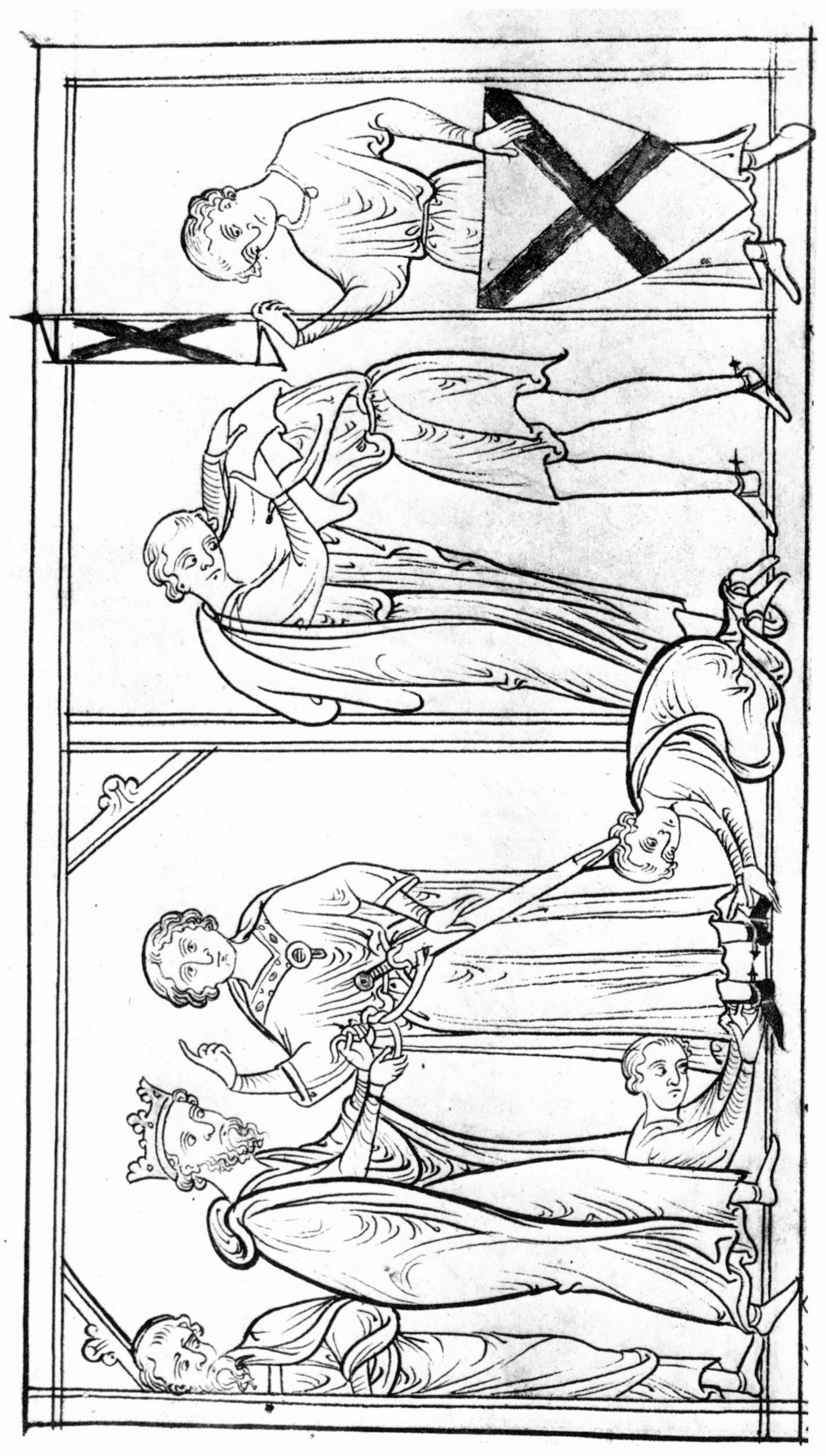

82

COLLECTIONS OF MATTHEW PARIS

Battle scene from Life of Offa

British Museum

Middle of 13th century

83

LIFE OF ST. EDWARD (THE CONFESSOR)

Blind beggars come to be healed

University Library, Cambridge

c. 1250

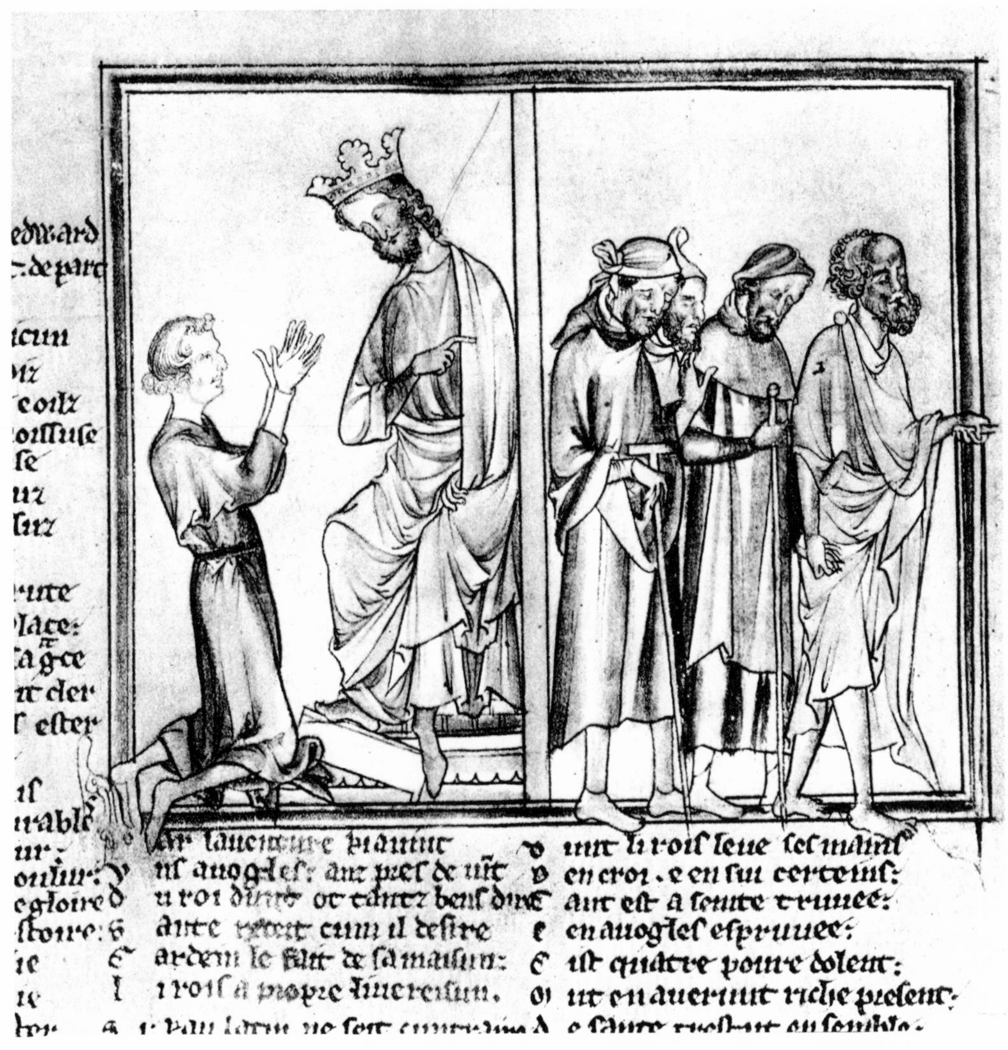

84

LIFE OF ST. EDWARD (THE CONFESSOR)

Two pilgrims return his ring

University Library, Cambridge

c. 1250

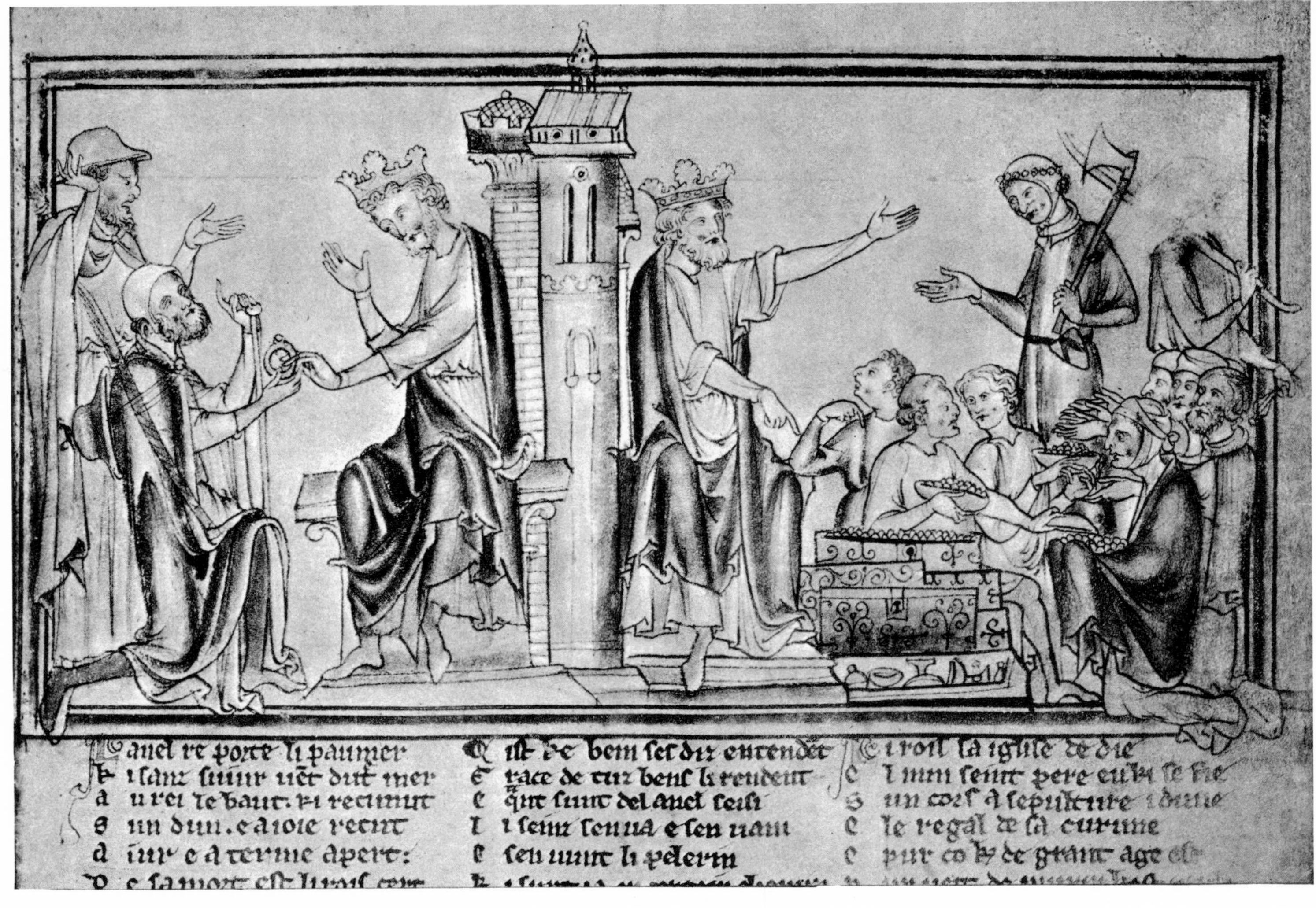
anel re porte li paumer
k isant suuir uet dut mer
a u rei de baut. ki recunut
s un dun. e a iole recut
d iur e a terme apert:
Q is de bein set dir entender
E race de tuz bens li rendeint
E qui sunt del anel seisi
L i seint seinna e sen nam
E seu uunt li pelerin
C i roil la iglise de die
E l nun seint pere eu ki se fie
S un cors a sepulture idune
E le regal de sa curune
E pur co ki de grant age est

85

WESTMINSTER PSALTER

St. Christopher, *British Museum*

(Drawing added in 13th century)

86

PSALTER OF ALPHONSO (Tenison Psalter)

Beatus page, *British Museum*

1284

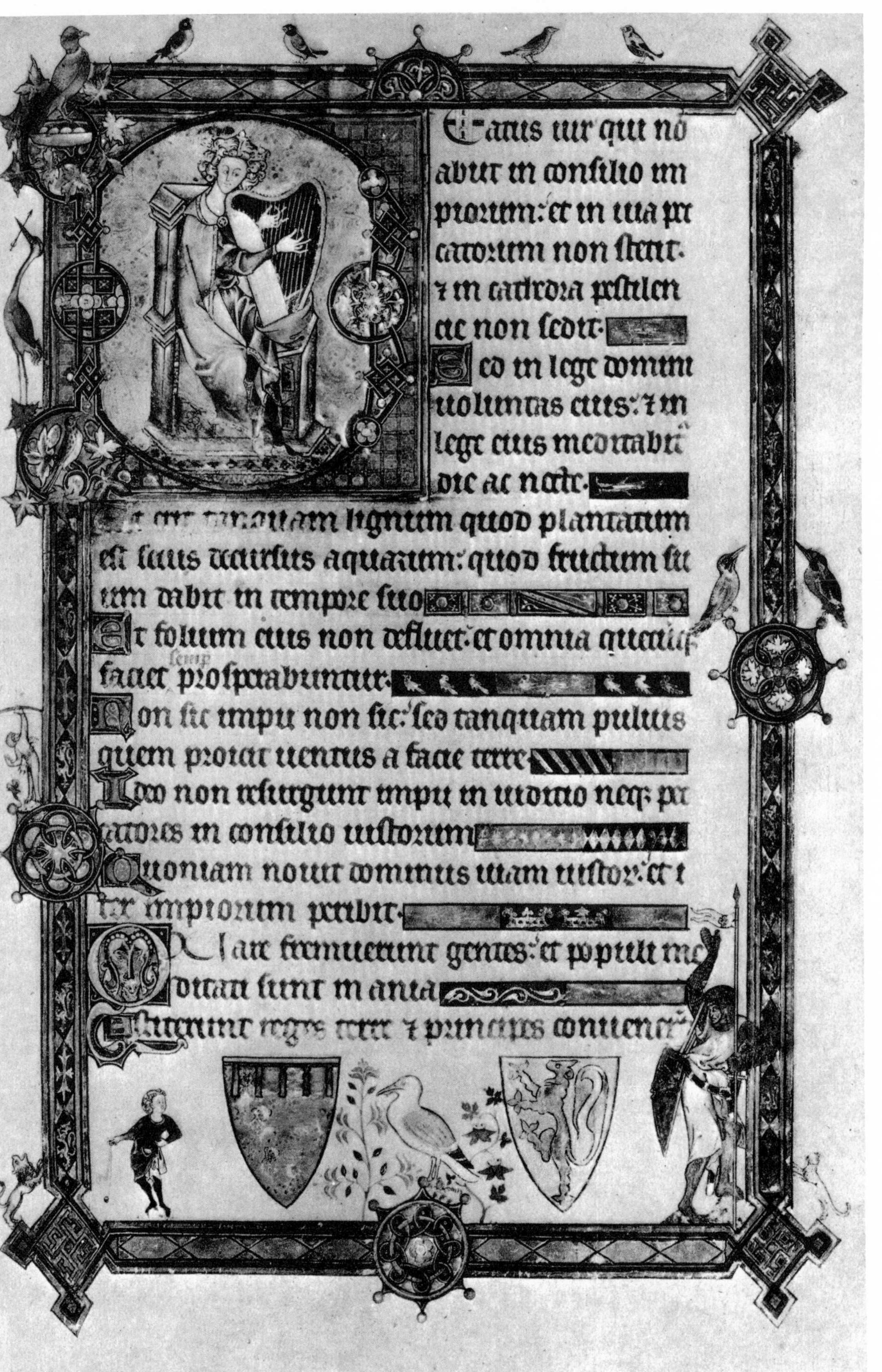

Beatus uir qui nō
abiit in consilio im
piorum: et in uia pec
catorum non stetit.
⁊ in cathedra pestilen
cie non sedit.
Sed in lege domini
uoluntas eius: ⁊ in
lege eius meditabitur
die ac nocte.
Et erit tanquam lignum quod plantatum
est secus decursus aquarum: quod fructum su
um dabit in tempore suo
Et folium eius non defluet: et omnia quecunque
faciet semp prosperabuntur.
Non sic impii non sic: sed tanquam puluis
quem proicit uentus a facie terre.
Ideo non resurgunt impii in iudicio neq; pec
catores in consilio iustorum
Quoniam nouit dominus uiam iustorum: et i
ter impiorum peribit.
Quare fremuerunt gentes: et populi me
ditati sunt inania
Astiterunt reges terre ⁊ principes conuenerunt

87

PSALTER OF ALPHONSO (Tenison Psalter)

Sts. Lucy, Mary Magdalen, Helena, and Radegund

British Museum

1284

88 a

PSALTER FROM HUTH COLLECTION

Last Judgment, *British Museum*

1280-1300

88 b

PSALTER FROM HUTH COLLECTION

Initial D, Psalm CIX. *British Museum*

1280-1300

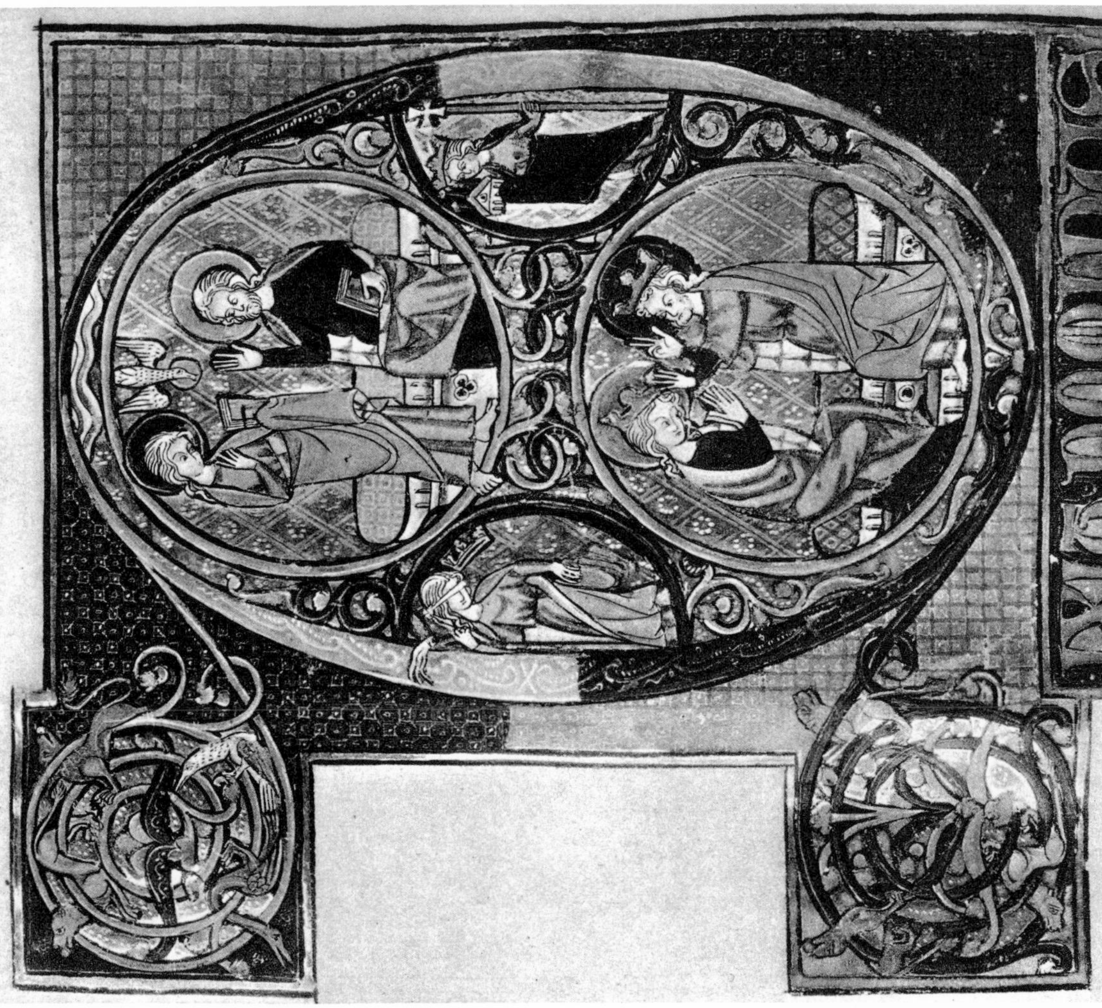

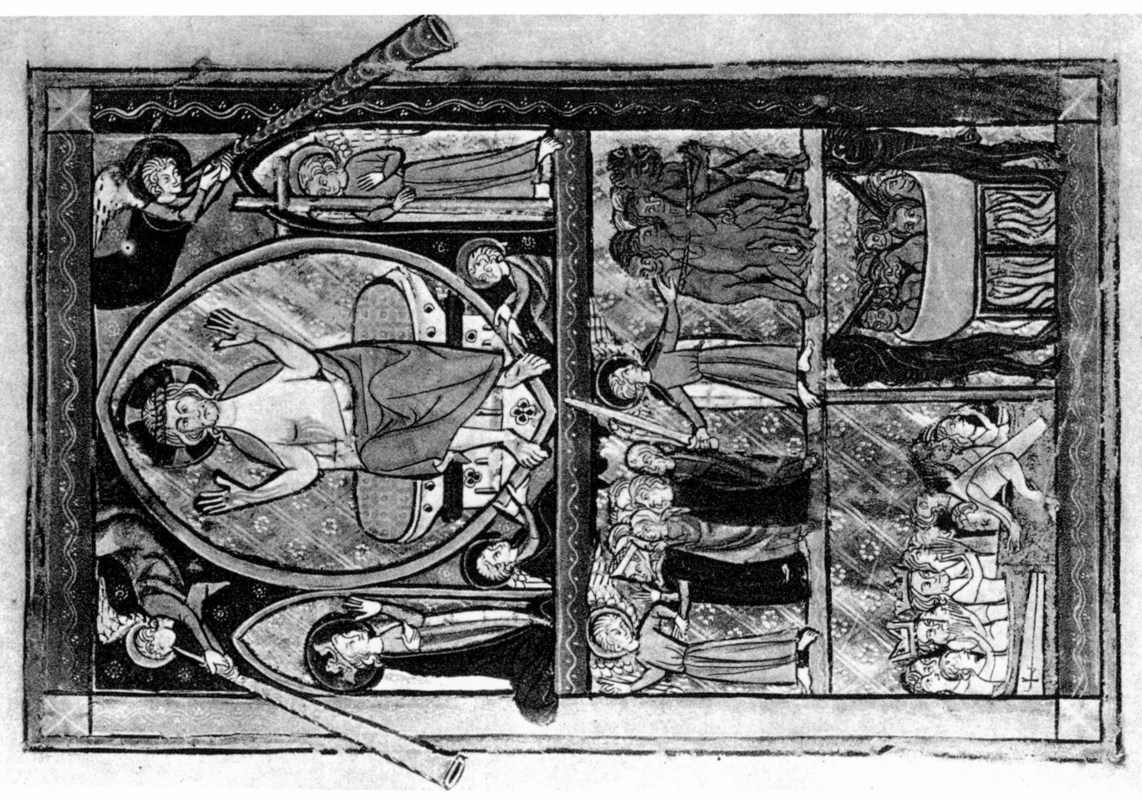

89

GRANDISON PSALTER

Baptism, Agony in the Garden

British Museum

Late 13th century

90 a

APOCALYPSE

The armies of horsemen, Rev. IX. 16.

Paris

Early 13th century

90 b

APOCALYPSE

Michael and his angels warring with the dragon

Paris

Early 13th century

91

APOCALYPSE

Two angels, Rev. XII. 10.

Bodleian Library, Oxford

1200-1250

92

TRINITY COLLEGE APOCALYPSE

Life of St. John

Trinity College, Cambridge

c. 1230

ci cumaunde domitien ke sein iohan seit issillez en le isle ke est apele pathmos.
ettez iohan
ki despit nos
deus en issil
en le isle ki
est apele par
mos.
ci est seint iohan mis en nef vers le isle ki est apel pathmos.

93

TRINITY COLLEGE APOCALYPSE

The scarlet woman, Rev. XVII. 3.

Trinity College, Cambridge

c. 1230

Veneis io uus
mustrerei la
dãpnaciun de
la graunt pu
teine. ke set sur
multes ewes.

94[a]

APOCALYPSE

Christ adored by the 24 Elders, Rev. IX. 10.

British Museum

Late 13th century

94[b]

APOCALYPSE

The rider on the white horse, Rev. VI. 2.

British Museum

Late 13th century

95 [a]

APOCALYPSE

The scarlet woman, Rev. XVII. 3.

British Museum

Late 13th century

95 [b]

APOCALYPSE

The dragon wars with the seed of the woman, Rev. XII. 17.

Dyson Perrins Collection

Middle of 13th century

96 a

APOCALYPSE

The scarlet woman, Rev. XVII. 3.

Paris

Late 13th century

96 b

APOCALYPSE

The vintage. Rev. XIV. 17.

Paris

Late 13th century

97 a

APOCALYPSE

The scarlet woman. Rev. XVII. 3.

Paris

Late 13th century

97 b

DOUCE APOCALYPSE

Fourth Angel sounding, Rev. VIII. 12.

Bodleian Library, Oxford

1270-1300

98 a

DE QUINCEY APOCALYPSE

Worship of the Beast, Rev. XIII. 4.

Lambeth Palace Library

Late 13th century

98 b

DE QUINCEY APOCALYPSE

Vintage Scene, Rev. XIV. 17.

Lambeth Palace Library

Late 13th century

99 [a]

APOCALYPSE

The rider on the pale horse, Rev. VI. 8.

British Museum

Early 14th century

99 [b]

APOCALYPSE

St. John kneeling before Christ

British Museum

Early 14th century

Ceo afferme les prophecies de cest liure a touz ceaux qe le oiront

100

APOCALYPSE

The rider on the white horse, Rev. VI. 2.

British Museum

Early 14th century

E ieo ui. k. lui aigneus out ouert un des
seaus. e. oi. k. un des quatre bestes me
dist. ausi cum uoice de toneire. uenez
ueer. E. ieo ui un blaũc cheual eissir.
e. cil. k. seent sure out un arc. e. corone li
est done. e. il eissi en uenchaũt p̃ ueintre.
Par le cheual blaũc. est
signefie seint eglise. k. est
nettez de peche p̃ baptes
me p̃ la mort ihu crist.
Cil ki seent sure. signefie le filz dieu.
Par le arc. est signefie seint escpt̃e

101

QUEEN MARY'S PSALTER

Psalm LI. Presentation. Initial

British Museum

Early 14th century

uid gloriaris
in malicia: qui
potens es in in-
iquitate.

102

QUEEN MARY'S PSALTER

Psalm CXVIII. Passion scenes

British Museum

Early 14th century

Da michi intellectum. ⁊ scrutabor
legem tuam: et custodiam illam in
toto corde meo.
Deduc me in semitā mandator

Edwardus.

103

PETERBOROUGH PSALTER (and BESTIARY)

St. Andrew and David

Corpus Christi College, Cambridge

Early 14th century

Andreas. Dauid.

104

PETERBOROUGH PSALTER (and BESTIARY)

Coronation of Virgin

Corpus Christi College, Cambridge

Early 14th century

105

ARUNDEL PSALTER (second part)

Tree of vices, British Museum

Before 1300

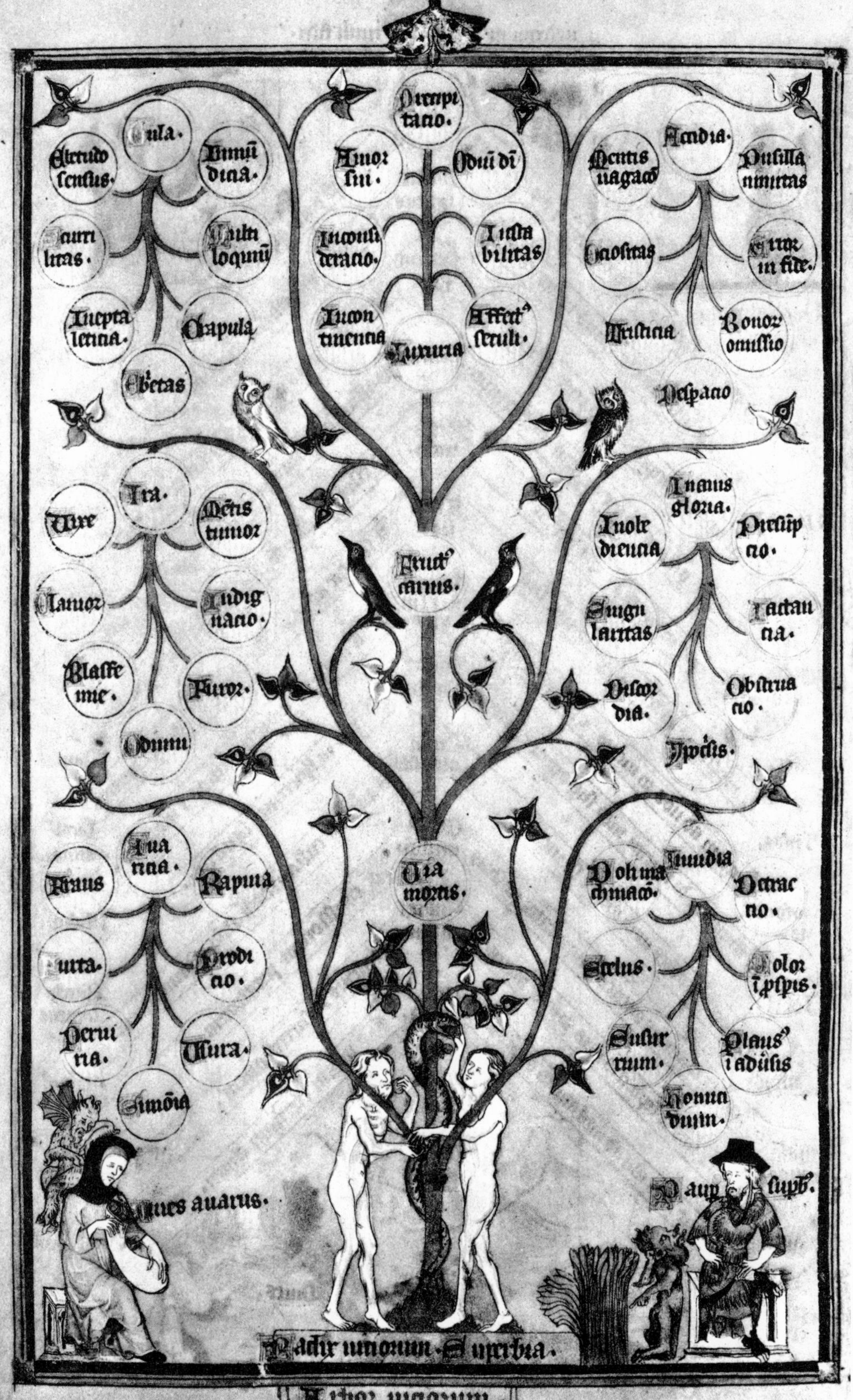

Arbor uiciorum.

106

ARUNDEL PSALTER (second part)

Christ enthroned with Evangelists

British Museum

Before 1300

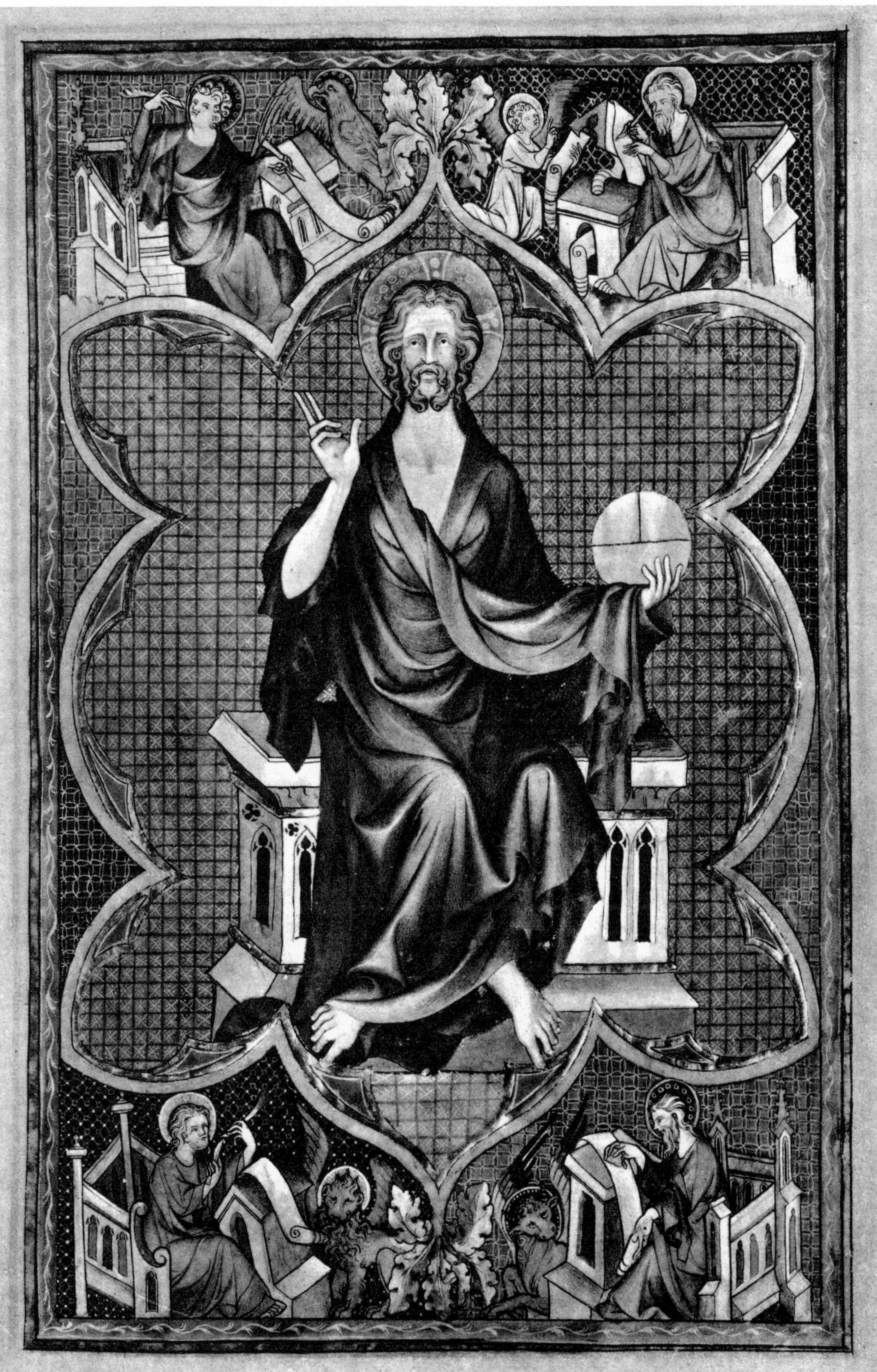

107

ARUNDEL PSALTER (second part)

Passion scenes, *British Museum*

Before 1300

INRI

108

ARUNDEL PSALTER (first part)

Psalm LXXX. Initial, David as musician

British Museum

1300-1308

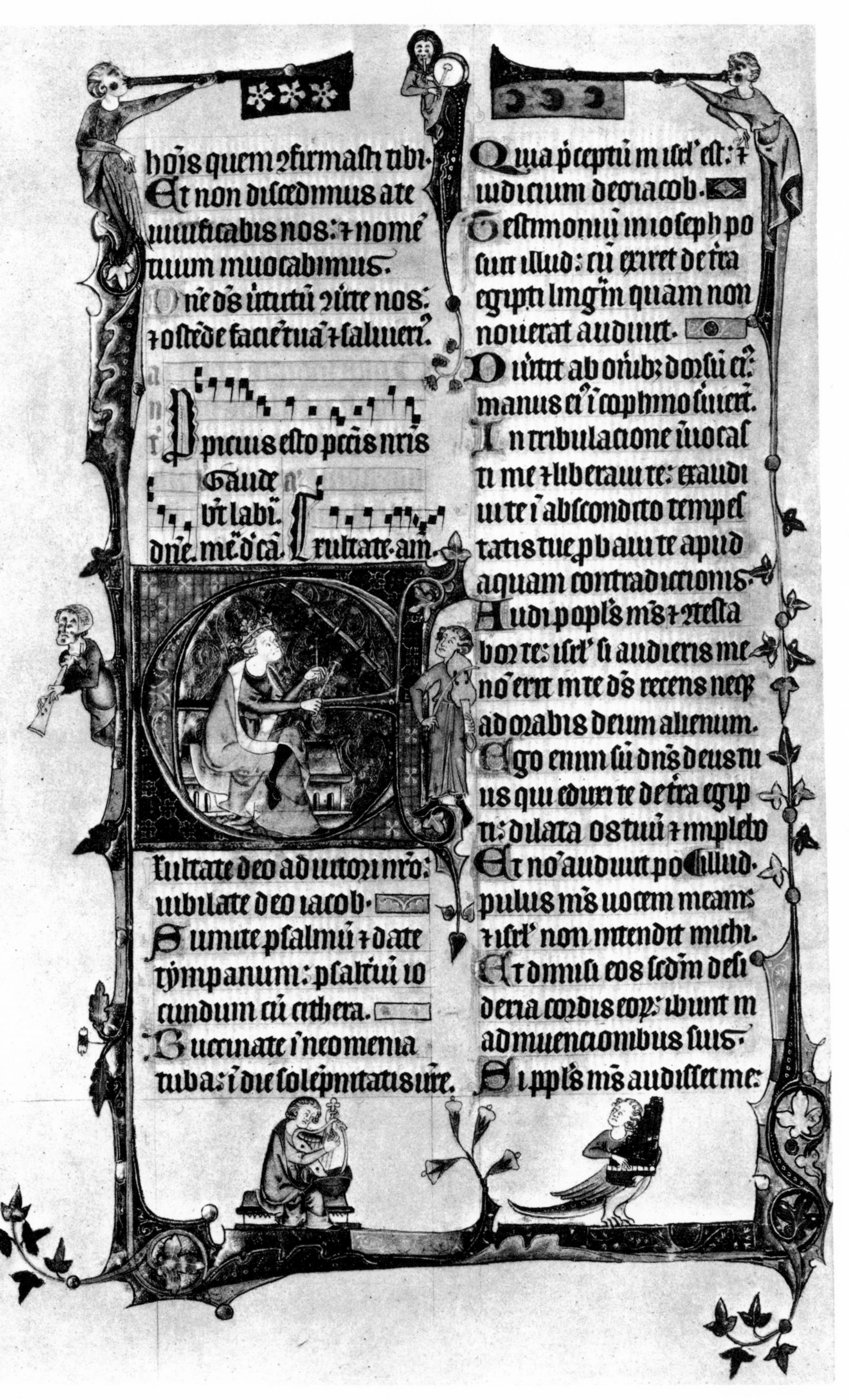

109

ORMESBY PSALTER

Psalm XXXVIII. Initial, Christ before Pilate (reduced)

Bodleian Library, Oxford

Early 14th century

ut deploramus: ualeamus euincere in
sultationes aduersantium uitiorū. per.
Dixi custodiam uias
meas: ut non delin
quam in lingua me
a. Posui ori meo cu
stodiam: cum con
sisteret aduersum me.
Obmutui ⁊ humiliatus sum ⁊ silui a bo
nis: ⁊ dolor meus renouatus est
Concaluit cor meum intra me: ⁊ in me
ditatione mea exardescet ignis.
Locutus sum in lingua mea: notū fac
michi domine finem meum,
Et numerum dierum meorum qui est:
ut sciam quid desit michi.
Ecce mensurabiles posuisti dies meos:
⁊ substancia mea tamquam nichilum ante te.

110

ORMESBY PSALTER

Second Beatus Page, David harping

Bodleian Library, Oxford

Early 14th century

abiit in consilio impiorū ⁊ in uia

III

GORLESTON PSALTER

Psalm CIX. Initial, The Trinity (reduced)

Dyson Perrins Collection

Before 1306

Dixit do
minus
dño me
o: sede a
dextris
meis.
Donec
ponam inimicos tuos: scabellum
pedum tuorum.
Virgam virtutis tue emittet dñs
ex syon: dñare ĩ medio ĩnimicoꝝ tuoꝝ.
Tecum principium in die virtutis
tue in splendoribꝫ scõꝝ: ex utero
ante luciferum genui te.
Iuravit dominus & non penitebit
eum: tu es sacerdos in eternum scdm

112

STOWE BREVIARY

Initial, St. Margaret

British Museum

1322-1325

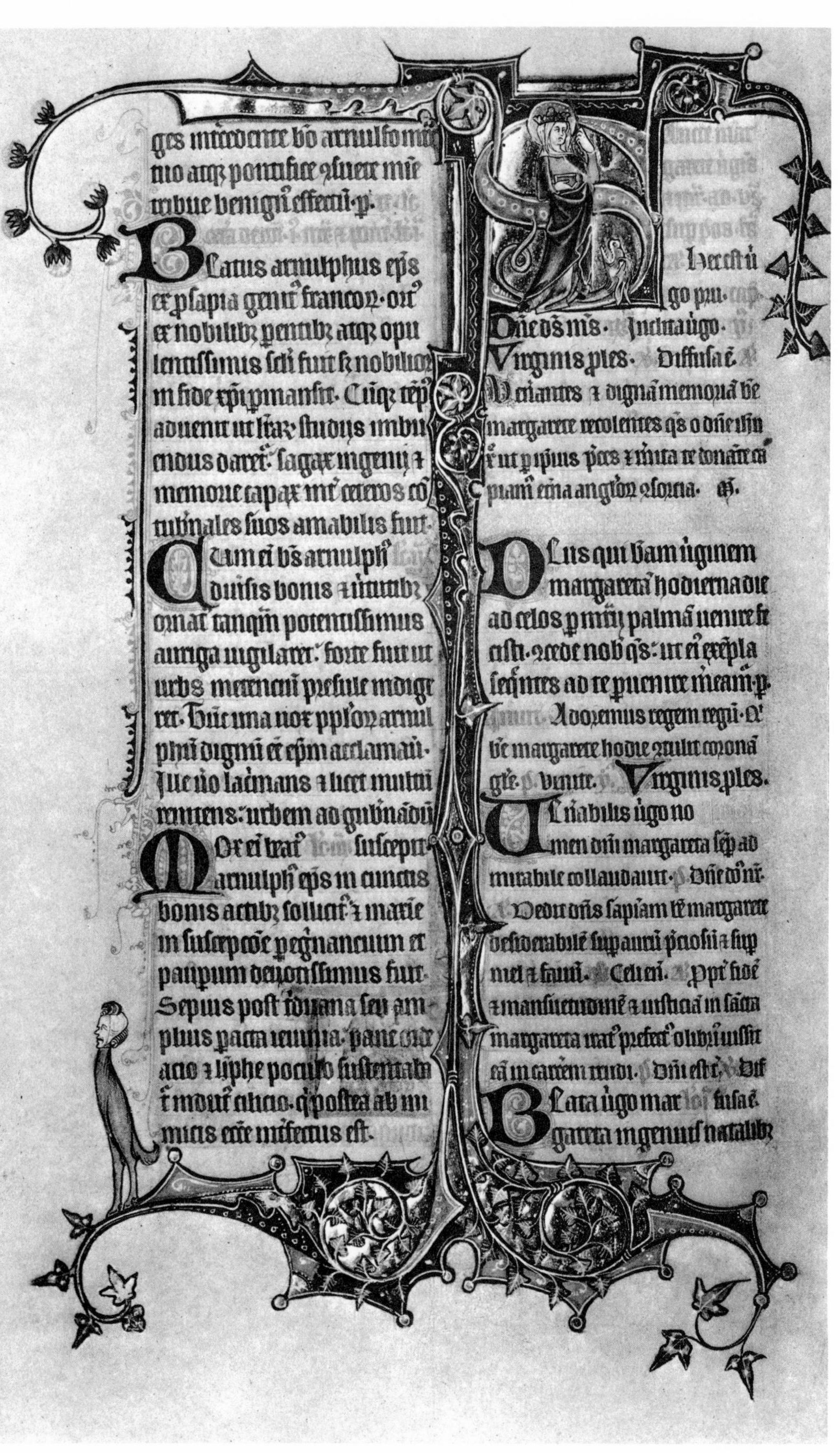

113

ST. OMER PSALTER

Beatus page, (slightly reduced)

Medallions, Scenes from Genesis

British Museum

c. 1322-1325

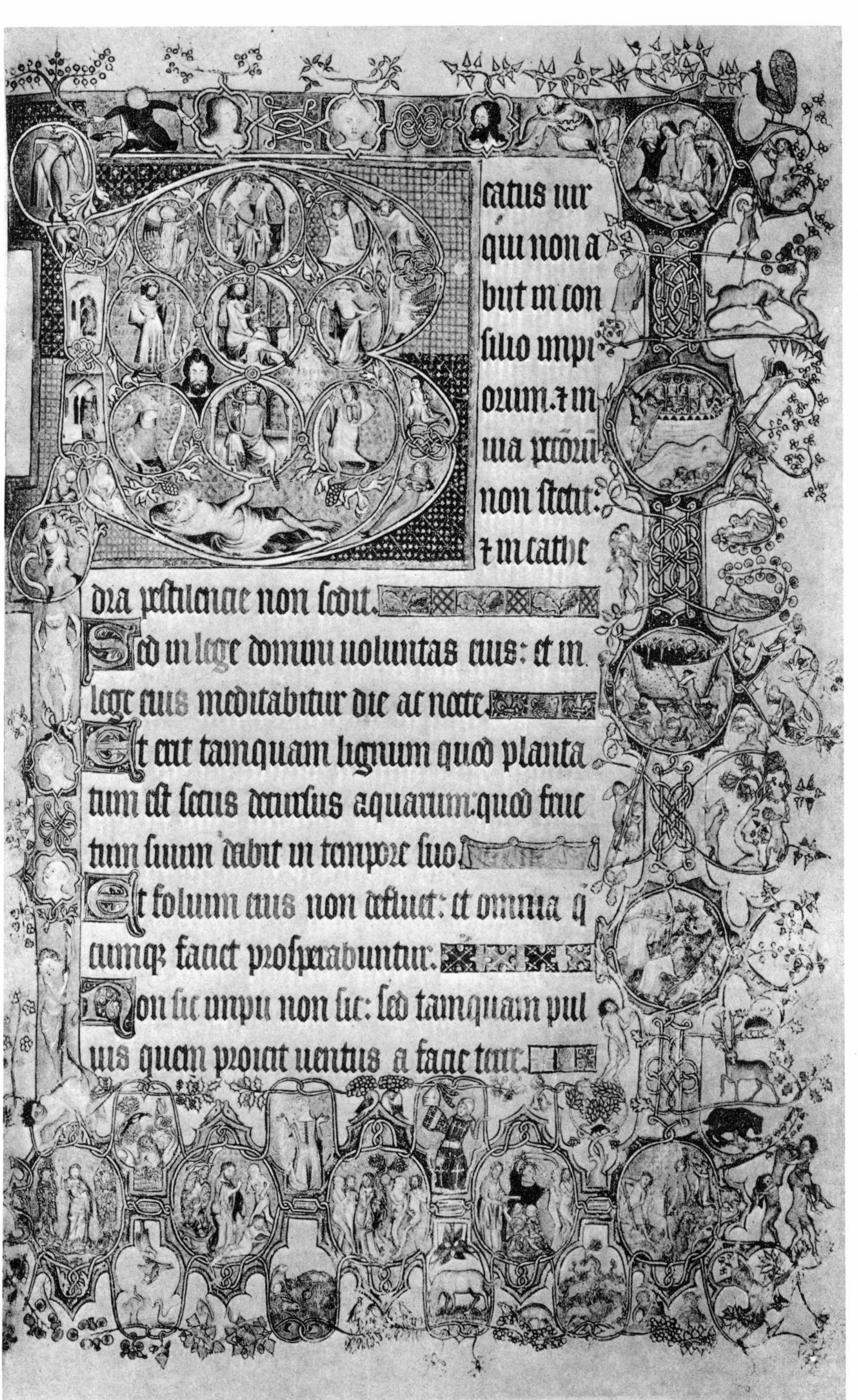

Beatus uir qui non abiit in consilio impiorum. et in uia peccatorum non stetit: et in cathedra pestilencie non sedit.
Sed in lege domini uoluntas eius: et in lege eius meditabitur die ac nocte.
Et erit tamquam lignum quod plantatum est secus decursus aquarum: quod fructum suum dabit in tempore suo.
Et folium eius non defluet: et omnia quecumque faciet prosperabuntur.
Non sic impii non sic: sed tamquam puluis quem proicit uentus a facie terre.

114

ST. OMER PSALTER

Psalm CIX. Initial, Last Judgment,

Medallions, Passion scenes.

British Museum

c. 1322-1325

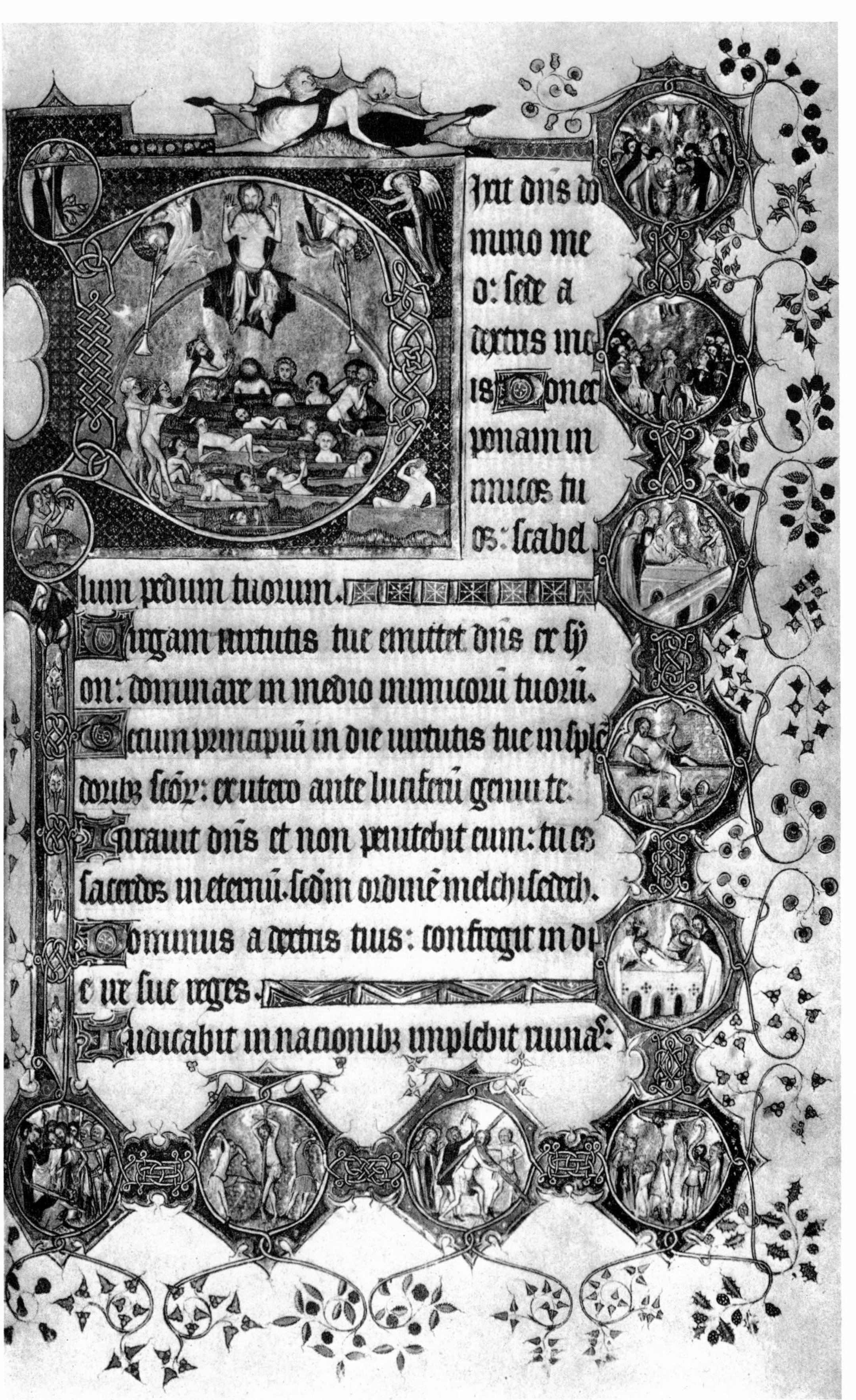

Dixit dñs do
mino meo: sede a
dextris me
is. Donec
ponam in
imicos tu
os: scabel
lum pedum tuorum.

Virgam virtutis tue emittet dñs ex sy
on: dominare in medio inimicorū tuorū.

Tecum principiū in die virtutis tue in splē
doribus scōr: ex utero ante luciferū genui te.

Iuravit dñs et non penitebit eum: tu es
sacerdos in eternū scđm ordinē melchisedech.

Dominus a dextris tuis: confregit in di
e ire sue reges.

Iudicabit in nationibus implebit ruinas:

115

PSALTER

Psalms II and III

All Souls' College, Oxford

Early 14th century

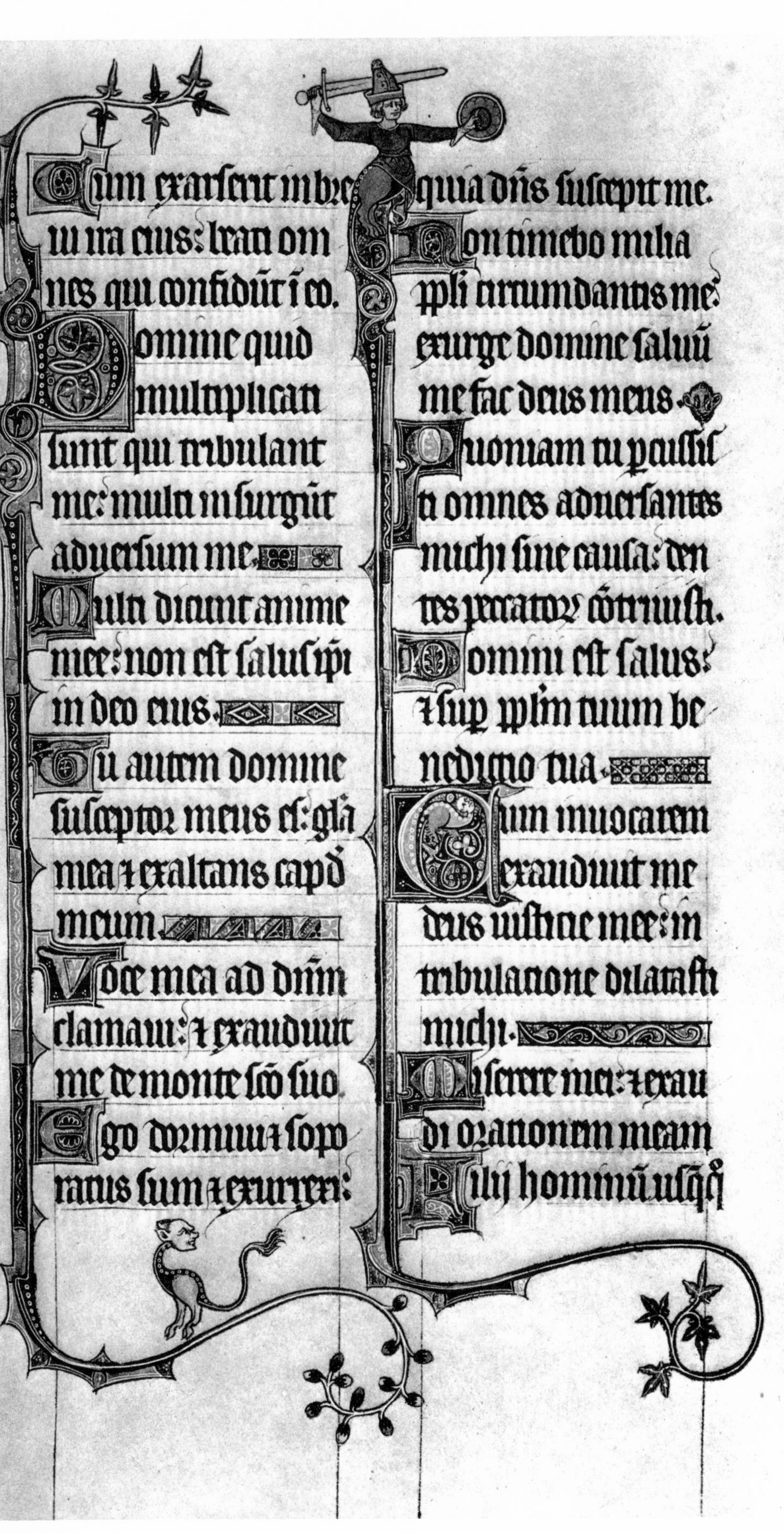

Cum exarserit in bre-
ui ira eius: beati om-
nes qui confidunt in eo.
Domine quid
multiplicati
sunt qui tribulant
me: multi insurgunt
aduersum me.
Multi dicunt anime
mee: non est salus ipsi
in deo eius.
Tu autem domine
susceptor meus es: gloria
mea et exaltans caput
meum.
Voce mea ad dominum
clamaui: et exaudiuit
me de monte sancto suo.
Ego dormiui et sop-
oratus sum et exurrexi:

quia dominus suscepit me.
Non timebo milia
populi circumdantis me:
exurge domine saluum
me fac deus meus.
Quoniam tu percussisti
omnes aduersantes
michi sine causa: den-
tes peccatorum contriuisti.
Domini est salus:
et super populum tuum be-
nedictio tua.
Cum inuocarem
exaudiuit me
deus iusticie mee: in
tribulatione dilatasti
michi.
Miserere mei: et exau-
di orationem meam.
Filii hominum usque

116

PSALTER

Psalm XCVII. Initial, Monks chanting

All Souls' College, Oxford.

Early 14th century

117

BOOK OF HOURS

Presentation of the Virgin in the Temple

British Museum

14th century

Aue ⁊ gaude uirgo maria
que a parentibꝫ ad templu̅
domini delata quindecim g
dus absqꝫ duce sup̄ uires eta
tis tue celerit' ascendisti Aue
B.M.

118

WYCLIFFE BIBLE

Page of Jeremiah

British Museum

End of 14th century

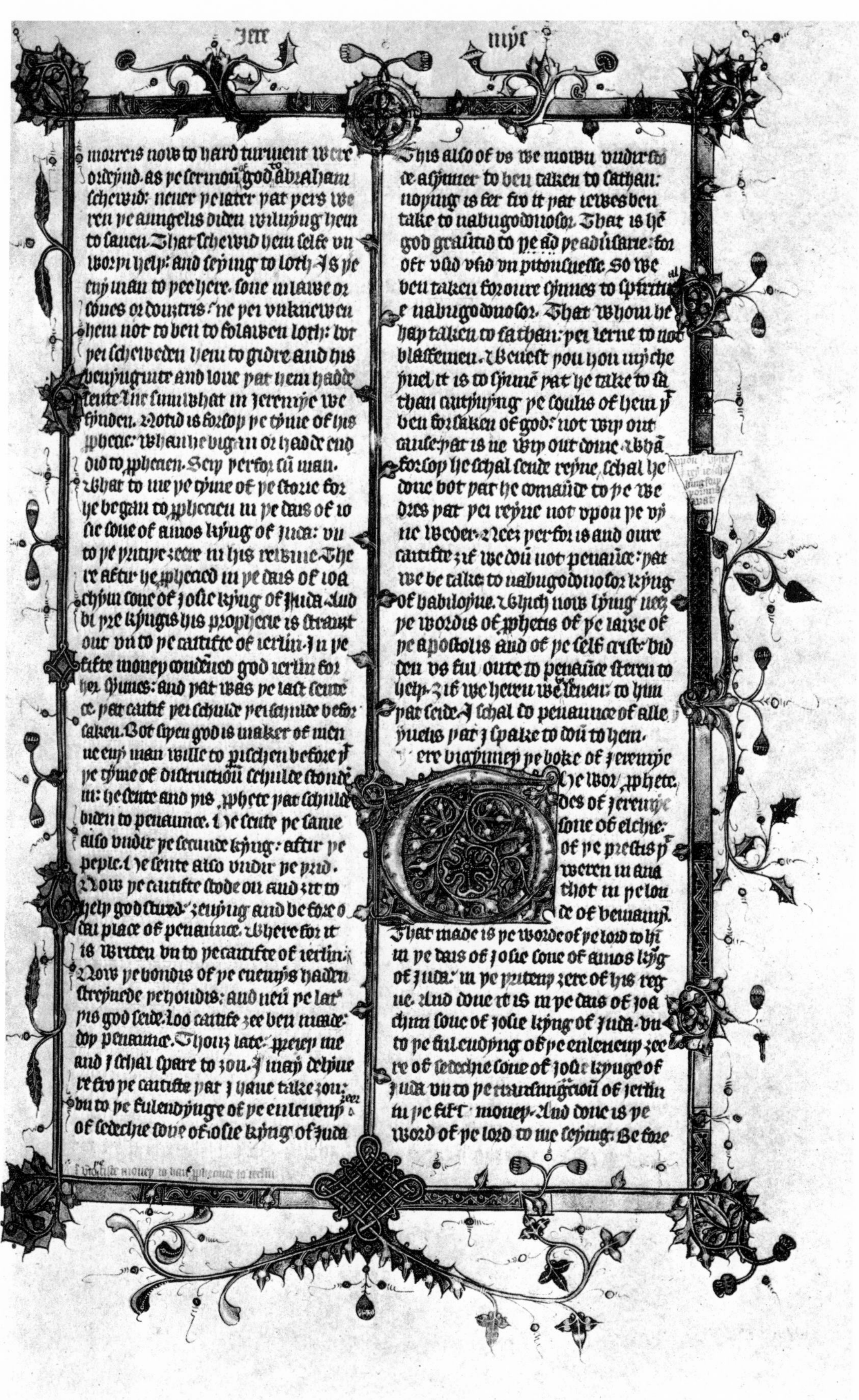

morteris now to hard turment were
ordeynd. as þe sermoun of god to Abraham
schewid: neuer þe later þat þei we
ren þe aungelis diden wilnyng hem
to sauen. That schewid hem selfe vn
worþi help: and seiyng to loth. I is þe
eny man to þee here. sone in lawe or
sones or douztris: ne þei vnknewen
hem not to ben to folawen loth: for
þei schewiden hem to gidre and his
benyngnite and loue þat hem hadde
sente. And sum what in Jeremye we
fynden. Noted is forsoþ þe tyme of his
prophecie: whanne he bigan or hadde end
id to prophecien. Seiþ þerfor sum man.
What to me þe tyme of þe storie for
he began to prophecien in þe dais of Io
sie sone of Amos kyng of Juda: vn
to þe þrittenþe zeer in his rewme. The
re after he prophecied in þe dais of Ioa
chym sone of Josie kyng of Juda. And
bi þre kyngis his prophecie is streizt
out vn to þe caitifte of Jerlm. In þe
fifte moneþ condempned god Jerlm for
her synnes: and þat was þe last sente
ce þat caitif þei schulde þei schulde be for
taken. Bot siþen god is maker of men
ne eny man wille to pischen before þe
þe tyme of distruccioun schulde stonde
in: he sente and þis prophete þat schulde
biden to penaunce. he sente þe same
also vnder þe secunde kyng: after þe
peple. he sente also vnder þe þrid.
Now þe caitifte stode on and zit to
help god stired: zeuyng and before o
ten place of penaunce. Where for it
is writen vn to þe caitifte of Jerlm.
Now þe bondis of þe enemys hadden
streyned þe hondis: and neu þe latter
þis god seide. loo caitife zee ben made:
doþ penaunce. Though late: preieþ me
and I schal spare to zou. I may deliue
re fro þe caitifte þat I haue take zou:
vn to þe fulendynge of þe enleuenþ zeer
of Sedechie sone of Josie kyng of Juda

This also of vs we mown vndirsto
de a synner to ben taken to Sathan:
noþing is fer fro it þat Iewes ben
take to Nabugodonosor. That is he
god grauntid to þe and þe aduersarie: for
oft vnd vnto vn pitousnesse. So we
ben taken for oure synnes to spiritu
e Nabugodonosor. That whom he
haþ taken to Sathan: þei lerne to not
blasfemen. Wenest þou hou myche
yuel it is to synne þat he take to Sa
than turmentyng þe soulis of hem þat
ben forsaken of god: not wiþ out
cause þat is ne wiþ out doome. Whanne
forsoþ he schal sende reyne schal he
done bot þat he comaunde to þe we
dres þat þei reyne not vpon þe vy
ne wedere. Ner þerfor is and oure
caitifte: zif we don not penaunce: þat
we be take to Nabugodonosor kyng
of Babiloyne. Which now lyuyng ner
þe wordis of prophetis of þe lawe of
þe apostolis and of þe self crist: bid
den vs ful oute to penaunce steren to
help. zif we heren we senen: to him
þat seide. I schal do penaunce of alle
yuelis þat I spake to don to hem.
Here bigynneþ þe boke of Jeremye

The wor prophete.
des of Jeremye
sone of Elchie:
of þe prestis þat
weren in Ana
thot in þe lon
de of Beniamyn.
That made is þe worde of þe lord to him
in þe dais of Josie sone of Amos kyng
of Juda: in þe þrittenþ zere of his reg
ne. And done it is in þe dais of Joa
chim sone of Josie kyng of Juda. vn
to þe fulendyng of þe enleuenþ zee
re of Sedechie sone of Josie kynge of
Juda vn to þe transmygracioun of Jerlm
in þe fift moneþ. And done is þe
word of þe lord to me seiyng. Be fore

119[a]

BIBLE OF RICHARD II

Abishag brought to David

British Museum

End of 14th century

119[b]

BIBLE OF RICHARD II.

Psalm LII. Initial, David mocked by enemies

British Museum

End of 14th century

120

BIBLE OF RICHARD II

Siege of Jerusalem, *British Museum*

End of 14th century

121

BIBLE OF RICHARD II

Initial A and Q with St. Jerome

British Museum

End of 14th century

[illegible] pessima est plaga tua. Omnes qui audierunt audicionem tuam: compresserunt manum super te. Quia super quem nō transiit malicia tua semper. Explicit liber Naum prophete. ¶ Incipit prologus sancti Jeronimi presbiteri in Abacuc prophetam.

Abacuc luctator fortissimus et rigidus stat super custodiā suam et figit gradum super municionem: ut xpm in cruce contempletur et dicat. Operuit celos gloria eius: et laude eius plena est terra. Splendor eius ut lux erit. cornua in manibus eius: ibi abscondita est fortitudo eius. Explicit primus prologus.

¶ Incipit secundus prologus in Abacuc prophetā.

Quatuor prophete in duodecim prophetarū volumine sunt. E quibus tres in principio lemma. id est pondus titulum habent. Naum Abacuc et Malachias. Quartus Zacharias in medio et circa finem duos huiuscemodi ponit titulos. Ex quibus unus est onus verbi domini in terra Adrach et Damasci requiei eius. Alter in fine onus verbi domini super israel. De Naum oracionibus tuis: iam liber editus est. De

122

CHICHELE BREVIARY

Decorated page, Initial, Annunciation

(slightly reduced)

Lambeth Palace Library

Early 15th century

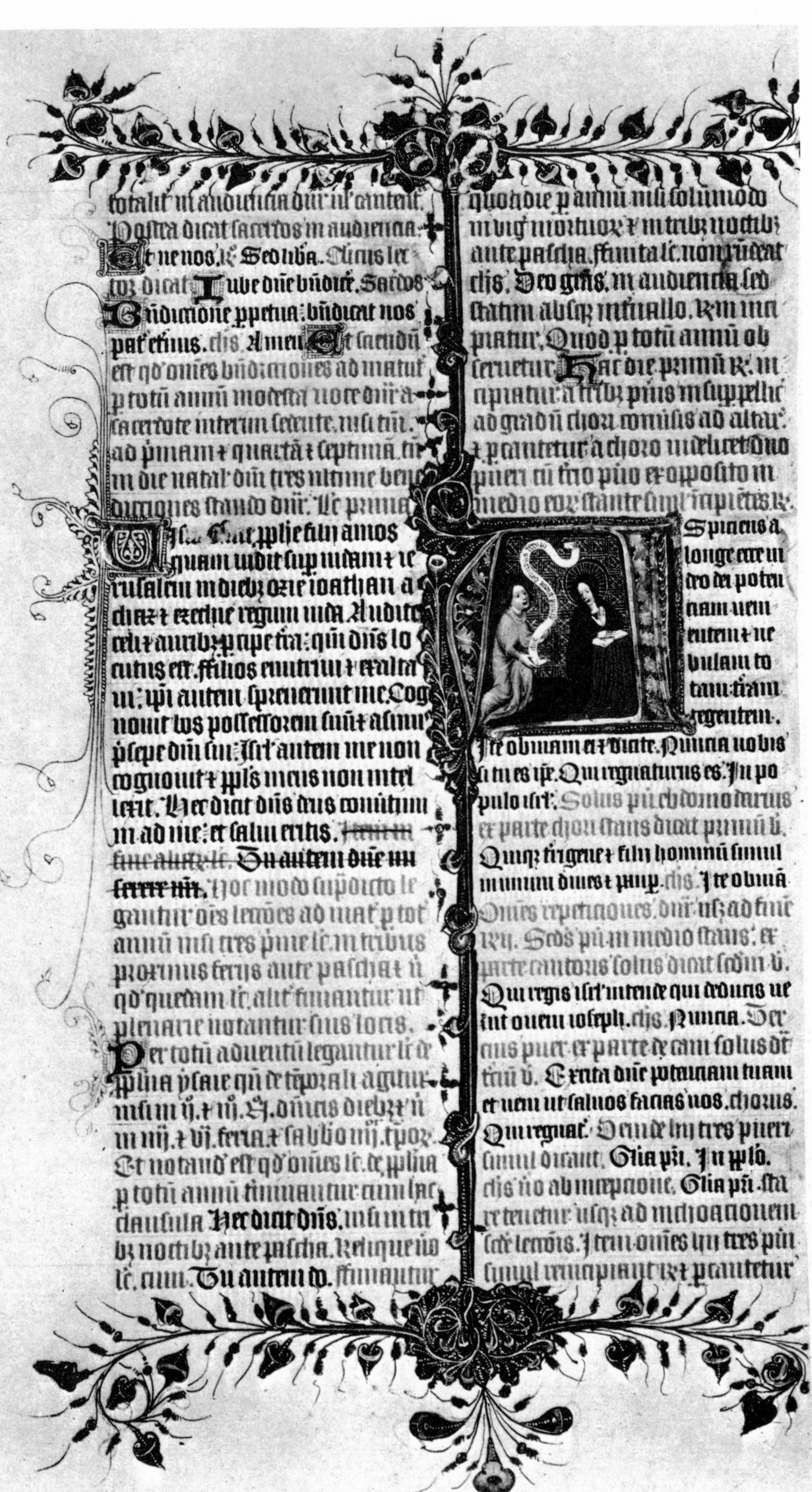

123 a

CHICHELE BREVIARY

Initial, David dancing before the Ark

Lambeth Palace Library

Early 15th century

123 b

PSALTER

Resurrection, *Lambeth Palace Library*

15th century

124

PSALTER

Page with border, *Lambeth Palace Library*

15th century

Deus in adiutori[um] meu[m].
Do[mi]ne ad adiuuan-
dum me festi[na]. Glo-ria
patri & filio & sp[irit]ui s[ancto].
Sicut er[at]. Alleluia.
Veni creator sp[irit]us mentes tuor[um] vi-
sita imple superna gr[ati]a que tu creasti
pectora. Memento salutis auctor quod
n[ost]ri quondam corporis ex illibata virgine nascendo forma[m] su[m]pseris. Maria plena gr[ati]e
mater m[isericordi]e tu nos ab hoste p[ro]tege in hora
mortis suscipe. Gloria tibi d[omi]ne qui.
Deus in no[m]i[n]e tuo saluu[m] me fac et i[n]
virtute tua iudica me. Deus ex-
audi orationem mea[m] auribus p[er]cipe v[er]ba oris
mei. Quoniam alieni insurrexerunt adversu[m]
me & fortes quesierunt a[n]i[m]am mea[m] & no[n]
proposuerunt deu[m] ante conspectu[m] suu[m]. Ecce
enim deus adiuuat me & dominus susceptor est anime mee. Averte mala inimicis
meis & in veritate tua disp[er]de illos. Vo

125

HOURS OF ELYSABETH YE QUENE

Crucifixion and border

Dyson Perrins Collection

c. 1410

[D]eus in adiutorium meum intende:
Domine ad adiuvandum me festi
na. Gloria patri. Sicut erat. ym
[ ]ou arator. Memento salutis.
Maria mater: Gloria tibi domine. ut supra. an.
Germinavit radix yesse. psalmus.
In convertendo dominus captivitatē syon:
facti sumus sicut consolati. Tunc repletum ē gau
dio os nostrum et lingua nostra exultacione. Tunc
dicent inter gentes magnificavit dominus facere
cum eis. Magnificavit dominus facere nobiscum

126

HOURS OF THE DUKE OF WARWICK

Christ before Pilate and border

Dyson Perrins Collection

First half of 15th century

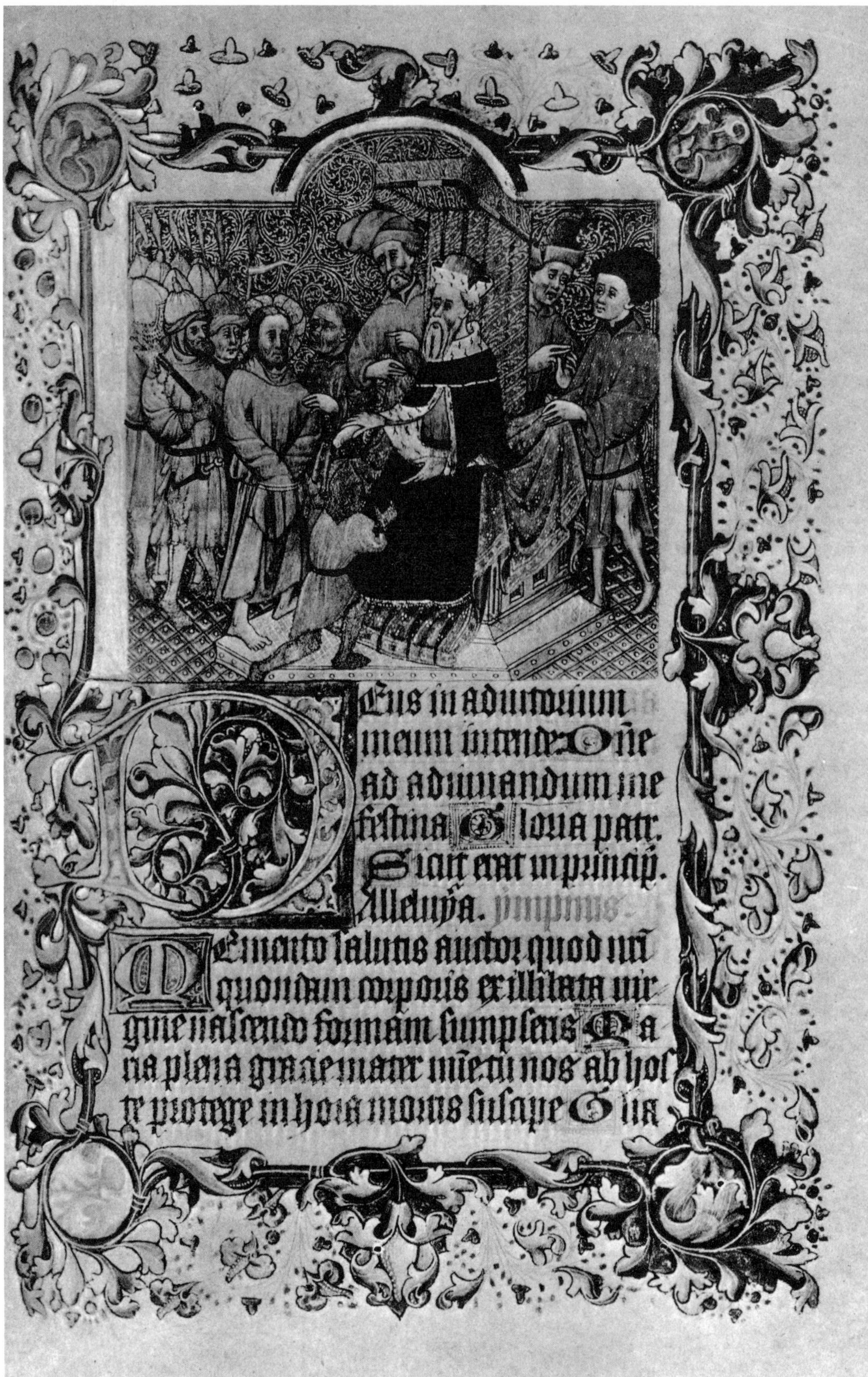
Eus in adiutorium
meum intende Dñe
ad adiuuandum me
festina Gloria patri.
Sicut erat in princip.
Alleluya. ympnus
Emento salutis auctor quod nri
quondam corporis ex illibata vir
gine nascendo formam sumpseris Ma
ria plena gracie mater mĩe tu nos ab hos
te protege in hora mortis suscipe Glia

127

LECTIONARY OF SIFERWAS

Page with border and miniature of the Circumcision

British Museum

c. 1400

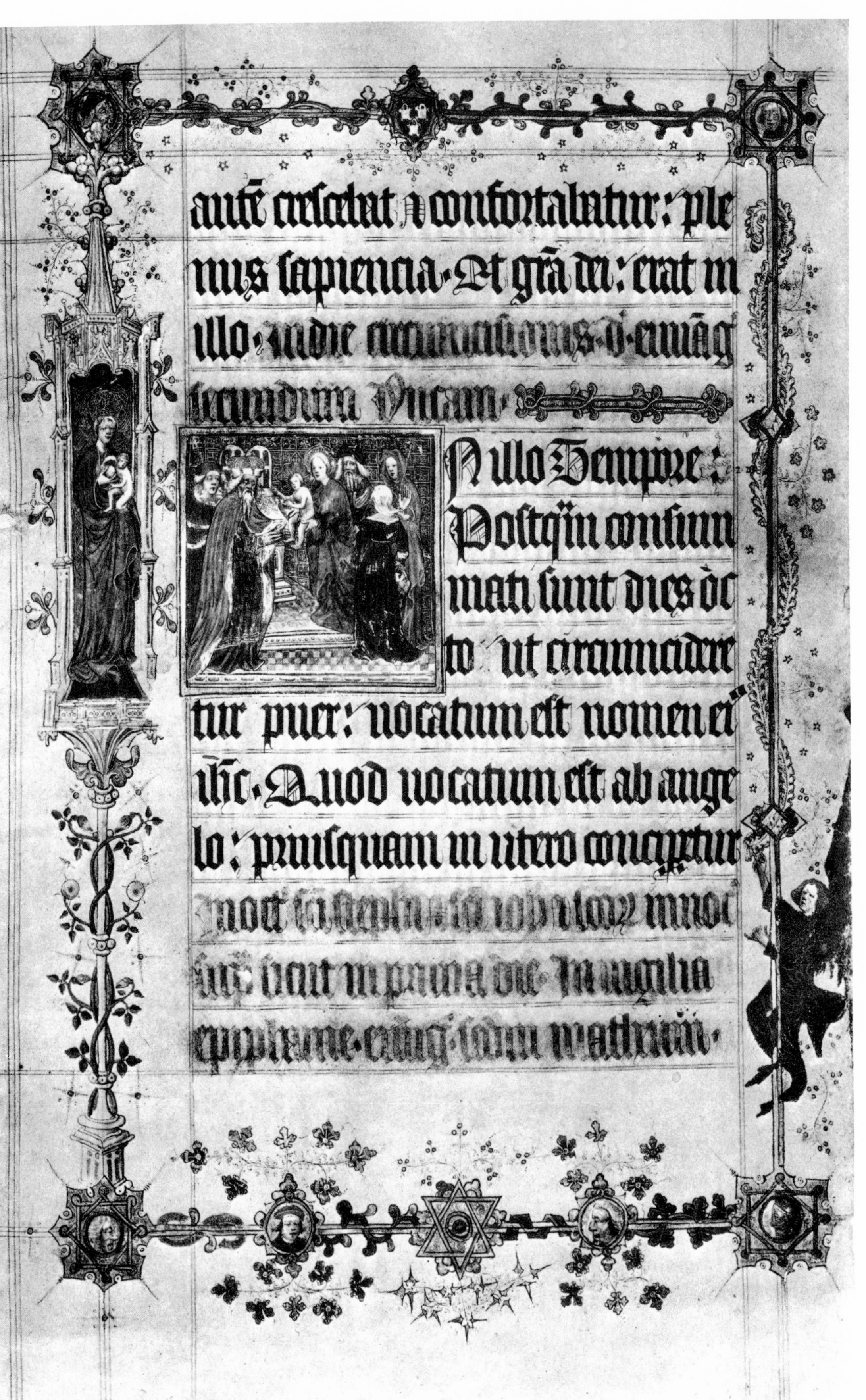

autē crescebat & confortabatur: ple
nus sapiencia. Et grā dei: erat in
illo. In die circumcisionis dn̄i. euāg
secundum lucam.
In illo tempore:
Postq̄m consum
mati sunt dies oc
to ut circumcidere
tur puer: vocatum est nomen ei'
ihc. Quod vocatum est ab ange
lo: priusquam in utero conciperetur.

128

EPISTLE OF OTHEA TO HECTOR

Perseus and Andromeda

St. John's College, Cambridge

c. 1450

and helpe. councell: in techinge hym where he is ygnoraunt. and helpe him: in confortynge his nown power. To thi suget: thou scholdest yif hym kepynge and chastisynge. kepynge: in kepynge hym from evil deedis. chastisynge: in chastisynge hym if that he haue doon amys. And to this prouerbe: Salamon seith in his prouerbis. Excogitat iustus de domo impii, vt detrahat impios a malo gaudium est facere iusticiam. Prouerbiorum. xxj° ca°.

Persyualle

Pegasus

Andromeda

Bellue

Texte.

Also remembre the of Persyualle
Whos name is knowen ouer alle
Through oute the worlde bothe softe and harde
The swifte hors Pegasus afterwarde

129

CHAUCER'S TROILUS

Frontispiece

Corpus Christi College, Cambridge

15th century